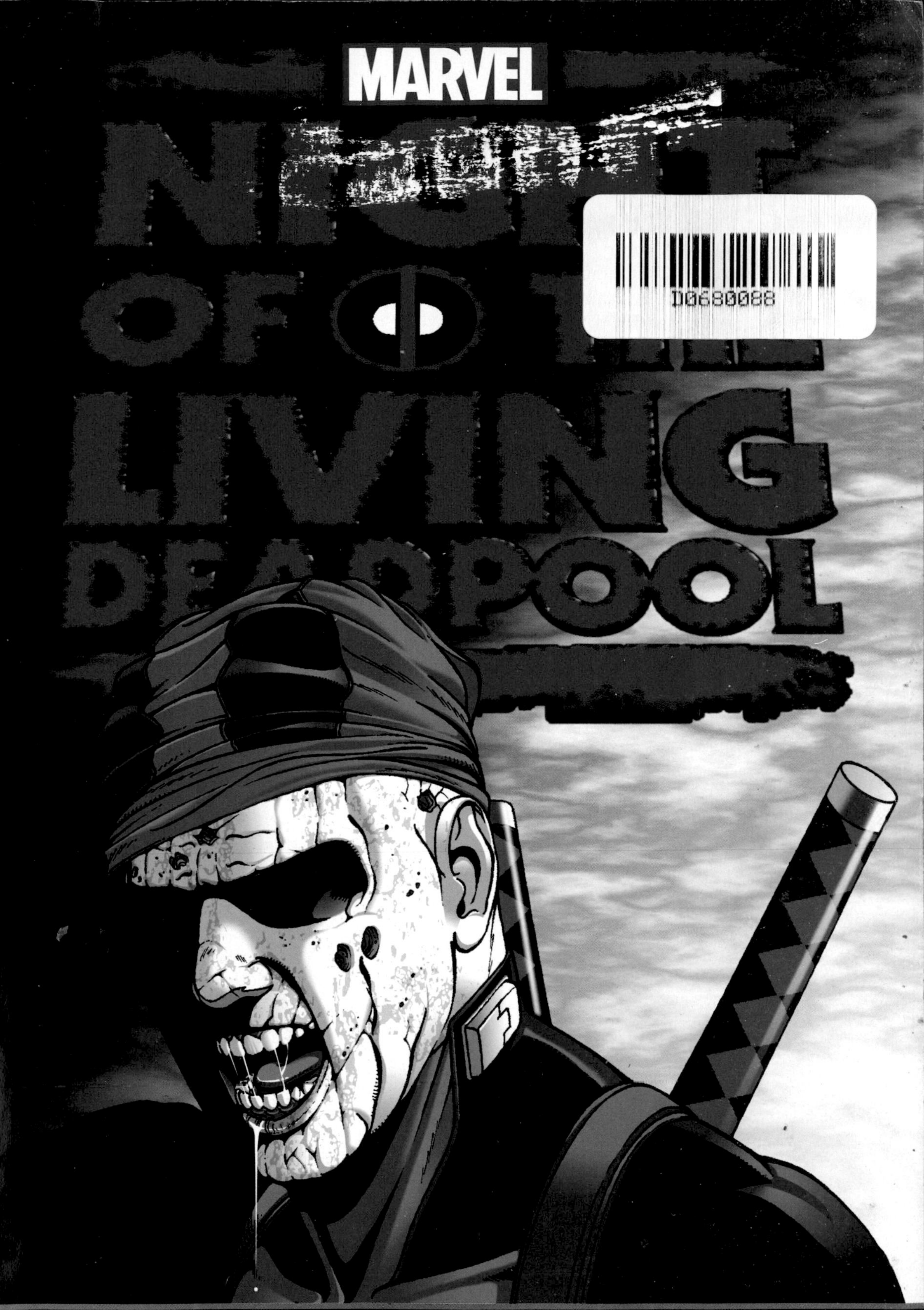
MARVEL
LIVING
DEADPOOL

NIGHT OF THE LIVING DEADPOOL. Contains material originally published [illegible] 2014. ISBN# 978-0-7851-9017-2. Published by MARVEL WORLDWIDE, INC., a subsidiary of MARVEL ENTERTAINMENT, LLC. OFFICE OF PUBLICA[illegible] arvel Characters, Inc. All rights reserved. All characters featured in this issue and the distinctive names and likenesses thereof, and all related in[illegible] of the names, characters, persons, and/or institutions in this magazine with those of any living or dead person or institution is intended, and a[illegible] **nada.** ALAN FINE, EVP - Office of the President, Marvel Worldwide, Inc. and EVP & CMO Marvel Characters B.V.; DAN BUCKLEY, Publisher & Pre[illegible] ve Officer; TOM BREVOORT, SVP of Publishing; DAVID BOGART, SVP of Operations & Procurement, Publishing; C.B. CEBULSKI, SVP of Creator & [illegible] M O'KEEFE, VP of Operations & Logistics; DAN CARR, Executive Director of Publishing Technology; SUSAN CRESPI, Editorial Operations Manager; [illegible] Emeritus. For information regarding advertising in Marvel Comics or on Marvel.com, please contact Niza Disla, Director of Marvel Partnerships, [illegible] 800-217-9158. **Manufactured between 4/18/2014 and 5/26/2014 by SOLISCO PRINTERS, SCOTT, QC, CANADA.**

10 9 8 7 6 5 4 3 2 1

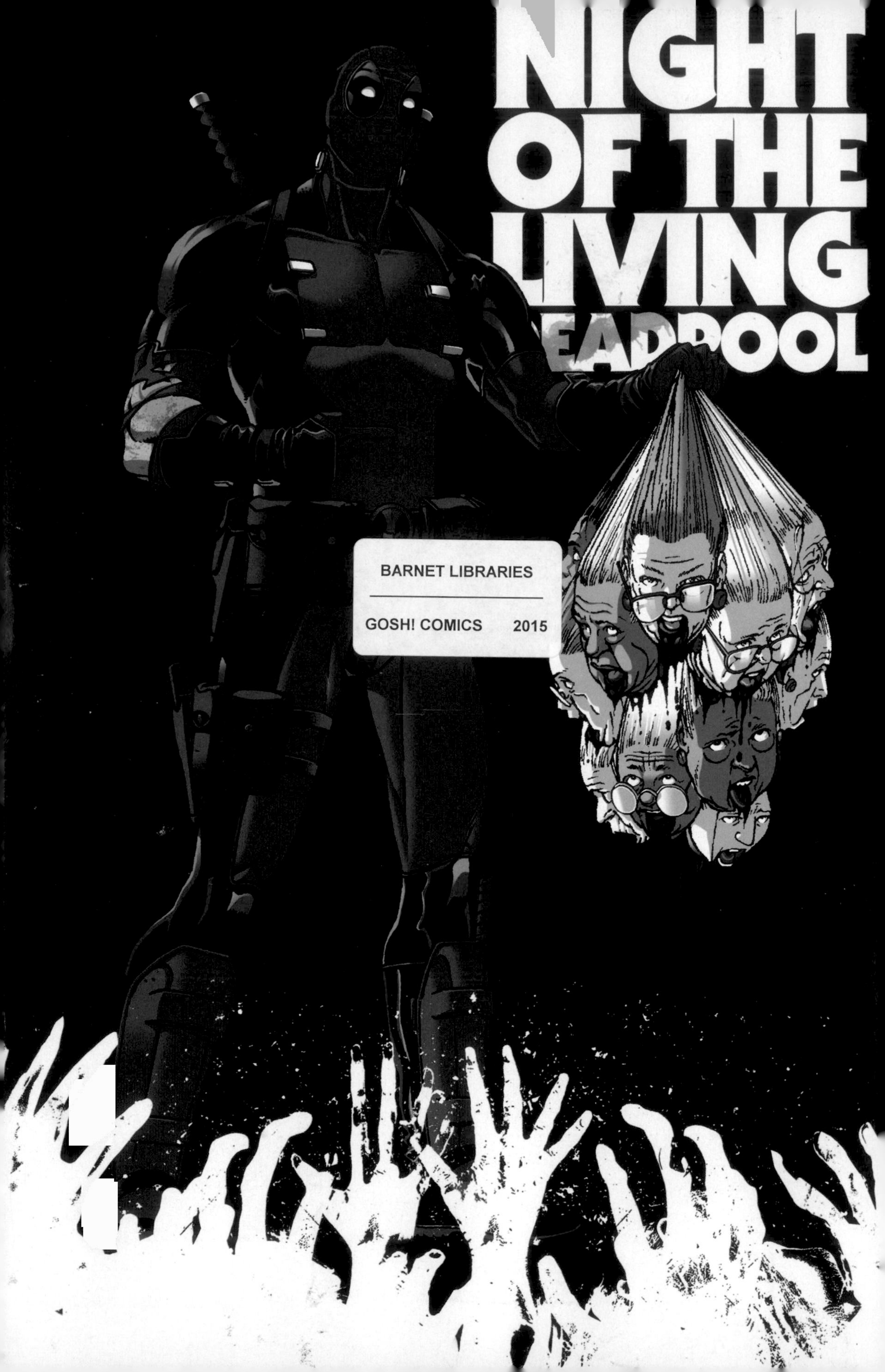
NIGHT
OF THE
LIVING
DEADPOOL

WRITER
CULLEN BUNN

ARTIST
RAMON ROSANAS

LETTERS
VC'S JOE SABINO

COVER ART
JAY SHAW

EDITOR
JORDAN D. WHITE

COLLECTION EDITOR
SARAH BRUNSTAD

ASSOCIATE MANAGING EDITOR
ALEX STARBUCK

EDITORS, SPECIAL PROJECTS
JENNIFER GRÜNWALD & MARK D. BEAZLEY

SENIOR EDITOR, SPECIAL PROJECTS
JEFF YOUNGQUIST

SVP PRINT, SALES & MARKETING
DAVID GABRIEL

BOOK DESIGN
NELSON RIBEIRO

EDITOR IN CHIEF
AXEL ALONSO

CHIEF CREATIVE OFFICER
JOE QUESADA

PUBLISHER
DAN BUCKLEY

EXECUTIVE PRODUCER
ALAN FINE

DEADPOOL CREATED BY ROB LIEFELD & FABIAN NICIEZA

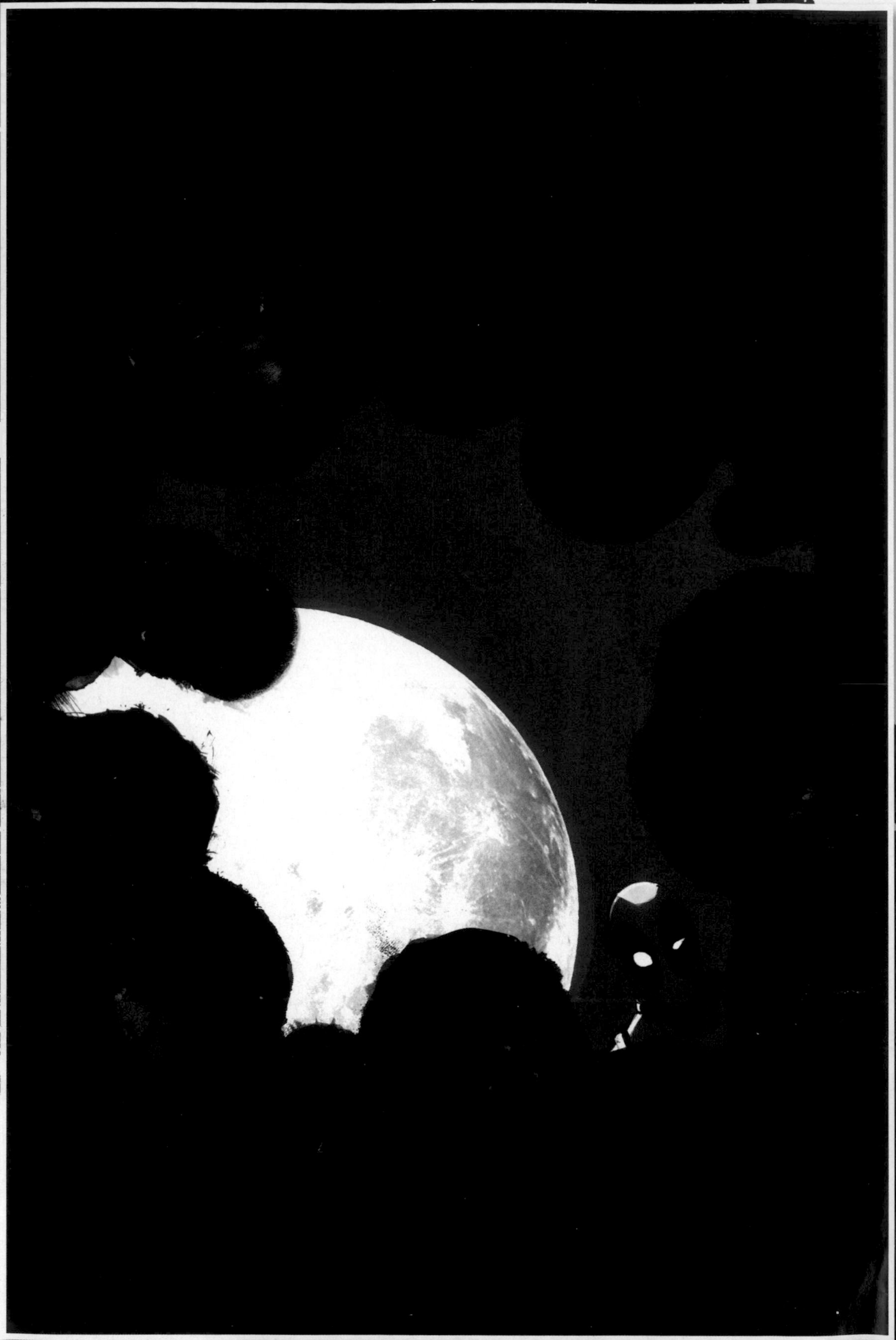

#1

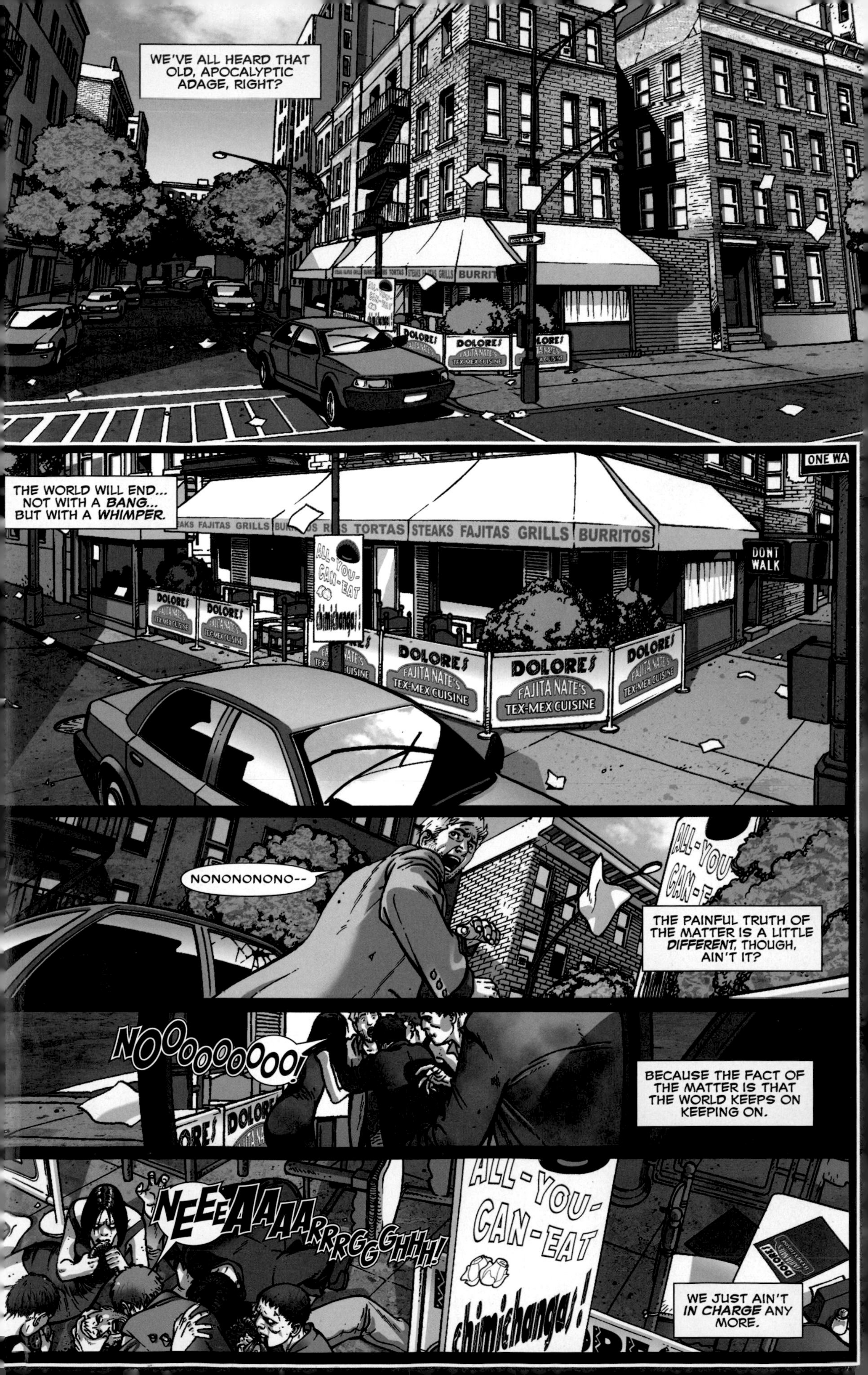

WE'VE ALL HEARD THAT OLD, APOCALYPTIC ADAGE, RIGHT?
THE WORLD WILL END... NOT WITH A *BANG*... BUT WITH A *WHIMPER*.
STEAKS FAJITAS GRILLS BURRITOS TORTAS
ALL-YOU-CAN-EAT chimichangas!
DOLORES FAJITA NATE'S TEX-MEX CUISINE
DONT WALK
ONE WAY
NONONONONO--
THE PAINFUL TRUTH OF THE MATTER IS A LITTLE *DIFFERENT*, THOUGH, AIN'T IT?
NOOOOOOOOO!
BECAUSE THE FACT OF THE MATTER IS THAT THE WORLD KEEPS ON KEEPING ON.
NEEEAAAARRRGGGHHH!
WE JUST AIN'T *IN CHARGE* ANY MORE.

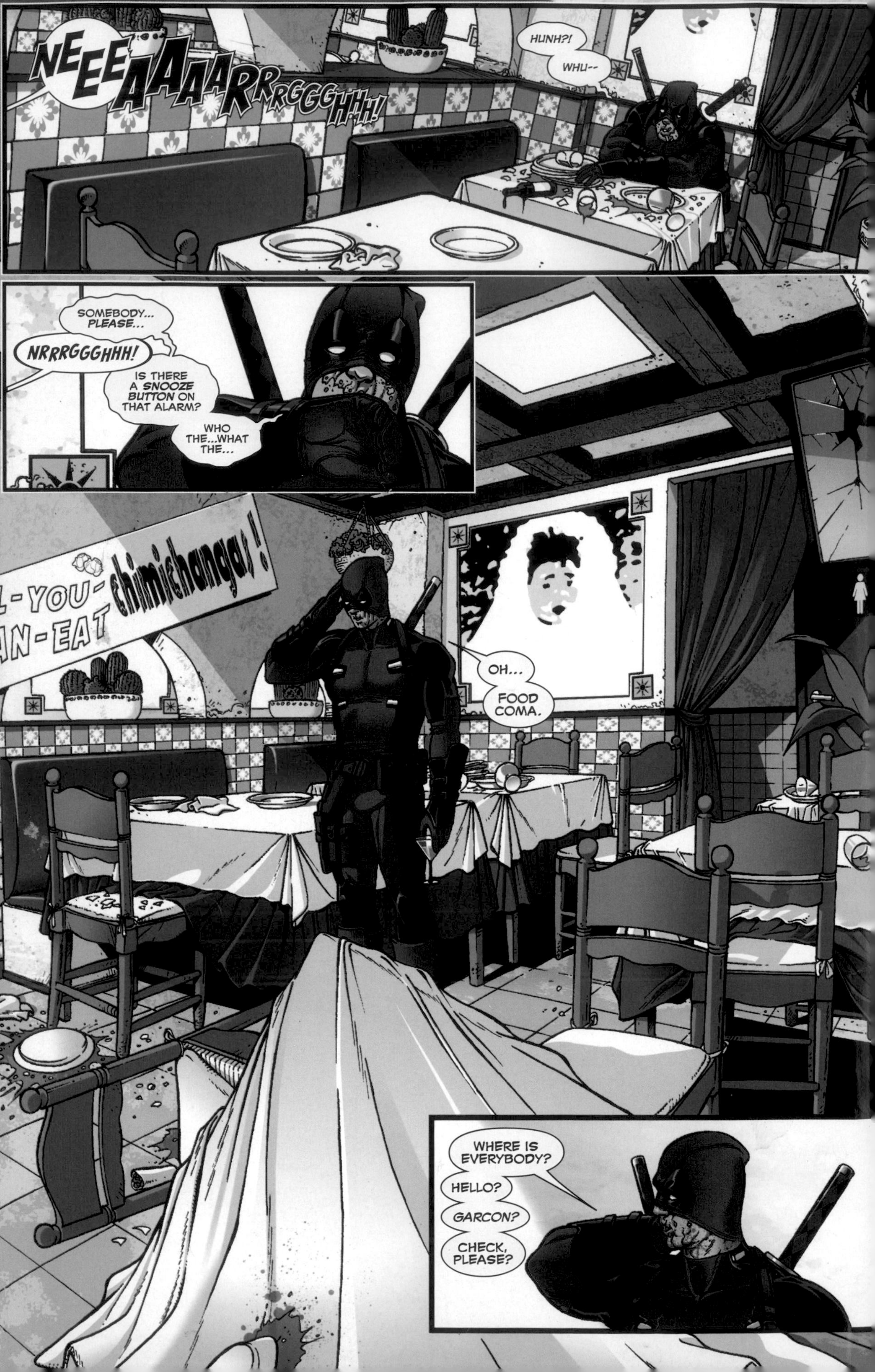
NEEEAAAARRRGGGHHH!
HUNH?!
WHU--
SOMEBODY... PLEASE...
NRRRGGGHHH!
IS THERE A SNOOZE BUTTON ON THAT ALARM?
WHO THE...WHAT THE...
L-YOU-AN-EAT chimichangas!
OH...
FOOD COMA.
WHERE IS EVERYBODY?
HELLO?
GARCON?
CHECK, PLEASE?

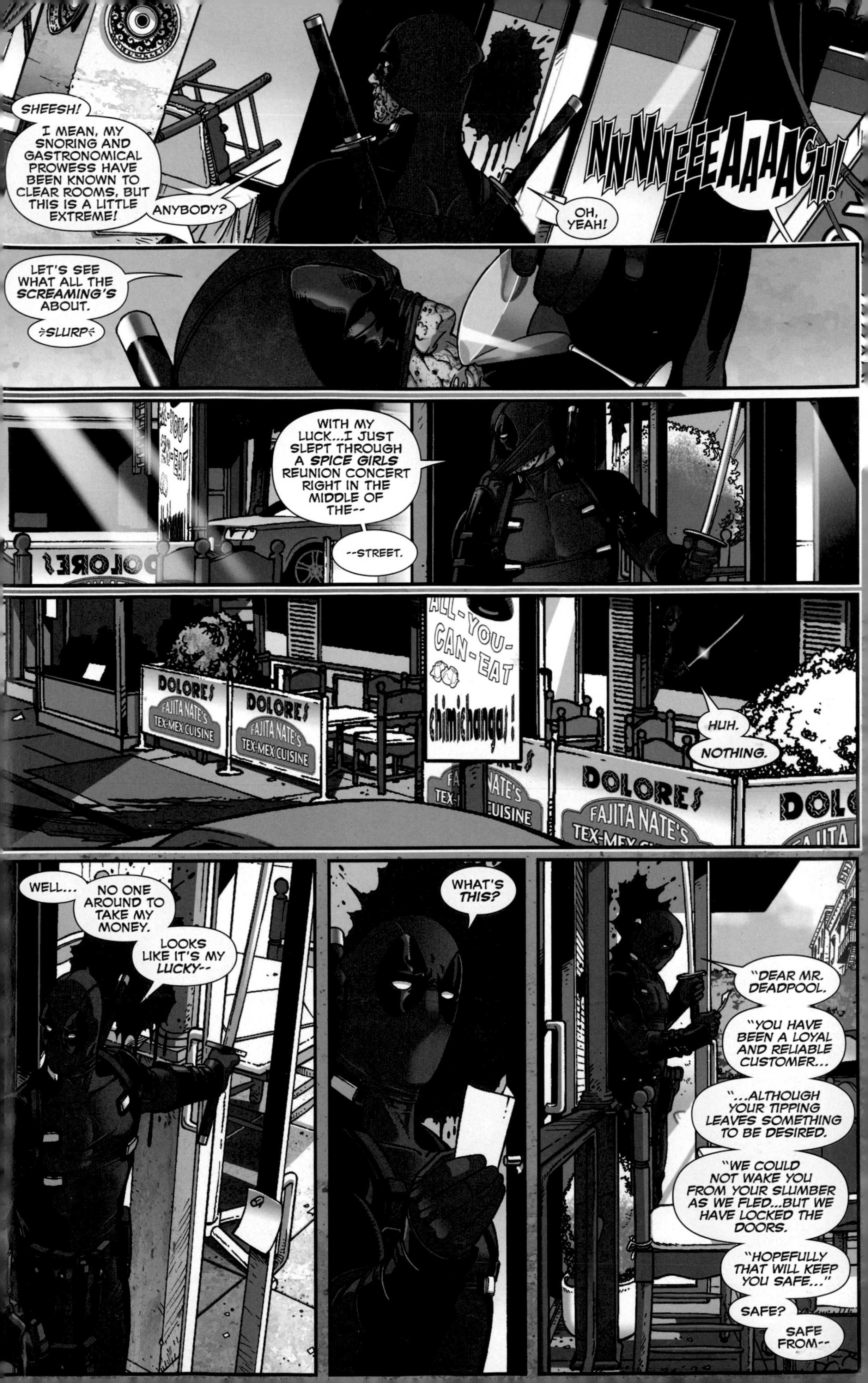
SHEESH!
I MEAN, MY SNORING AND GASTRONOMICAL PROWESS HAVE BEEN KNOWN TO CLEAR ROOMS, BUT THIS IS A LITTLE EXTREME!
ANYBODY?
NNNNEEEAAAAGH!
OH, YEAH!
LET'S SEE WHAT ALL THE SCREAMING'S ABOUT.
SLURP
WITH MY LUCK...I JUST SLEPT THROUGH A SPICE GIRLS REUNION CONCERT RIGHT IN THE MIDDLE OF THE--
--STREET.
DOLORES
DOLORES
FAJITA NATE'S
TEX-MEX CUISINE
DOLORES
FAJITA NATE'S
TEX-MEX CUISINE
ALL-YOU-CAN-EAT
chimichangas!
HUH.
NOTHING.
DOLORES
FAJITA NATE'S
TEX-MEX
WELL...
NO ONE AROUND TO TAKE MY MONEY.
LOOKS LIKE IT'S MY LUCKY--
WHAT'S THIS?
"DEAR MR. DEADPOOL.
"YOU HAVE BEEN A LOYAL AND RELIABLE CUSTOMER...
"...ALTHOUGH YOUR TIPPING LEAVES SOMETHING TO BE DESIRED.
"WE COULD NOT WAKE YOU FROM YOUR SLUMBER AS WE FLED...BUT WE HAVE LOCKED THE DOORS.
"HOPEFULLY THAT WILL KEEP YOU SAFE..."
SAFE?
SAFE FROM--

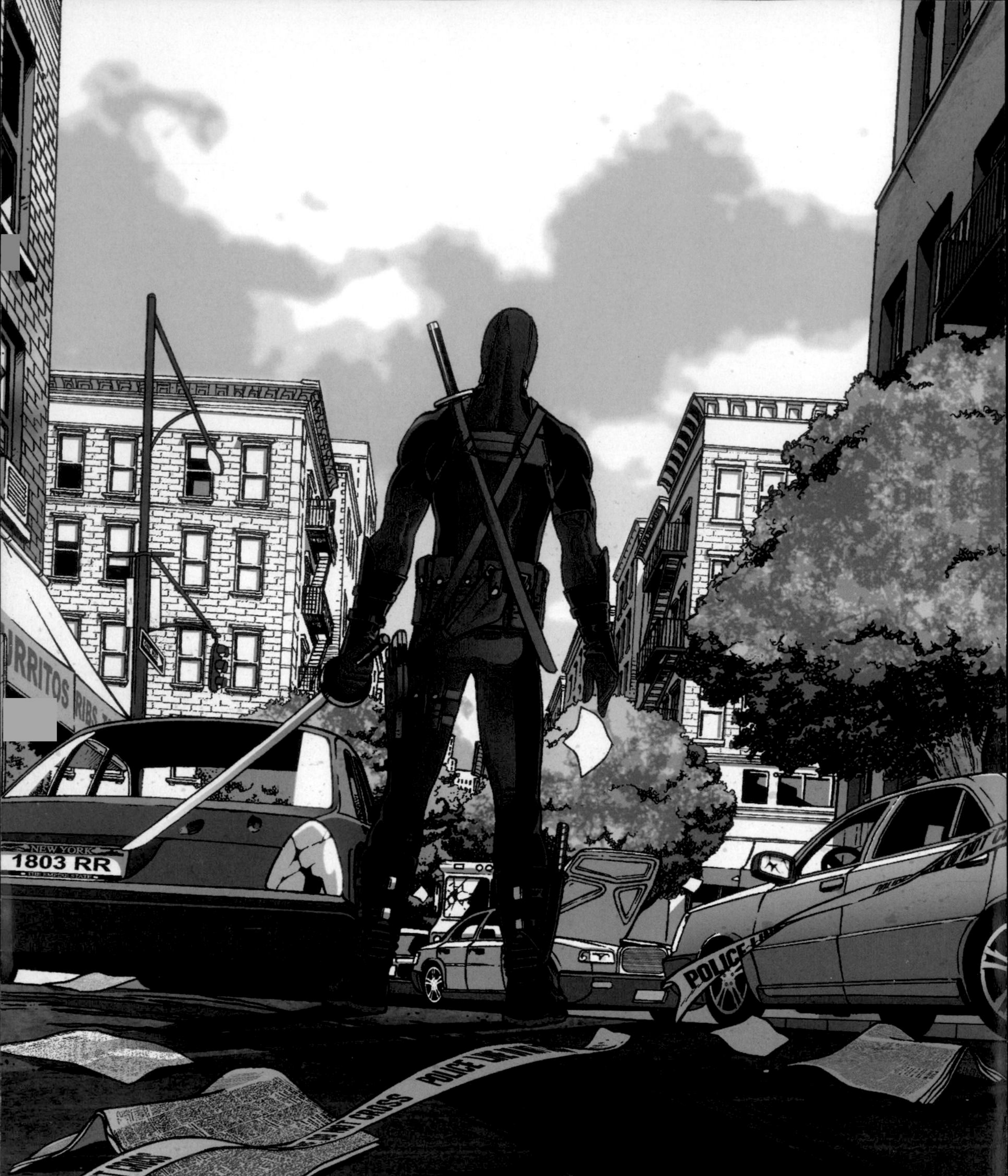
NEW YORK
1803 RR
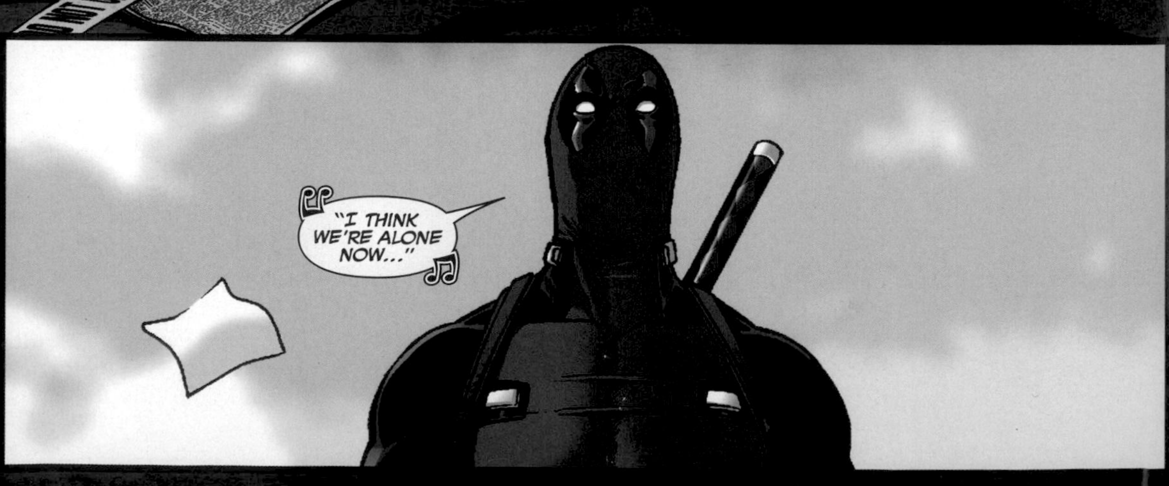
"I THINK WE'RE ALONE NOW..."

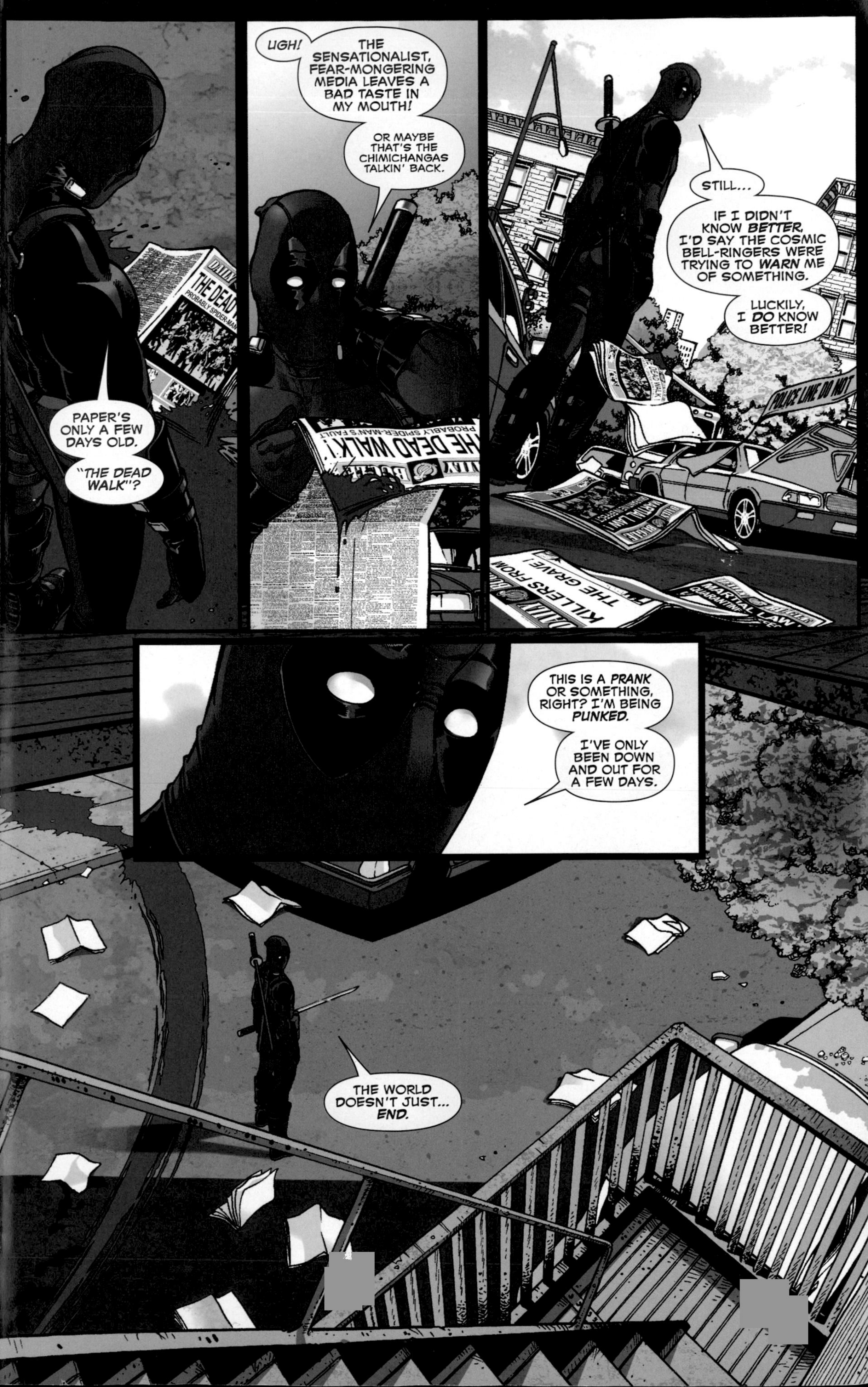

PAPER'S ONLY A FEW DAYS OLD.
"THE DEAD WALK"?
UGH!
THE SENSATIONALIST, FEAR-MONGERING MEDIA LEAVES A BAD TASTE IN MY MOUTH!
OR MAYBE THAT'S THE CHIMICHANGAS TALKIN' BACK.
PROBABLY SPIDER-MAN'S FAULT
STILL...
IF I DIDN'T KNOW BETTER, I'D SAY THE COSMIC BELL-RINGERS WERE TRYING TO WARN ME OF SOMETHING.
LUCKILY, I DO KNOW BETTER!
POLICE LINE DO NOT
MARTIAL LAW
KILLERS FROM THE GRAVE!
THIS IS A PRANK OR SOMETHING, RIGHT? I'M BEING PUNKED.
I'VE ONLY BEEN DOWN AND OUT FOR A FEW DAYS.
THE WORLD DOESN'T JUST... END.

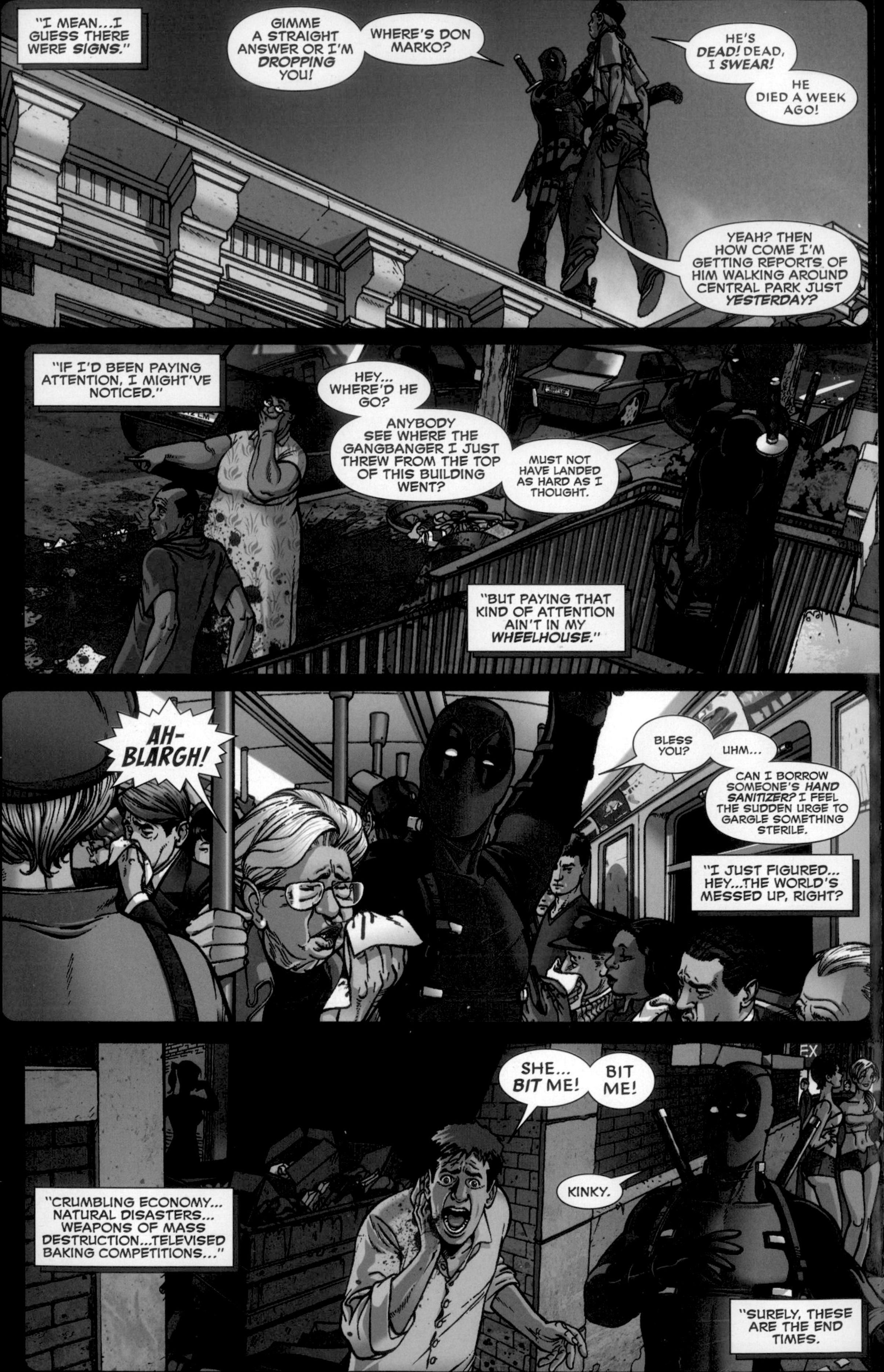
"I MEAN...I GUESS THERE WERE SIGNS."
GIMME A STRAIGHT ANSWER OR I'M DROPPING YOU!
WHERE'S DON MARKO?
HE'S DEAD! DEAD, I SWEAR!
HE DIED A WEEK AGO!
YEAH? THEN HOW COME I'M GETTING REPORTS OF HIM WALKING AROUND CENTRAL PARK JUST YESTERDAY?
"IF I'D BEEN PAYING ATTENTION, I MIGHT'VE NOTICED."
HEY... WHERE'D HE GO?
ANYBODY SEE WHERE THE GANGBANGER I JUST THREW FROM THE TOP OF THIS BUILDING WENT?
MUST NOT HAVE LANDED AS HARD AS I THOUGHT.
"BUT PAYING THAT KIND OF ATTENTION AIN'T IN MY WHEELHOUSE."
AH-BLARGH!
BLESS YOU?
UHM...
CAN I BORROW SOMEONE'S HAND SANITIZER? I FEEL THE SUDDEN URGE TO GARGLE SOMETHING STERILE.
"I JUST FIGURED... HEY...THE WORLD'S MESSED UP, RIGHT?
"CRUMBLING ECONOMY... NATURAL DISASTERS... WEAPONS OF MASS DESTRUCTION...TELEVISED BAKING COMPETITIONS..."
SHE... BIT ME!
BIT ME!
KINKY.
"SURELY, THESE ARE THE END TIMES.

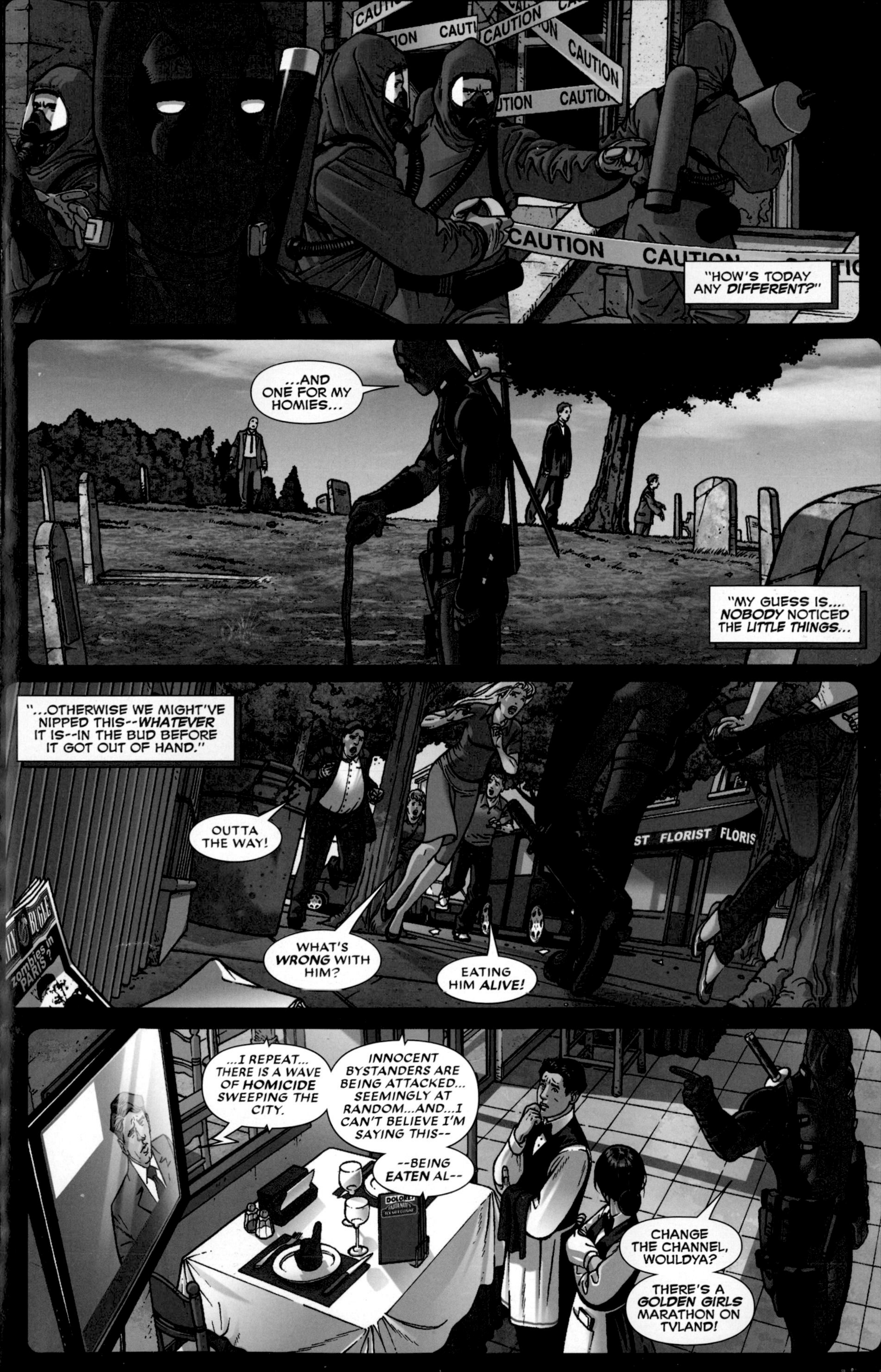
CAUTION
"HOW'S TODAY ANY *DIFFERENT?*"
...AND ONE FOR MY HOMIES...
"MY GUESS IS... *NOBODY* NOTICED THE *LITTLE THINGS*...
"...OTHERWISE WE MIGHT'VE NIPPED THIS--*WHATEVER* IT IS--IN THE BUD BEFORE IT GOT OUT OF HAND."
OUTTA THE WAY!
FLORIST FLORIST
WHAT'S *WRONG* WITH HIM?
EATING HIM *ALIVE!*
BUGLE
ZOMBIES IN PARIS?
...I REPEAT... THERE IS A WAVE OF *HOMICIDE* SWEEPING THE CITY.
INNOCENT BYSTANDERS ARE BEING ATTACKED... SEEMINGLY AT RANDOM...AND...I CAN'T BELIEVE I'M SAYING THIS--
--BEING *EATEN* AL--
CHANGE THE CHANNEL, WOULDYA?
THERE'S A *GOLDEN GIRLS* MARATHON ON TVLAND!

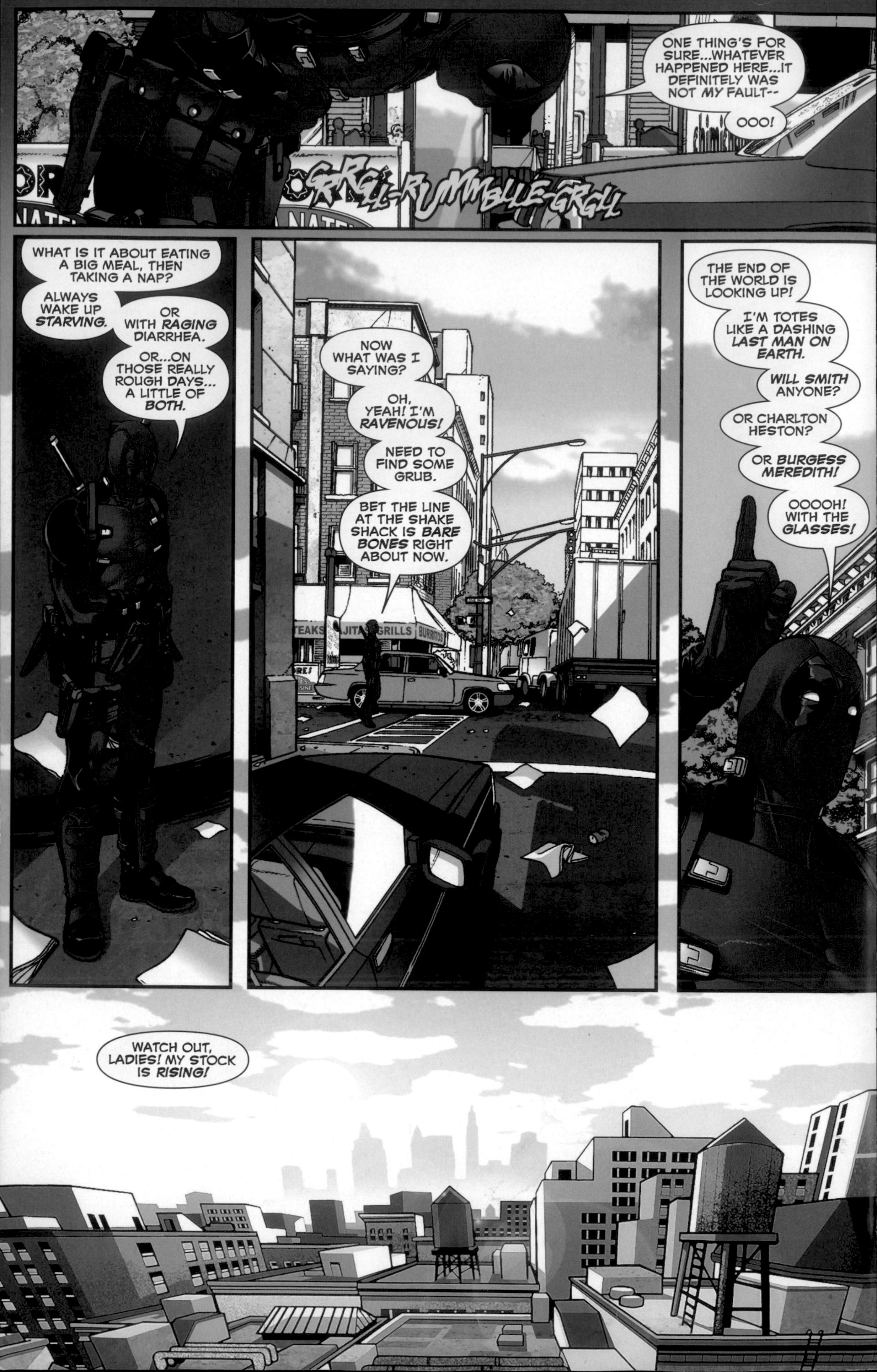

ONE THING'S FOR SURE...WHATEVER HAPPENED HERE...IT DEFINITELY WAS NOT MY FAULT--
OOO!
GRGL-RUMMBLLE-GRGL
WHAT IS IT ABOUT EATING A BIG MEAL, THEN TAKING A NAP?
ALWAYS WAKE UP STARVING.
OR WITH RAGING DIARRHEA.
OR...ON THOSE REALLY ROUGH DAYS... A LITTLE OF BOTH.
NOW WHAT WAS I SAYING?
OH, YEAH! I'M RAVENOUS!
NEED TO FIND SOME GRUB.
BET THE LINE AT THE SHAKE SHACK IS BARE BONES RIGHT ABOUT NOW.
STEAKS
FAJITAS
GRILLS
BURRITOS
THE END OF THE WORLD IS LOOKING UP!
I'M TOTES LIKE A DASHING LAST MAN ON EARTH.
WILL SMITH ANYONE?
OR CHARLTON HESTON?
OR BURGESS MEREDITH!
OOOOH! WITH THE GLASSES!
WATCH OUT, LADIES! MY STOCK IS RISING!

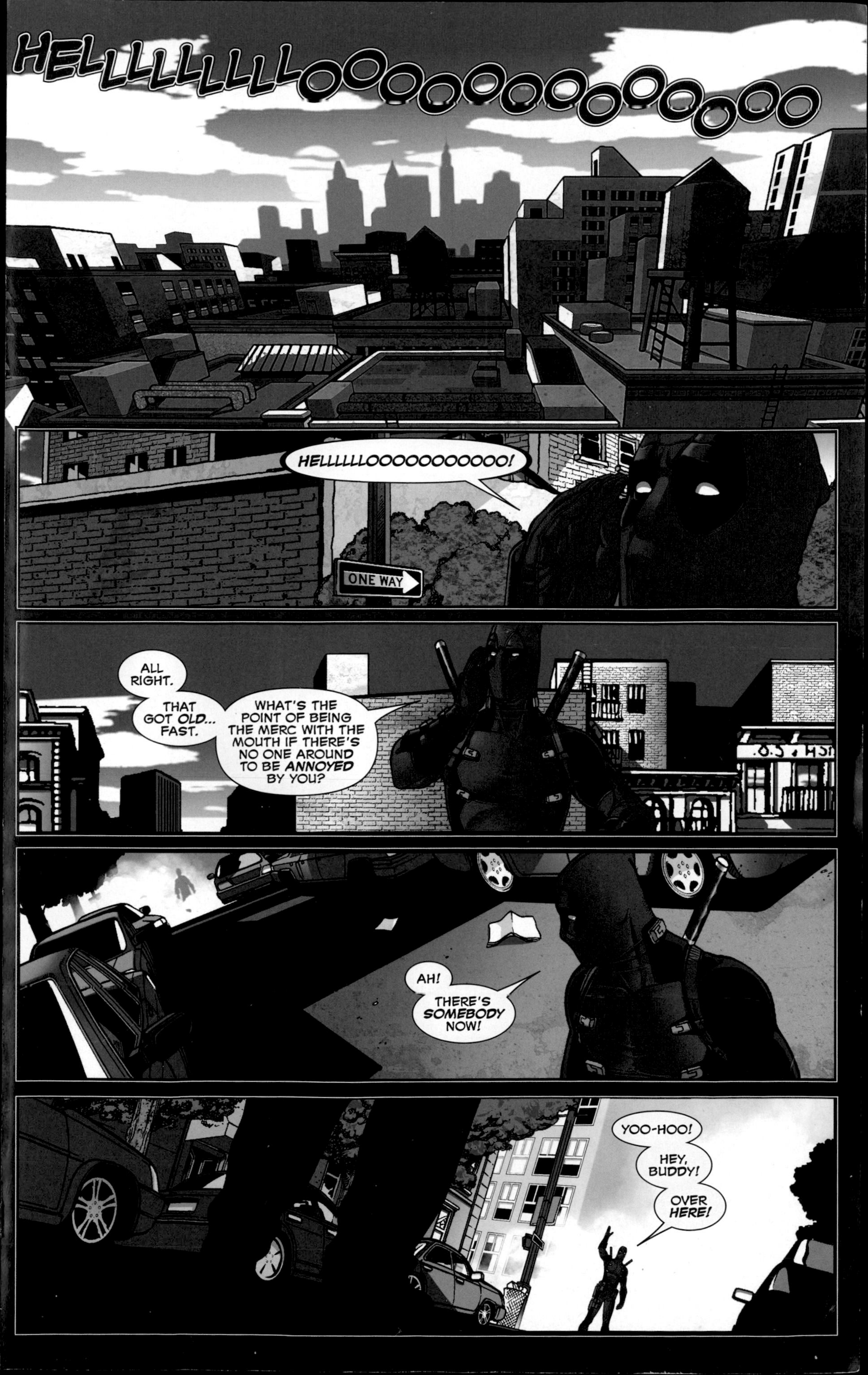
HELLLLLLLLLLOOOOOOOOOOOOOOO
HELLLLLLLOOOOOOOOOOOO!
ONE WAY
ALL RIGHT.
THAT GOT OLD... FAST.
WHAT'S THE POINT OF BEING THE MERC WITH THE MOUTH IF THERE'S NO ONE AROUND TO BE ANNOYED BY YOU?
AH!
THERE'S SOMEBODY NOW!
YOO-HOO!
HEY, BUDDY!
OVER HERE!

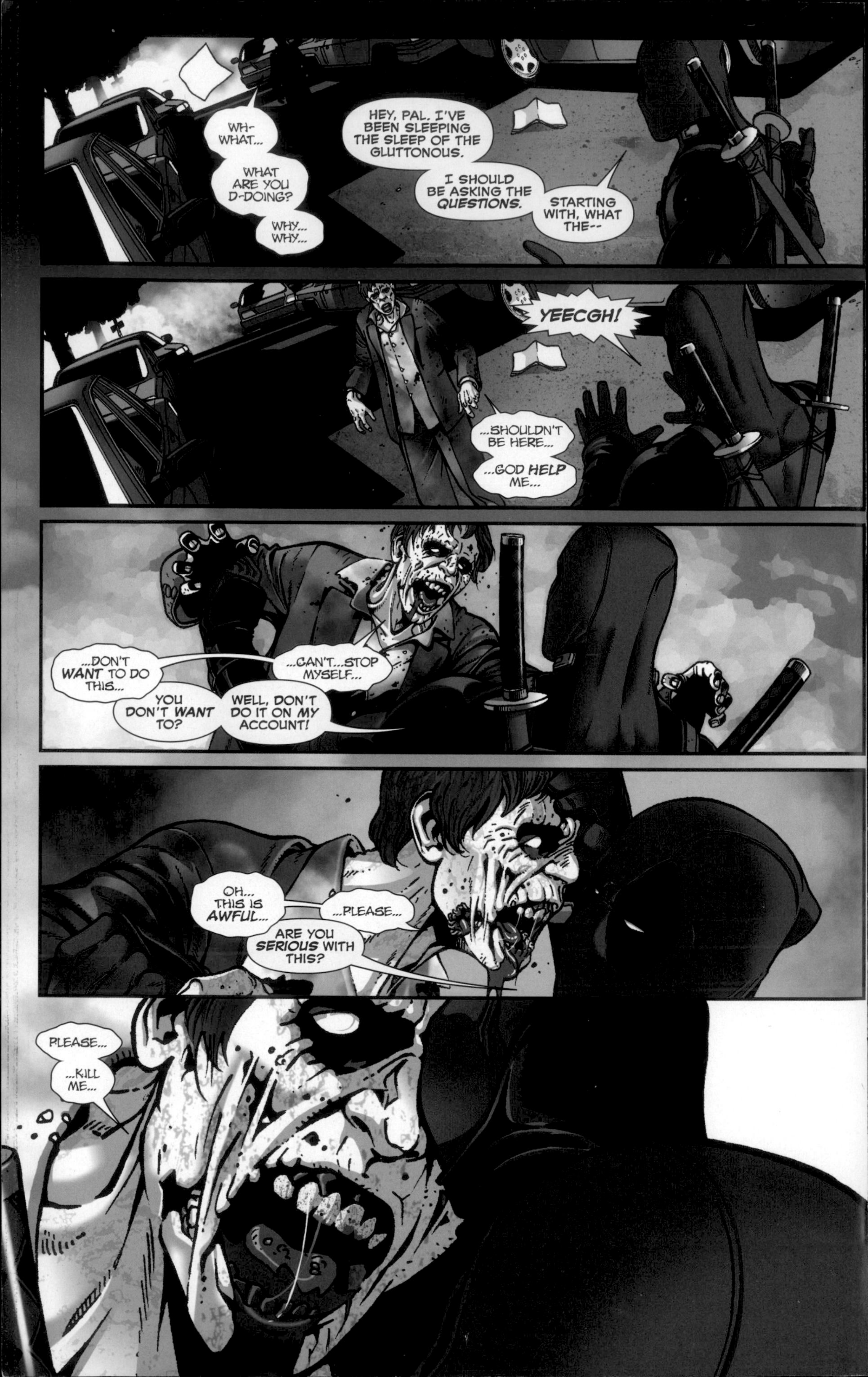
WH-WHAT...
WHAT ARE YOU D-DOING?
WHY... WHY...
HEY, PAL. I'VE BEEN SLEEPING THE SLEEP OF THE GLUTTONOUS.
I SHOULD BE ASKING THE *QUESTIONS.*
STARTING WITH, WHAT THE--
YEECGH!
...SHOULDN'T BE HERE...
...GOD *HELP* ME...
...DON'T *WANT* TO DO THIS...
...CAN'T...STOP MYSELF...
YOU DON'T *WANT* TO?
WELL, DON'T DO IT ON *MY* ACCOUNT!
OH... THIS IS *AWFUL...*
...PLEASE...
ARE YOU *SERIOUS* WITH THIS?
PLEASE...
...KILL ME...

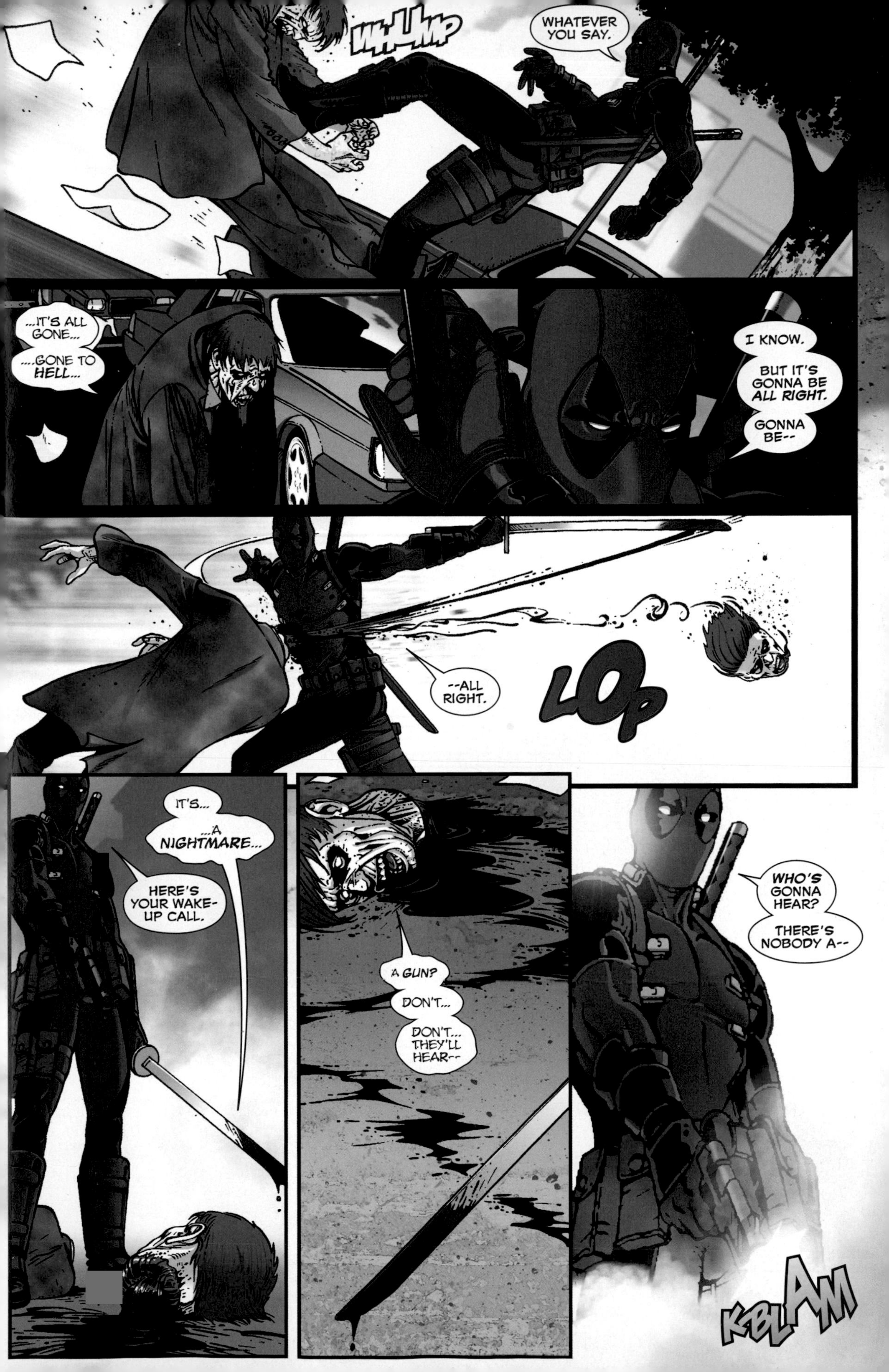
WHUMP
WHATEVER YOU SAY.
...IT'S ALL GONE...
...GONE TO HELL...
I KNOW.
BUT IT'S GONNA BE ALL RIGHT.
GONNA BE--
--ALL RIGHT.
LOP
IT'S...
...A NIGHTMARE...
HERE'S YOUR WAKE-UP CALL.
A GUN?
DON'T...
DON'T... THEY'LL HEAR--
WHO'S GONNA HEAR?
THERE'S NOBODY A--
KBLAM

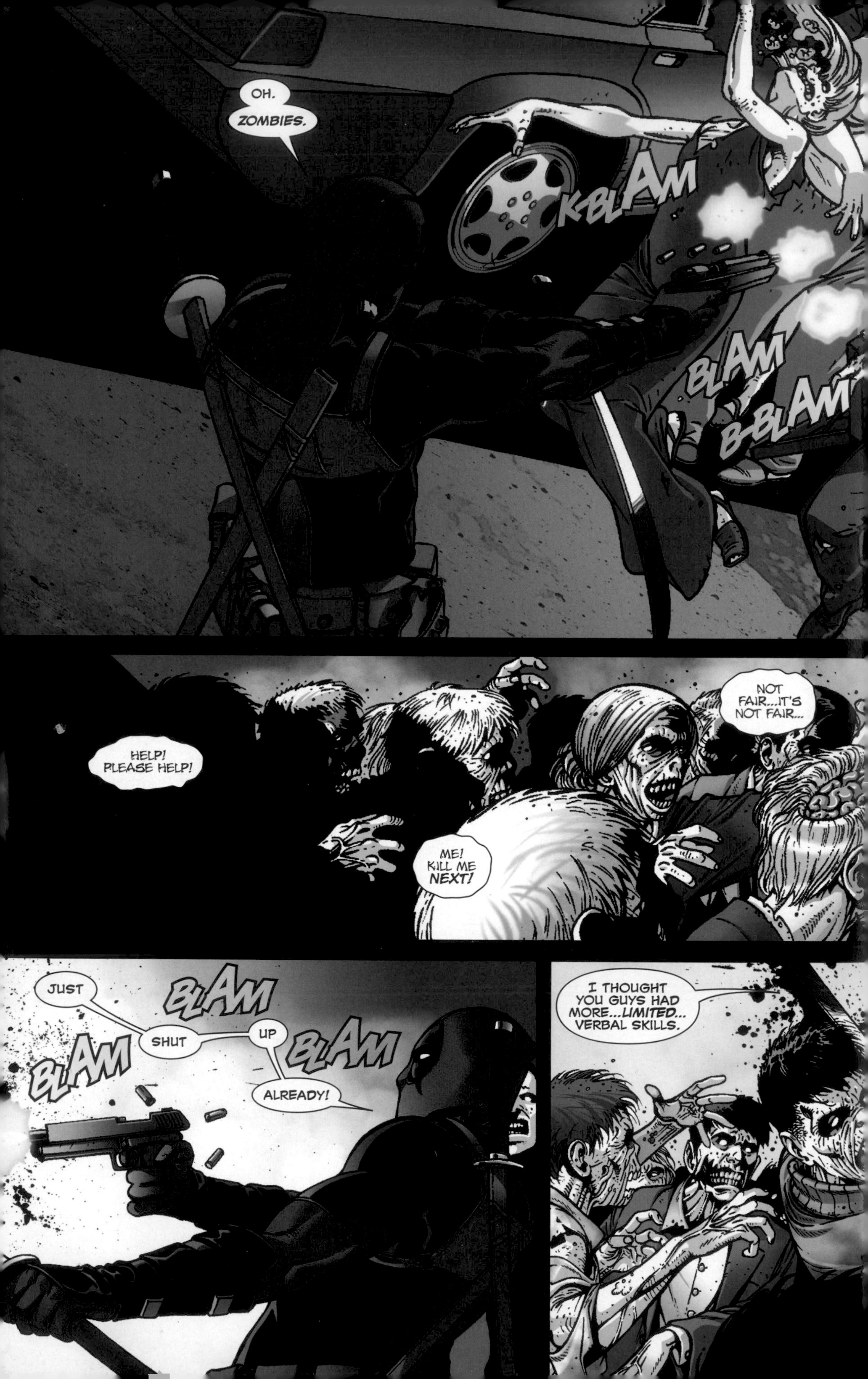
OH.
ZOMBIES.
K-BLAM
BLAM
B-BLAM
HELP! PLEASE HELP!
NOT FAIR...IT'S NOT FAIR...
ME! KILL ME NEXT!
JUST
SHUT
UP
ALREADY!
BLAM
BLAM
BLAM
I THOUGHT YOU GUYS HAD MORE...LIMITED... VERBAL SKILLS.

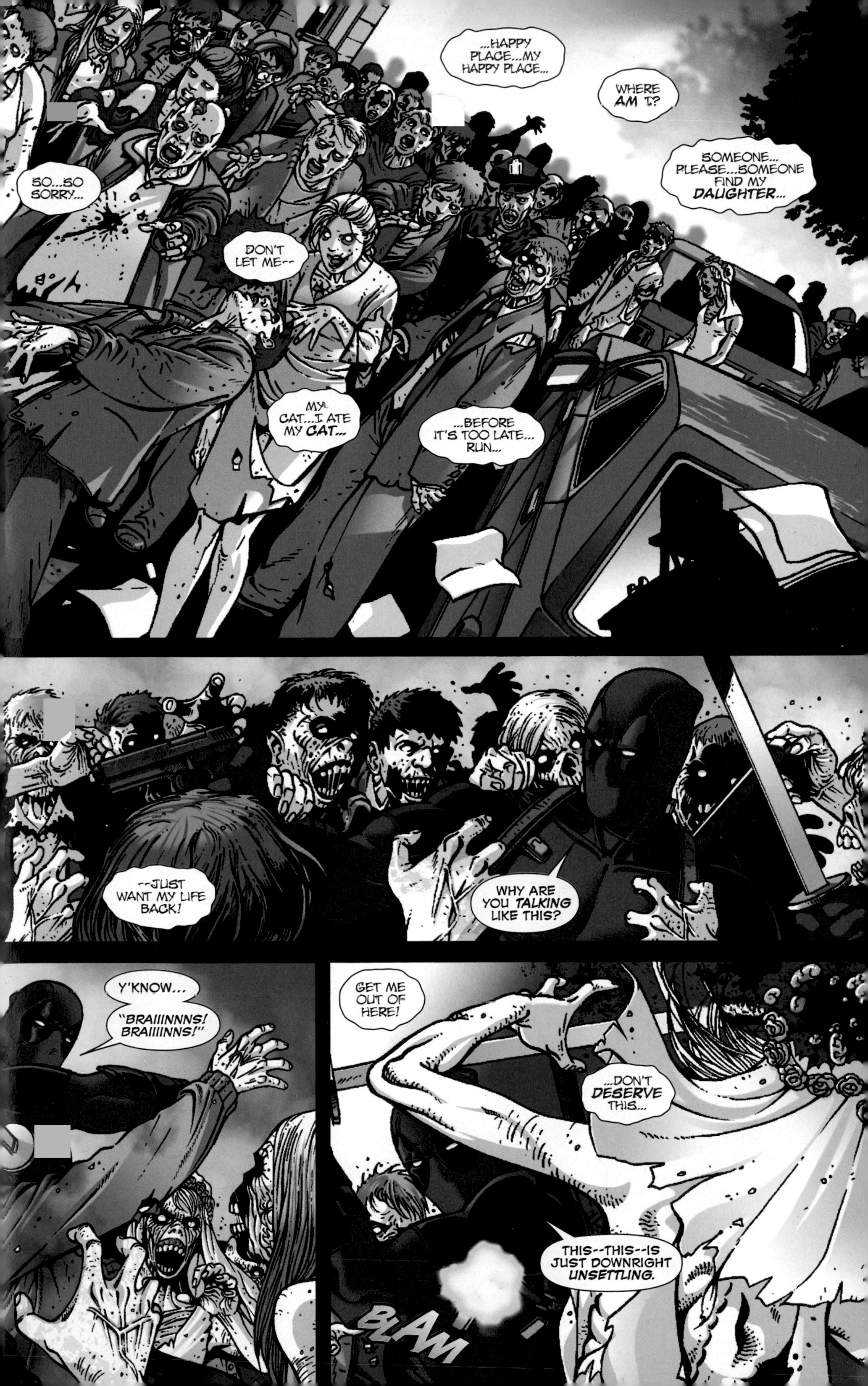
...HAPPY PLACE...MY HAPPY PLACE...
WHERE AM I?
SOMEONE... PLEASE...SOMEONE FIND MY DAUGHTER...
SO...SO SORRY...
DON'T LET ME--
MY CAT...I ATE MY CAT...
...BEFORE IT'S TOO LATE... RUN...
--JUST WANT MY LIFE BACK!
WHY ARE YOU TALKING LIKE THIS?
Y'KNOW...
"BRAIIINNNS! BRAIIIINNS!"
GET ME OUT OF HERE!
...DON'T DESERVE THIS...
THIS--THIS--IS JUST DOWNRIGHT UNSETTLING.
BLAM

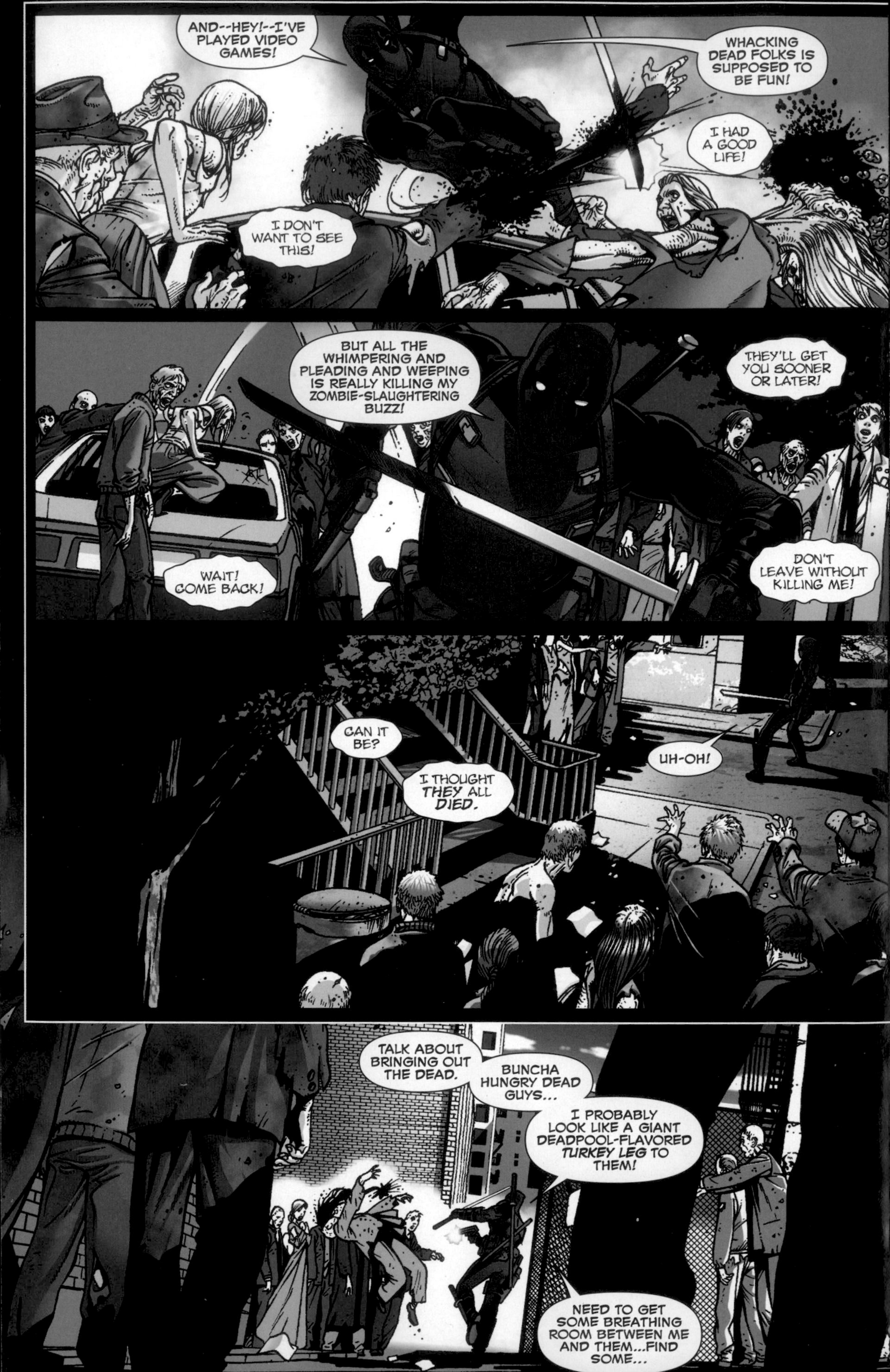
AND--HEY!--I'VE PLAYED VIDEO GAMES!
WHACKING DEAD FOLKS IS SUPPOSED TO BE FUN!
I HAD A GOOD LIFE!
I DON'T WANT TO SEE THIS!
BUT ALL THE WHIMPERING AND PLEADING AND WEEPING IS REALLY KILLING MY ZOMBIE-SLAUGHTERING BUZZ!
THEY'LL GET YOU SOONER OR LATER!
WAIT! COME BACK!
DON'T LEAVE WITHOUT KILLING ME!
CAN IT BE?
I THOUGHT THEY ALL DIED.
UH-OH!
TALK ABOUT BRINGING OUT THE DEAD.
BUNCHA HUNGRY DEAD GUYS...
I PROBABLY LOOK LIKE A GIANT DEADPOOL-FLAVORED TURKEY LEG TO THEM!
NEED TO GET SOME BREATHING ROOM BETWEEN ME AND THEM...FIND SOME...

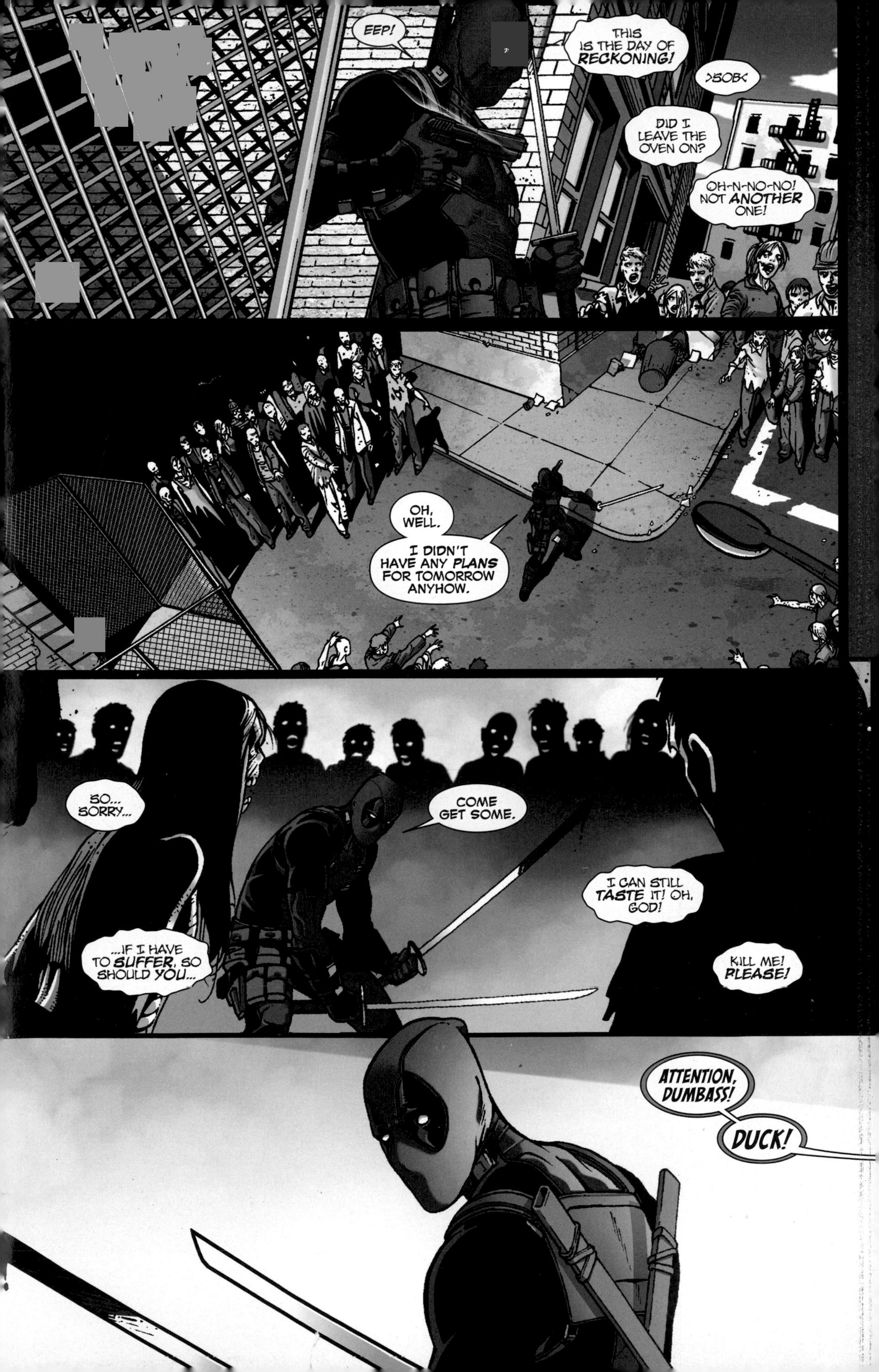

EEP!
THIS IS THE DAY OF RECKONING!
>SOB<
DID I LEAVE THE OVEN ON?
OH-N-NO-NO! NOT ANOTHER ONE!
OH, WELL.
I DIDN'T HAVE ANY PLANS FOR TOMORROW ANYHOW.
SO... SORRY...
COME GET SOME.
...IF I HAVE TO SUFFER, SO SHOULD YOU...
I CAN STILL TASTE IT! OH, GOD!
KILL ME! PLEASE!
ATTENTION, DUMBASS!
DUCK!

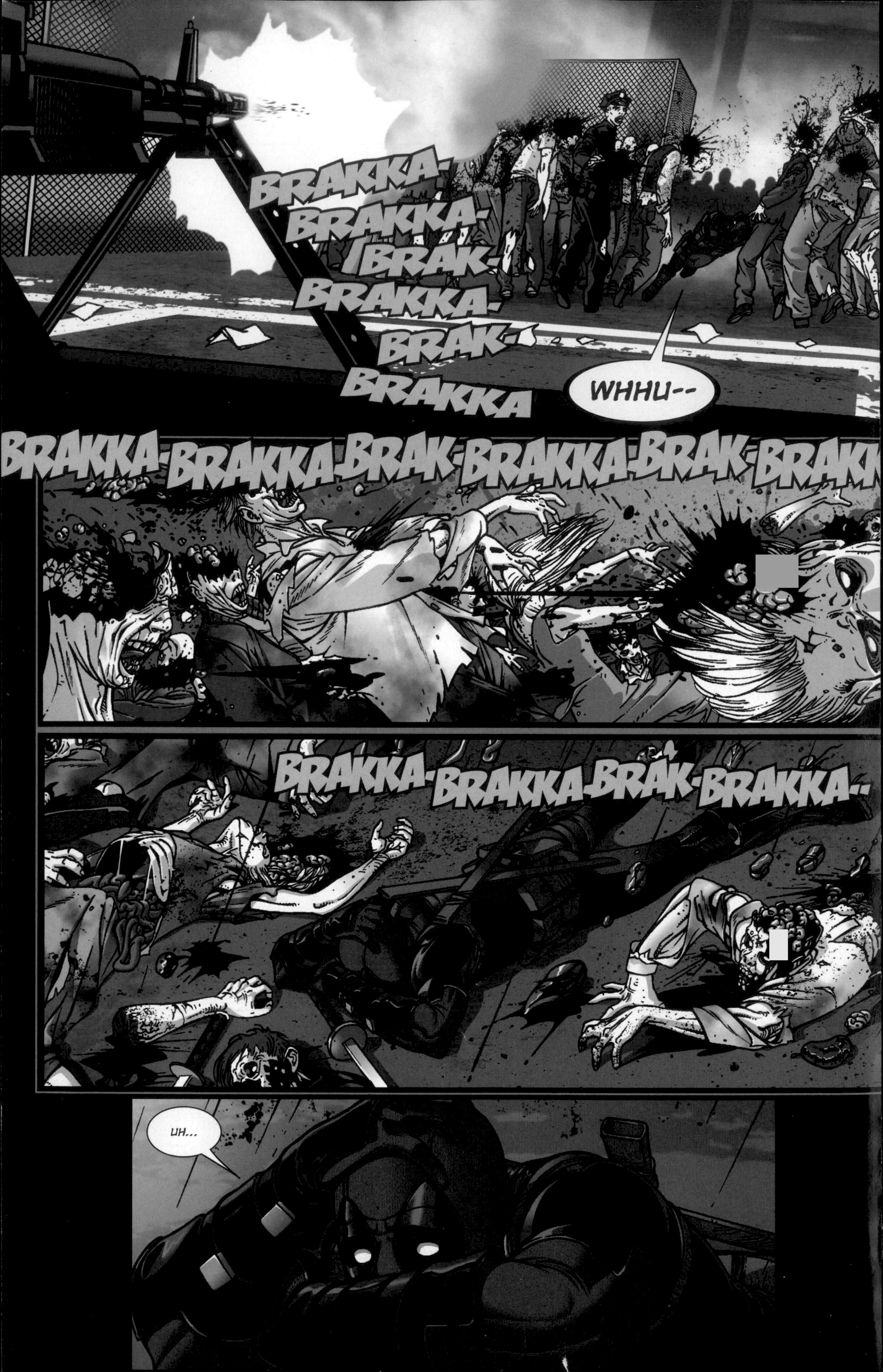
BRAKKA-
BRAKKA-
BRAK-
BRAKKA-
BRAK-
BRAKKA
WHHU--
BRAKKA-BRAKKA-BRAK-BRAKKA-BRAK-BRAKK
BRAKKA-BRAKKA-BRAK-BRAKKA-
UH...

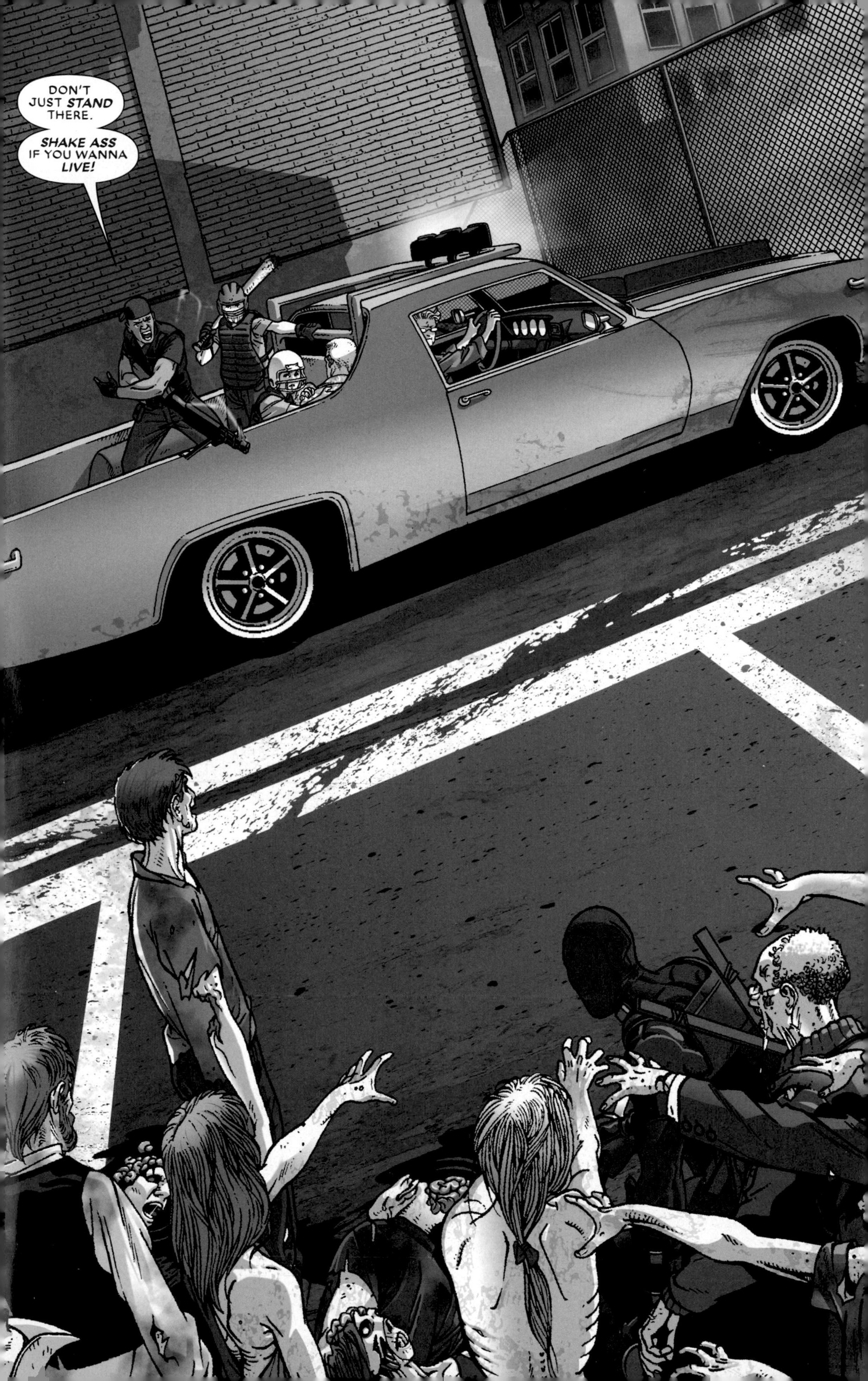
DON'T JUST STAND THERE.
SHAKE ASS IF YOU WANNA LIVE!

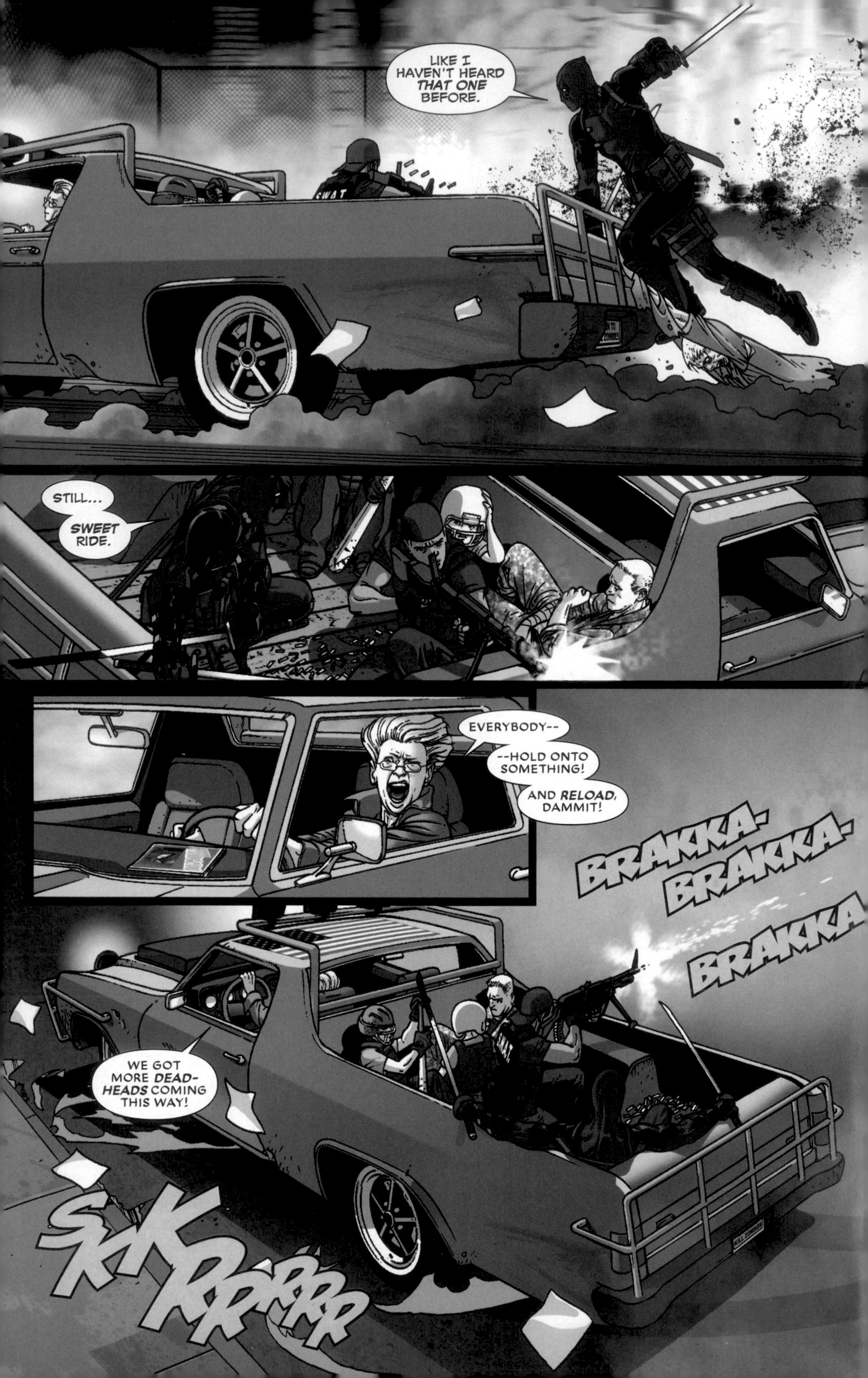
LIKE I HAVEN'T HEARD THAT ONE BEFORE.
STILL... SWEET RIDE.
EVERYBODY--
--HOLD ONTO SOMETHING!
AND RELOAD, DAMMIT!
BRAKKA-
BRAKKA-
BRAKKA
WE GOT MORE DEAD-HEADS COMING THIS WAY!
SKKRRRRR

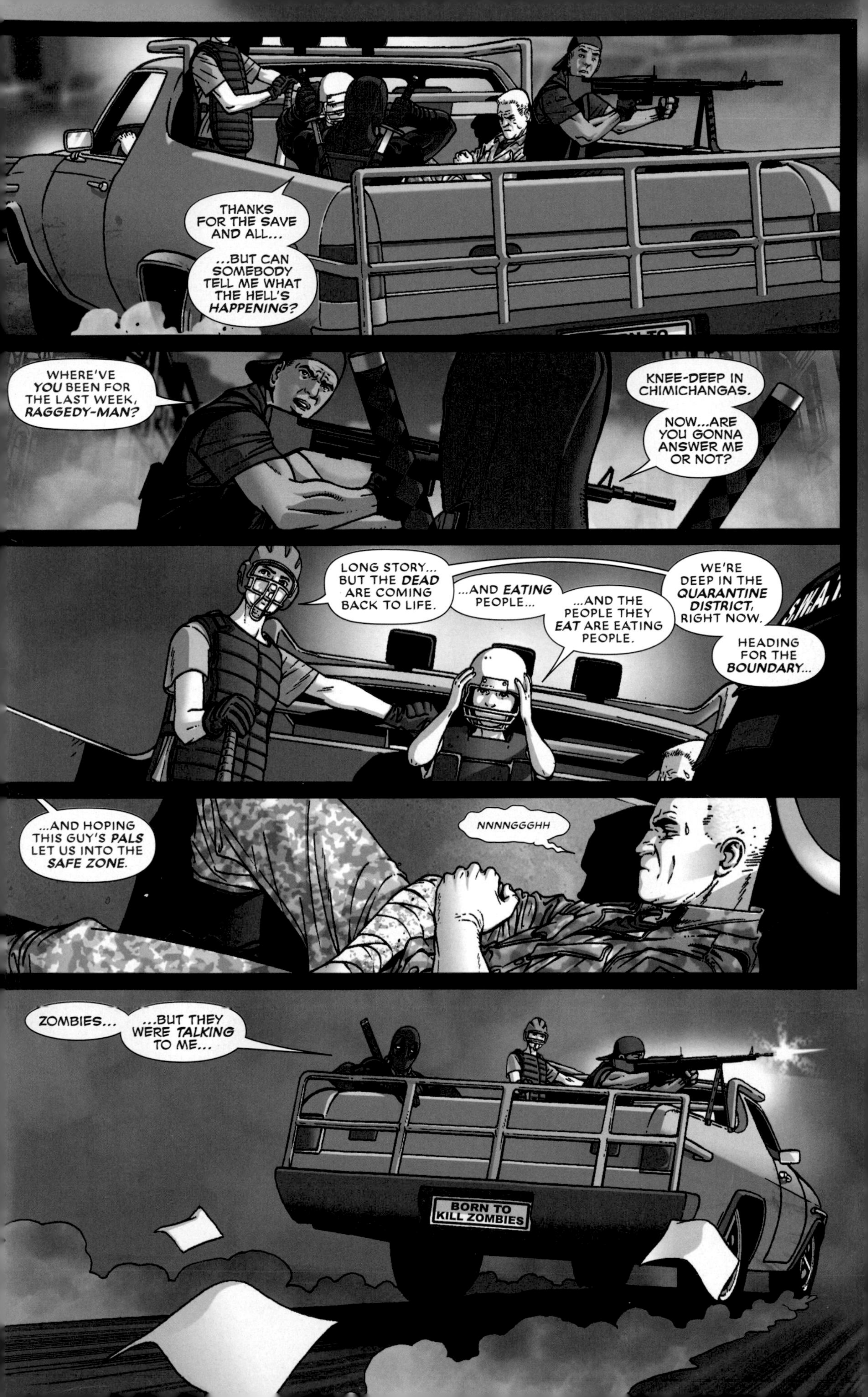
THANKS FOR THE SAVE AND ALL...
...BUT CAN SOMEBODY TELL ME WHAT THE HELL'S HAPPENING?
WHERE'VE YOU BEEN FOR THE LAST WEEK, RAGGEDY-MAN?
KNEE-DEEP IN CHIMICHANGAS.
NOW...ARE YOU GONNA ANSWER ME OR NOT?
LONG STORY... BUT THE DEAD ARE COMING BACK TO LIFE.
...AND EATING PEOPLE...
...AND THE PEOPLE THEY EAT ARE EATING PEOPLE.
WE'RE DEEP IN THE QUARANTINE DISTRICT, RIGHT NOW.
HEADING FOR THE BOUNDARY...
...AND HOPING THIS GUY'S PALS LET US INTO THE SAFE ZONE.
NNNNGGGHH
ZOMBIES...
...BUT THEY WERE TALKING TO ME...
BORN TO KILL ZOMBIES

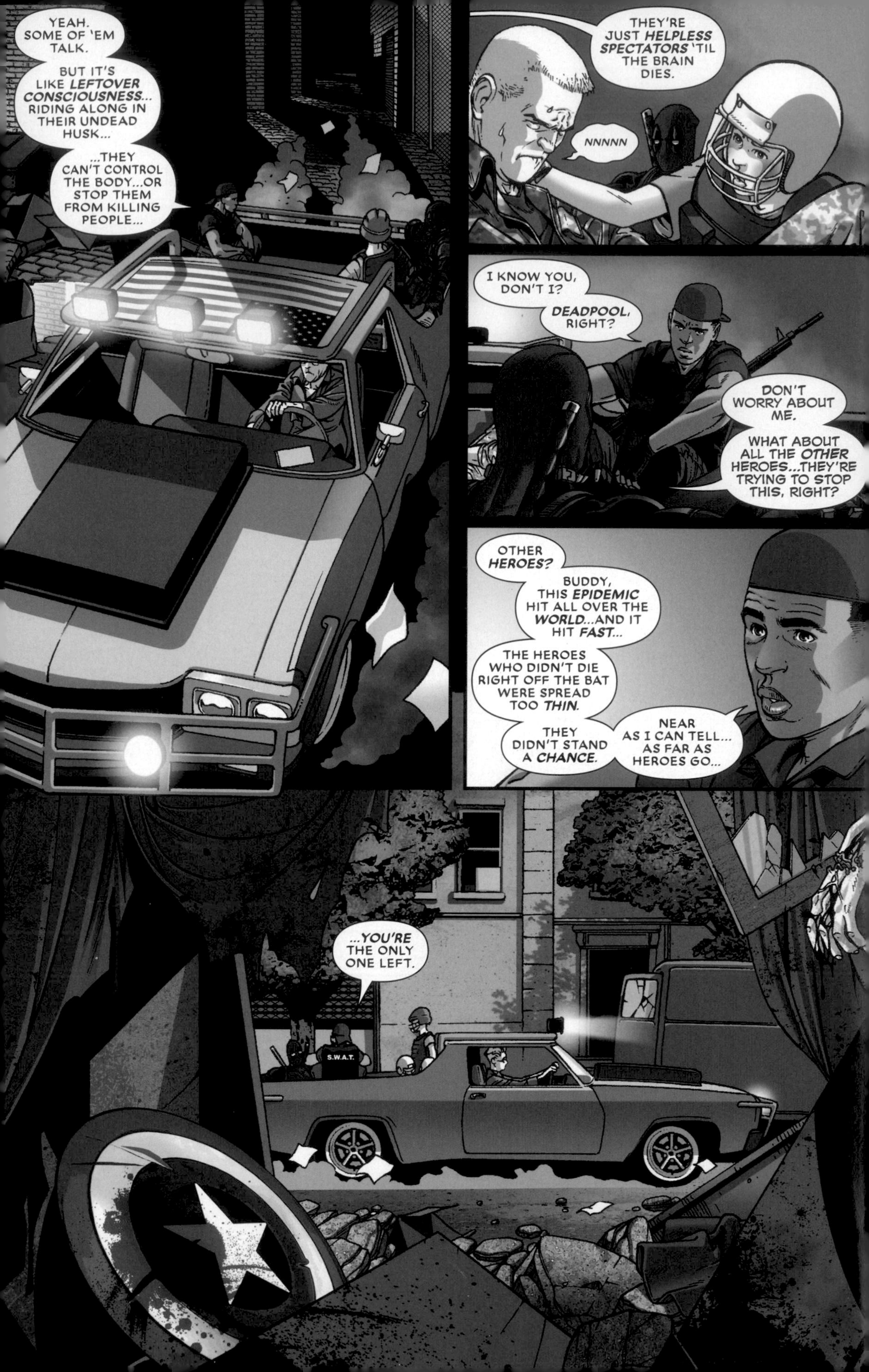
YEAH. SOME OF 'EM TALK.
BUT IT'S LIKE LEFTOVER CONSCIOUSNESS... RIDING ALONG IN THEIR UNDEAD HUSK...
...THEY CAN'T CONTROL THE BODY...OR STOP THEM FROM KILLING PEOPLE...
THEY'RE JUST HELPLESS SPECTATORS 'TIL THE BRAIN DIES.
NNNNN
I KNOW YOU, DON'T I?
DEADPOOL, RIGHT?
DON'T WORRY ABOUT ME.
WHAT ABOUT ALL THE OTHER HEROES...THEY'RE TRYING TO STOP THIS, RIGHT?
OTHER HEROES?
BUDDY, THIS EPIDEMIC HIT ALL OVER THE WORLD...AND IT HIT FAST...
THE HEROES WHO DIDN'T DIE RIGHT OFF THE BAT WERE SPREAD TOO THIN.
THEY DIDN'T STAND A CHANCE.
NEAR AS I CAN TELL... AS FAR AS HEROES GO...
...YOU'RE THE ONLY ONE LEFT.
S.W.A.T.

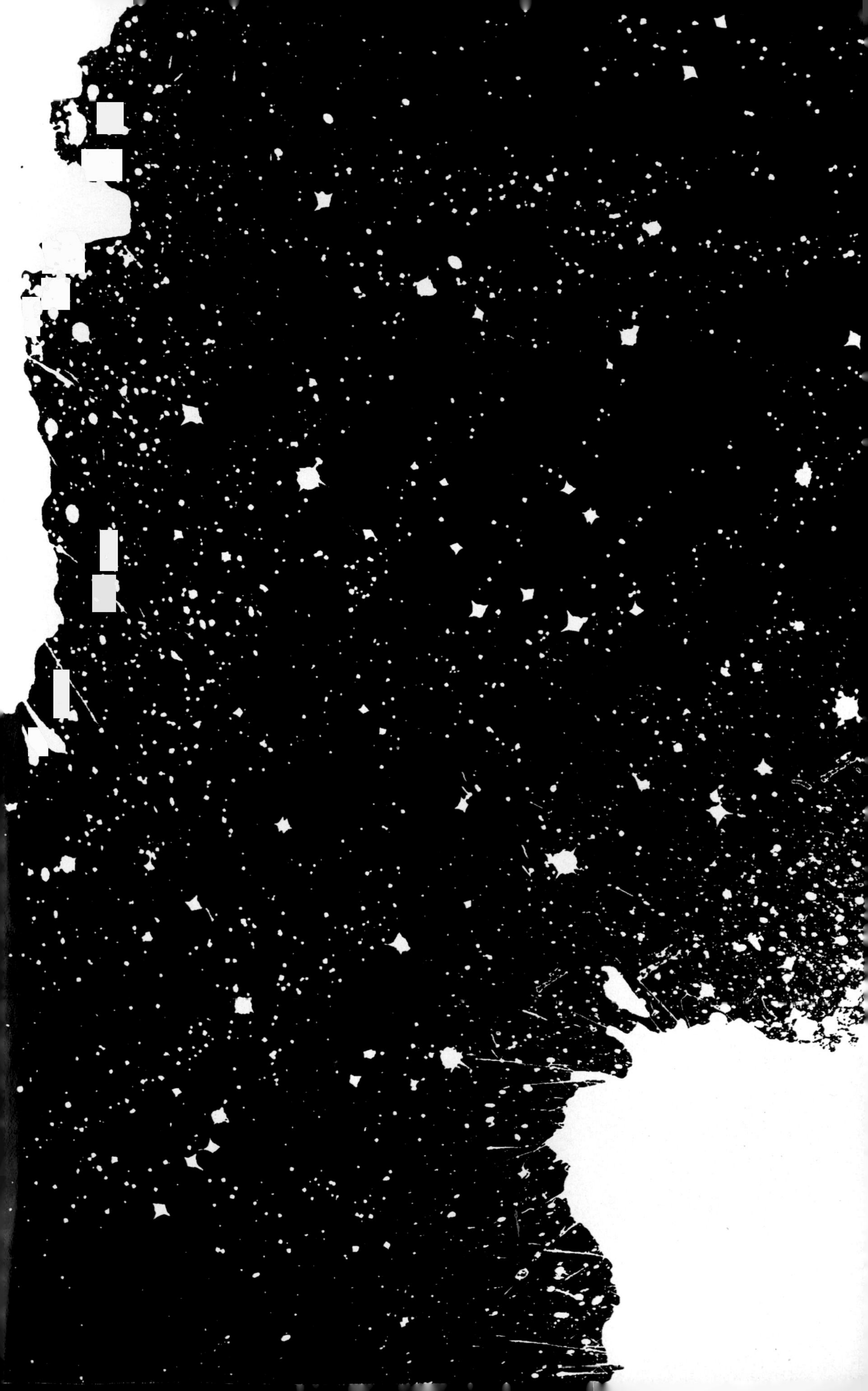

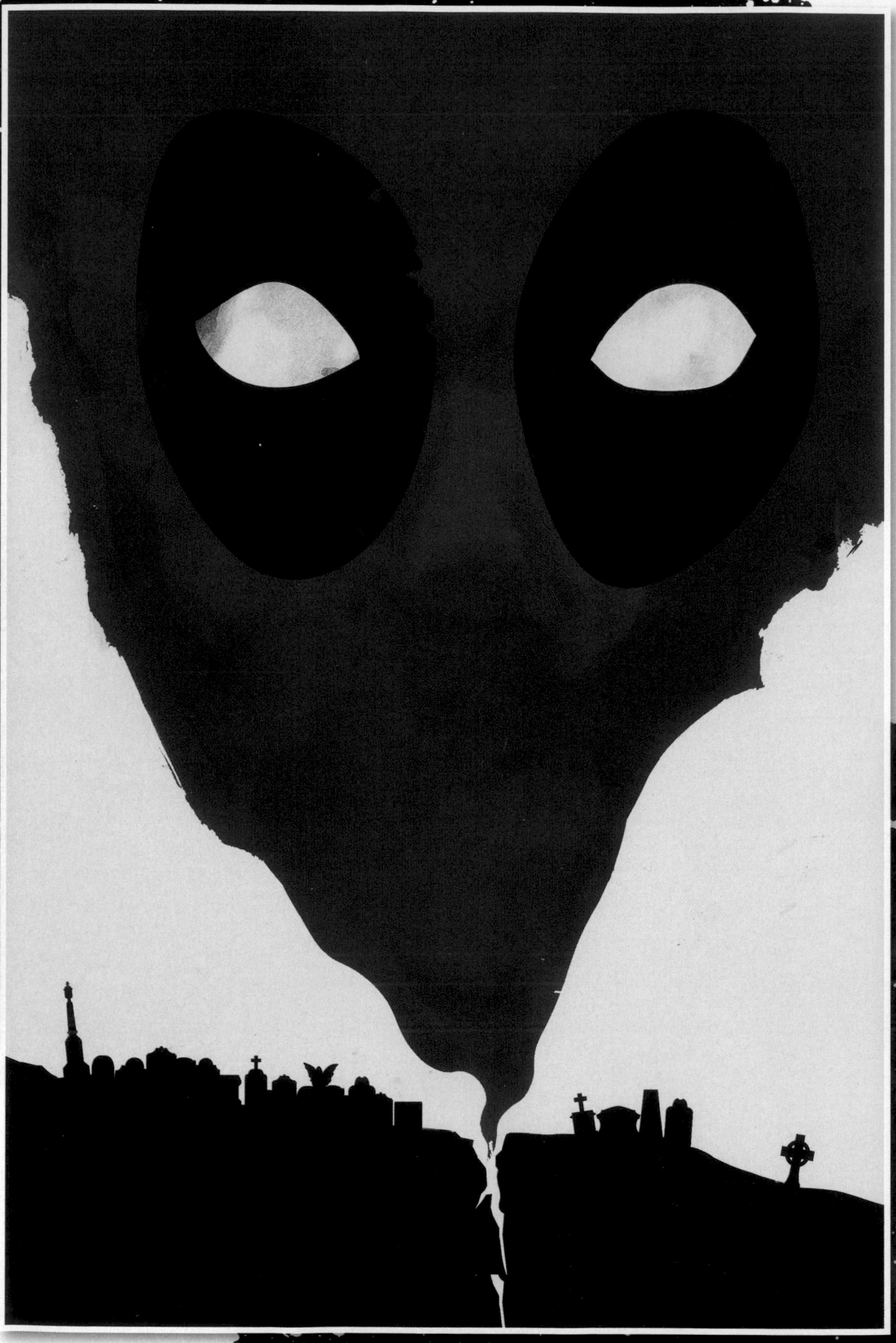

#2

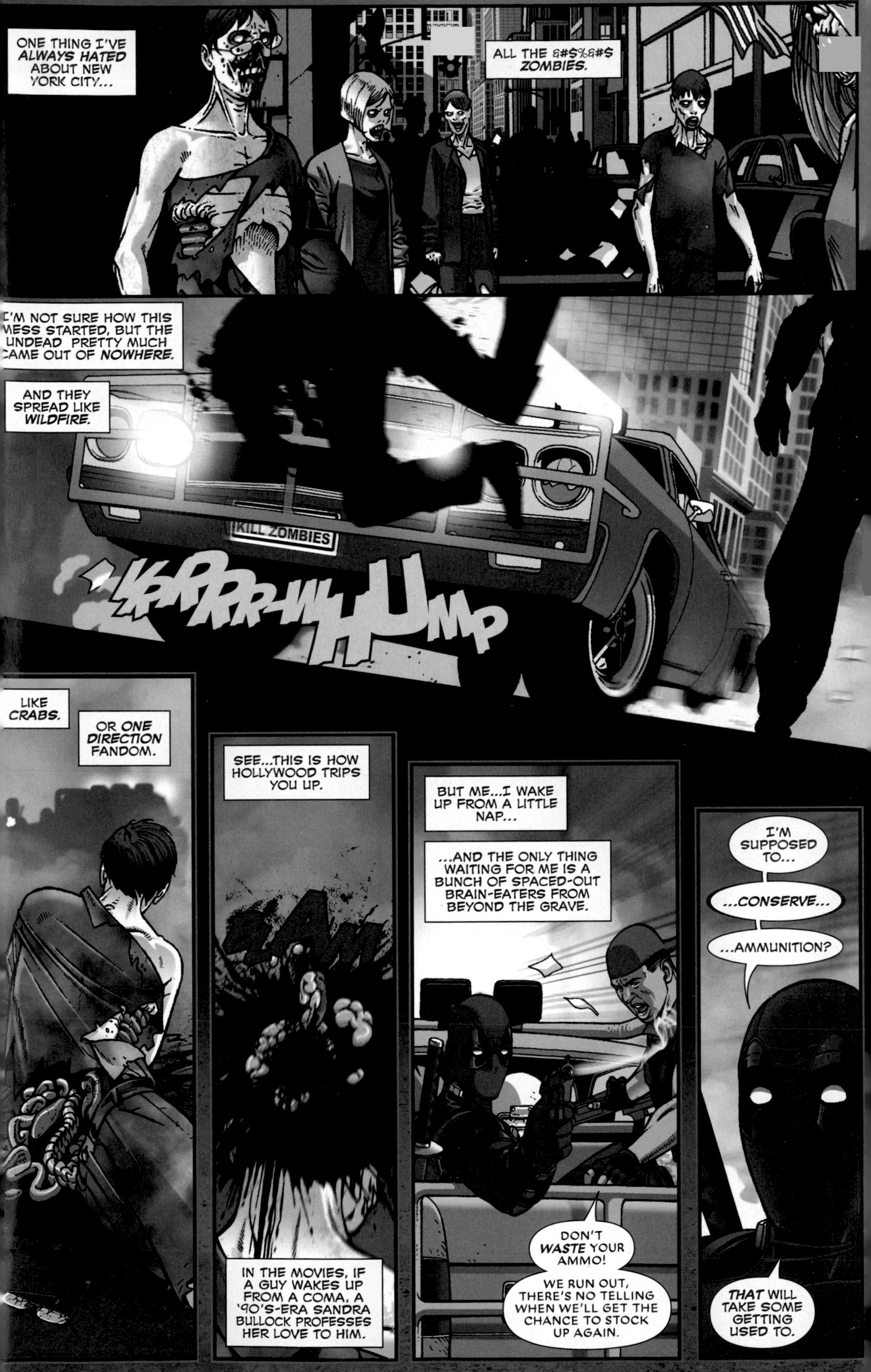
ONE THING I'VE ALWAYS HATED ABOUT NEW YORK CITY...
ALL THE &#$%&#$ ZOMBIES.
I'M NOT SURE HOW THIS MESS STARTED, BUT THE UNDEAD PRETTY MUCH CAME OUT OF NOWHERE.
AND THEY SPREAD LIKE WILDFIRE.
KILL ZOMBIES
KRRRR-WHUMP
LIKE CRABS.
OR ONE DIRECTION FANDOM.
SEE...THIS IS HOW HOLLYWOOD TRIPS YOU UP.
IN THE MOVIES, IF A GUY WAKES UP FROM A COMA, A '90'S-ERA SANDRA BULLOCK PROFESSES HER LOVE TO HIM.
BUT ME...I WAKE UP FROM A LITTLE NAP...
...AND THE ONLY THING WAITING FOR ME IS A BUNCH OF SPACED-OUT BRAIN-EATERS FROM BEYOND THE GRAVE.
DON'T WASTE YOUR AMMO!
WE RUN OUT, THERE'S NO TELLING WHEN WE'LL GET THE CHANCE TO STOCK UP AGAIN.
I'M SUPPOSED TO...
...CONSERVE...
...AMMUNITION?
THAT WILL TAKE SOME GETTING USED TO.

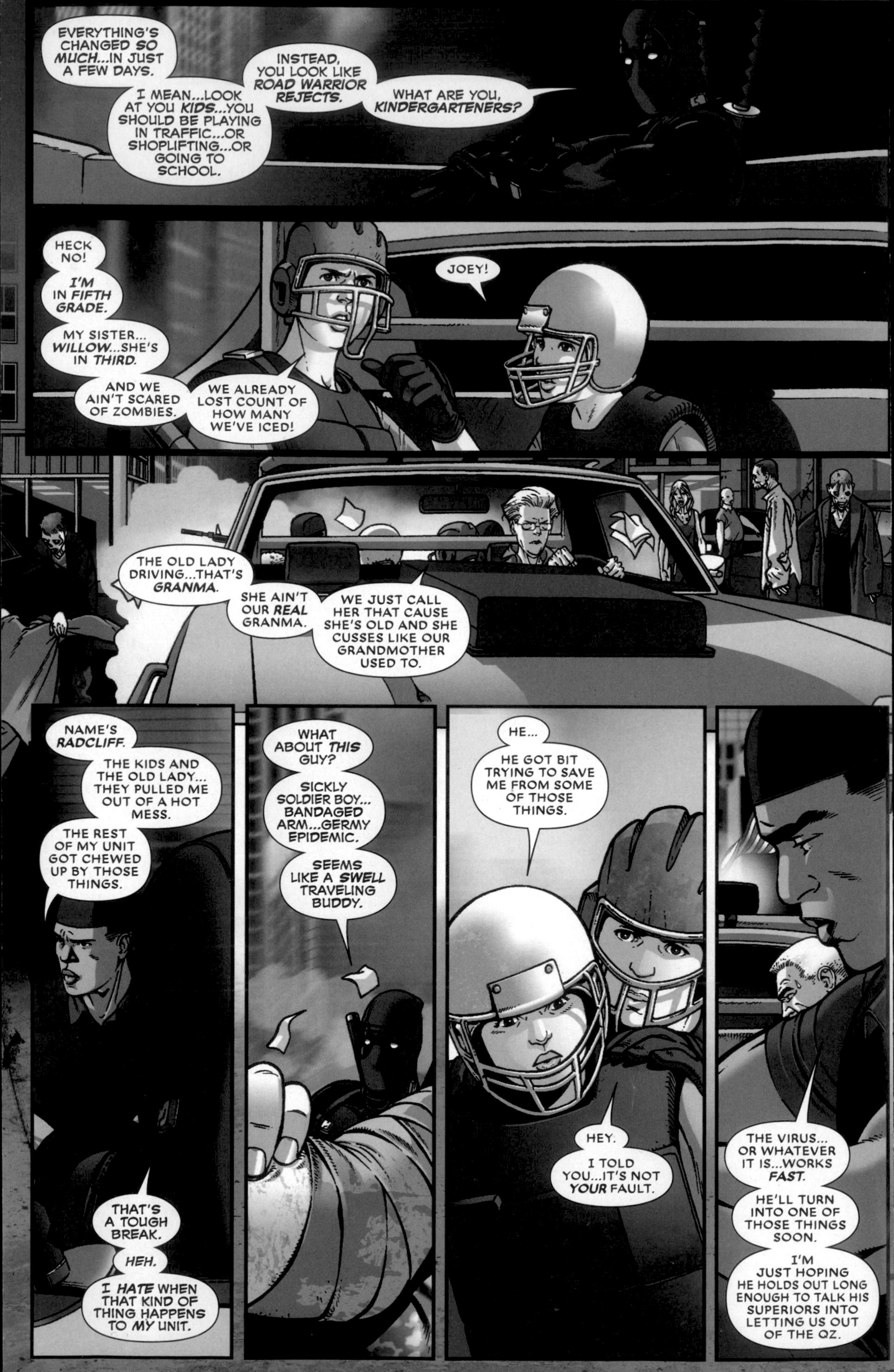

EVERYTHING'S CHANGED SO MUCH...IN JUST A FEW DAYS.
I MEAN...LOOK AT YOU KIDS...YOU SHOULD BE PLAYING IN TRAFFIC...OR SHOPLIFTING...OR GOING TO SCHOOL.
INSTEAD, YOU LOOK LIKE ROAD WARRIOR REJECTS.
WHAT ARE YOU, KINDERGARTENERS?
HECK NO!
I'M IN FIFTH GRADE.
MY SISTER... WILLOW...SHE'S IN THIRD.
AND WE AIN'T SCARED OF ZOMBIES.
WE ALREADY LOST COUNT OF HOW MANY WE'VE ICED!
JOEY!
THE OLD LADY DRIVING...THAT'S GRANMA.
SHE AIN'T OUR REAL GRANMA.
WE JUST CALL HER THAT CAUSE SHE'S OLD AND SHE CUSSES LIKE OUR GRANDMOTHER USED TO.
NAME'S RADCLIFF.
THE KIDS AND THE OLD LADY... THEY PULLED ME OUT OF A HOT MESS.
THE REST OF MY UNIT GOT CHEWED UP BY THOSE THINGS.
THAT'S A TOUGH BREAK.
HEH.
I HATE WHEN THAT KIND OF THING HAPPENS TO MY UNIT.
WHAT ABOUT THIS GUY?
SICKLY SOLDIER BOY... BANDAGED ARM...GERMY EPIDEMIC.
SEEMS LIKE A SWELL TRAVELING BUDDY.
HE...
HE GOT BIT TRYING TO SAVE ME FROM SOME OF THOSE THINGS.
HEY.
I TOLD YOU...IT'S NOT YOUR FAULT.
THE VIRUS... OR WHATEVER IT IS...WORKS FAST.
HE'LL TURN INTO ONE OF THOSE THINGS SOON.
I'M JUST HOPING HE HOLDS OUT LONG ENOUGH TO TALK HIS SUPERIORS INTO LETTING US OUT OF THE QZ.

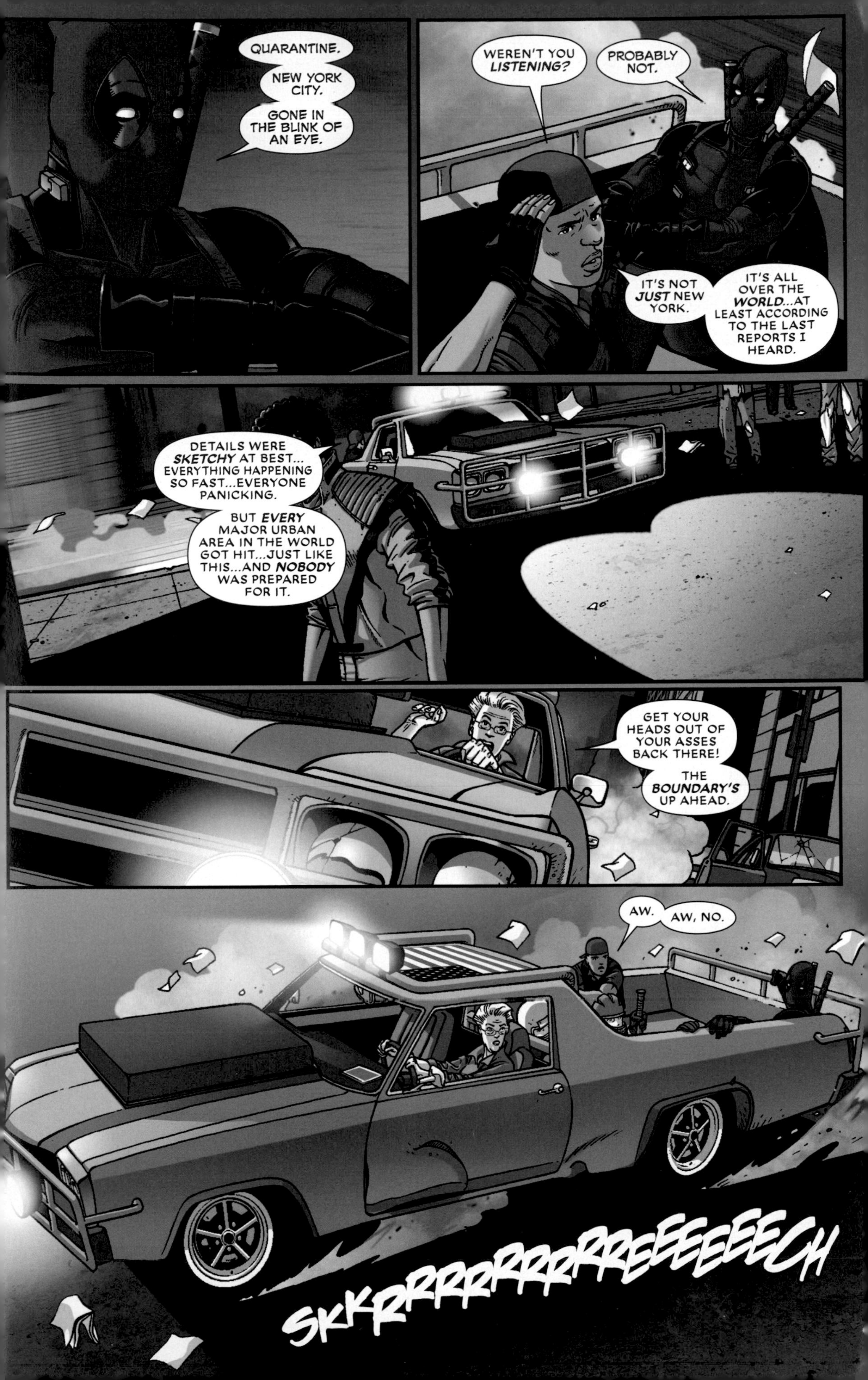
QUARANTINE.
NEW YORK CITY.
GONE IN THE BLINK OF AN EYE.
WEREN'T YOU LISTENING?
PROBABLY NOT.
IT'S NOT JUST NEW YORK.
IT'S ALL OVER THE WORLD...AT LEAST ACCORDING TO THE LAST REPORTS I HEARD.
DETAILS WERE SKETCHY AT BEST... EVERYTHING HAPPENING SO FAST...EVERYONE PANICKING.
BUT EVERY MAJOR URBAN AREA IN THE WORLD GOT HIT...JUST LIKE THIS...AND NOBODY WAS PREPARED FOR IT.
GET YOUR HEADS OUT OF YOUR ASSES BACK THERE!
THE BOUNDARY'S UP AHEAD.
AW.
AW, NO.
SKKRRRRRRRRREEEEEEECH

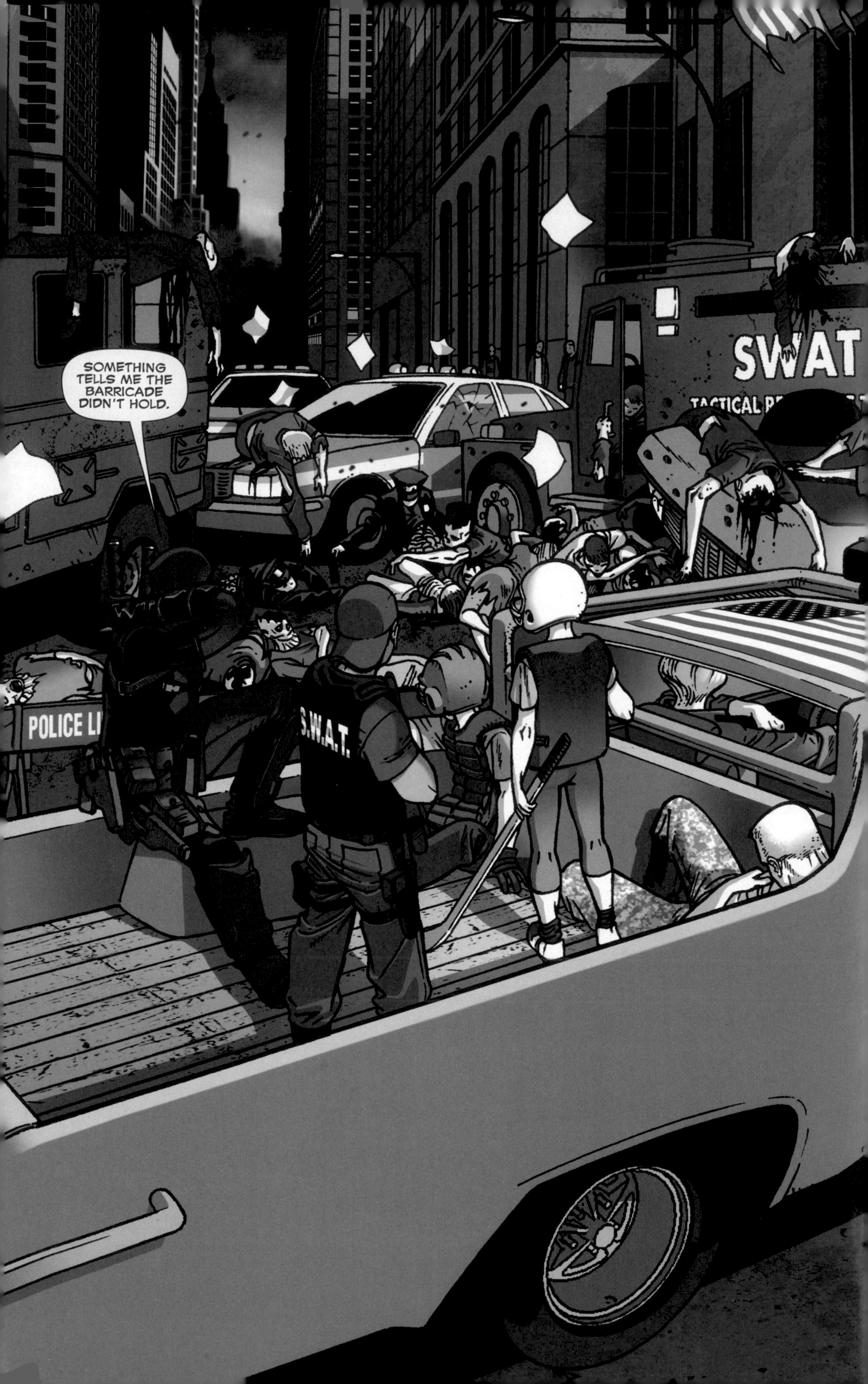
SOMETHING TELLS ME THE BARRICADE DIDN'T HOLD.
SWAT
S.W.A.T.
POLICE LI

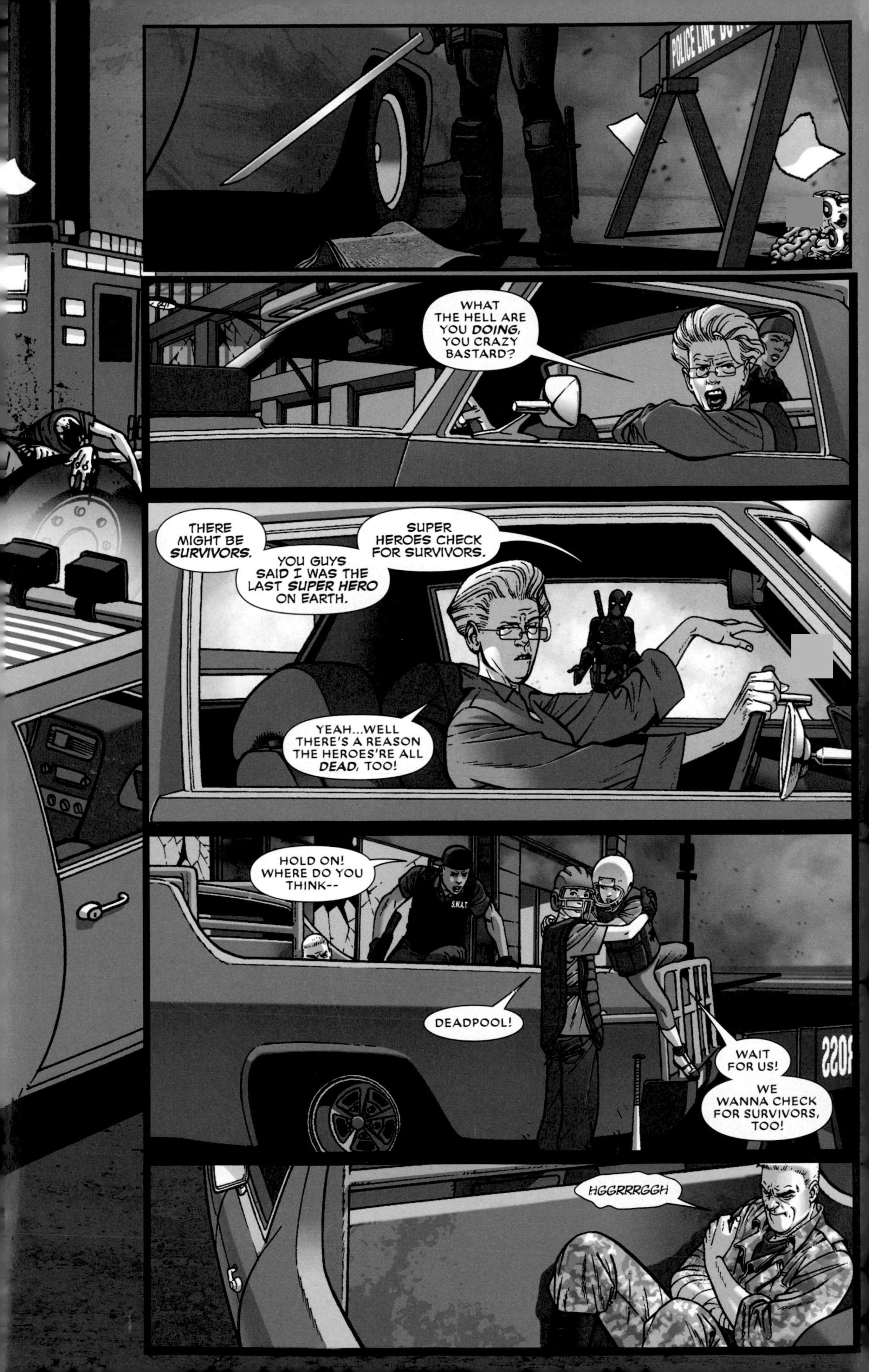
POLICE LINE DO N
WHAT THE HELL ARE YOU DOING, YOU CRAZY BASTARD?
THERE MIGHT BE SURVIVORS.
SUPER HEROES CHECK FOR SURVIVORS.
YOU GUYS SAID I WAS THE LAST SUPER HERO ON EARTH.
YEAH...WELL THERE'S A REASON THE HEROES'RE ALL DEAD, TOO!
HOLD ON! WHERE DO YOU THINK--
S.W.A.T.
DEADPOOL!
WAIT FOR US!
WE WANNA CHECK FOR SURVIVORS, TOO!
HGGRRRGGH

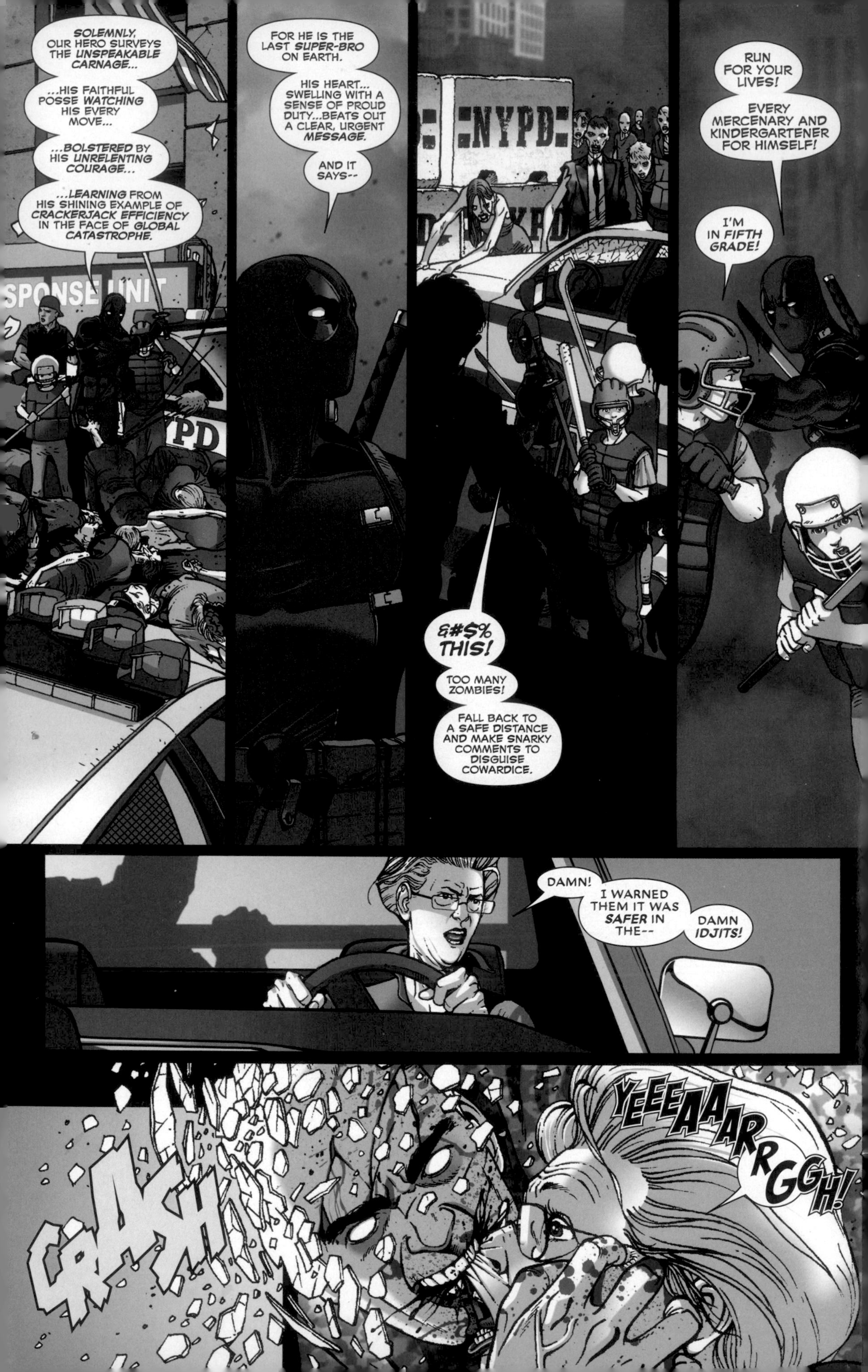
SOLEMNLY, OUR HERO SURVEYS THE UNSPEAKABLE CARNAGE...
...HIS FAITHFUL POSSE WATCHING HIS EVERY MOVE...
...BOLSTERED BY HIS UNRELENTING COURAGE...
...LEARNING FROM HIS SHINING EXAMPLE OF CRACKERJACK EFFICIENCY IN THE FACE OF GLOBAL CATASTROPHE.
SPONSE UNIT
PD
FOR HE IS THE LAST SUPER-BRO ON EARTH.
HIS HEART... SWELLING WITH A SENSE OF PROUD DUTY...BEATS OUT A CLEAR, URGENT MESSAGE.
AND IT SAYS--
NYPD
&#$% THIS!
TOO MANY ZOMBIES!
FALL BACK TO A SAFE DISTANCE AND MAKE SNARKY COMMENTS TO DISGUISE COWARDICE.
RUN FOR YOUR LIVES!
EVERY MERCENARY AND KINDERGARTENER FOR HIMSELF!
I'M IN FIFTH GRADE!
DAMN!
I WARNED THEM IT WAS SAFER IN THE--
DAMN IDJITS!
CRASH
YEEEAAARRGGH!

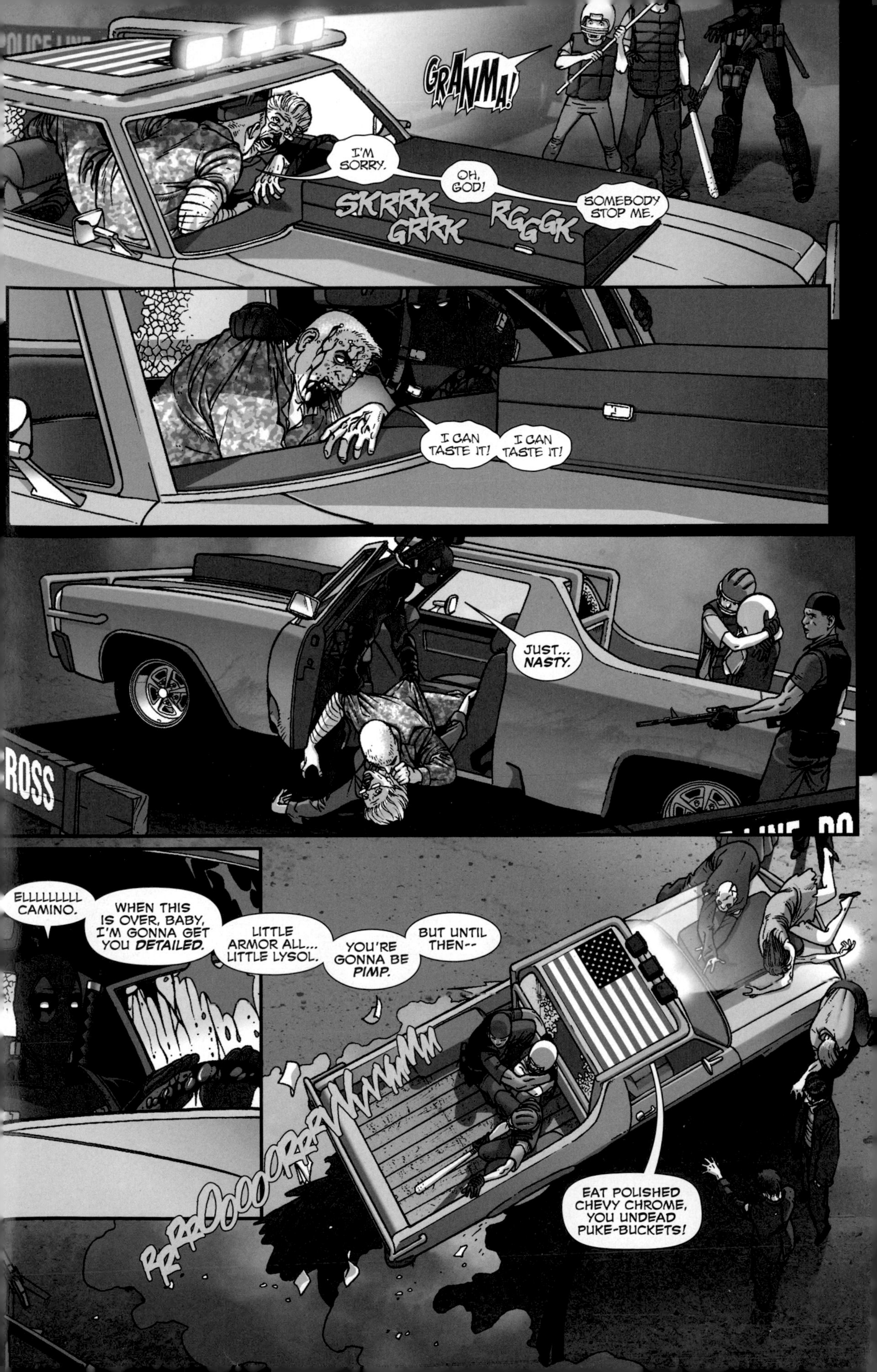
GRANMA!
I'M SORRY.
OH, GOD!
SOMEBODY STOP ME.
SKRRK GRRK
RGGGK
I CAN TASTE IT!
I CAN TASTE IT!
JUST... NASTY.
ROSS
ELLLLLLLLL CAMINO.
WHEN THIS IS OVER, BABY, I'M GONNA GET YOU DETAILED.
LITTLE ARMOR ALL... LITTLE LYSOL.
YOU'RE GONNA BE PIMP.
BUT UNTIL THEN--
RRRROOOOORRRVVVMMMMM
EAT POLISHED CHEVY CHROME, YOU UNDEAD PUKE-BUCKETS!

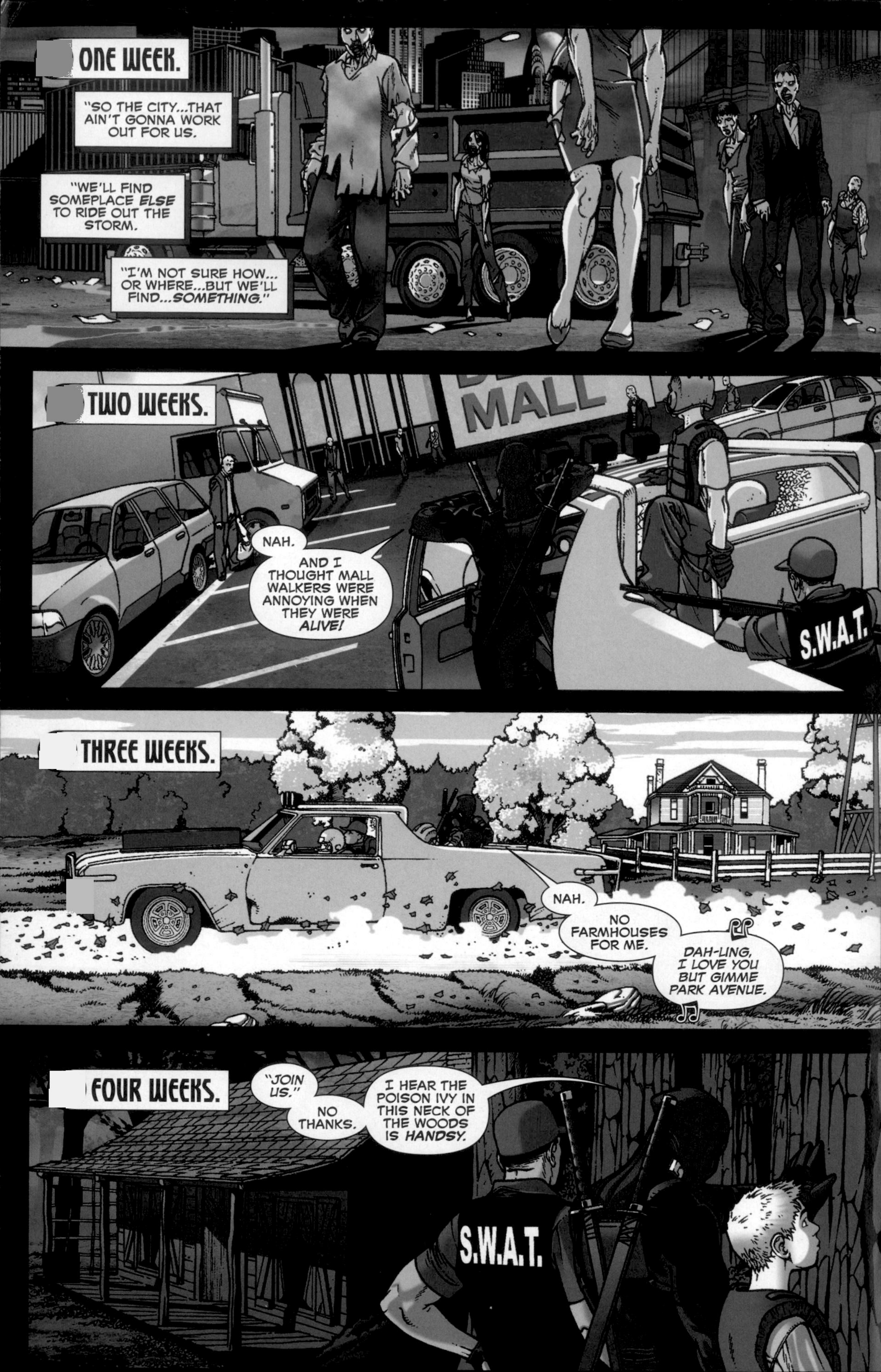
ONE WEEK.
"SO THE CITY...THAT AIN'T GONNA WORK OUT FOR US.
"WE'LL FIND SOMEPLACE *ELSE* TO RIDE OUT THE STORM.
"I'M NOT SURE HOW... OR WHERE...BUT WE'LL FIND...*SOMETHING*."
TWO WEEKS.
MALL
NAH.
AND I THOUGHT MALL WALKERS WERE ANNOYING WHEN THEY WERE *ALIVE!*
S.W.A.T.
THREE WEEKS.
NAH.
NO FARMHOUSES FOR ME.
DAH-LING, I LOVE YOU BUT GIMME PARK AVENUE.
FOUR WEEKS.
"JOIN US."
NO THANKS.
I HEAR THE POISON IVY IN THIS NECK OF THE WOODS IS *HANDSY*.
S.W.A.T.

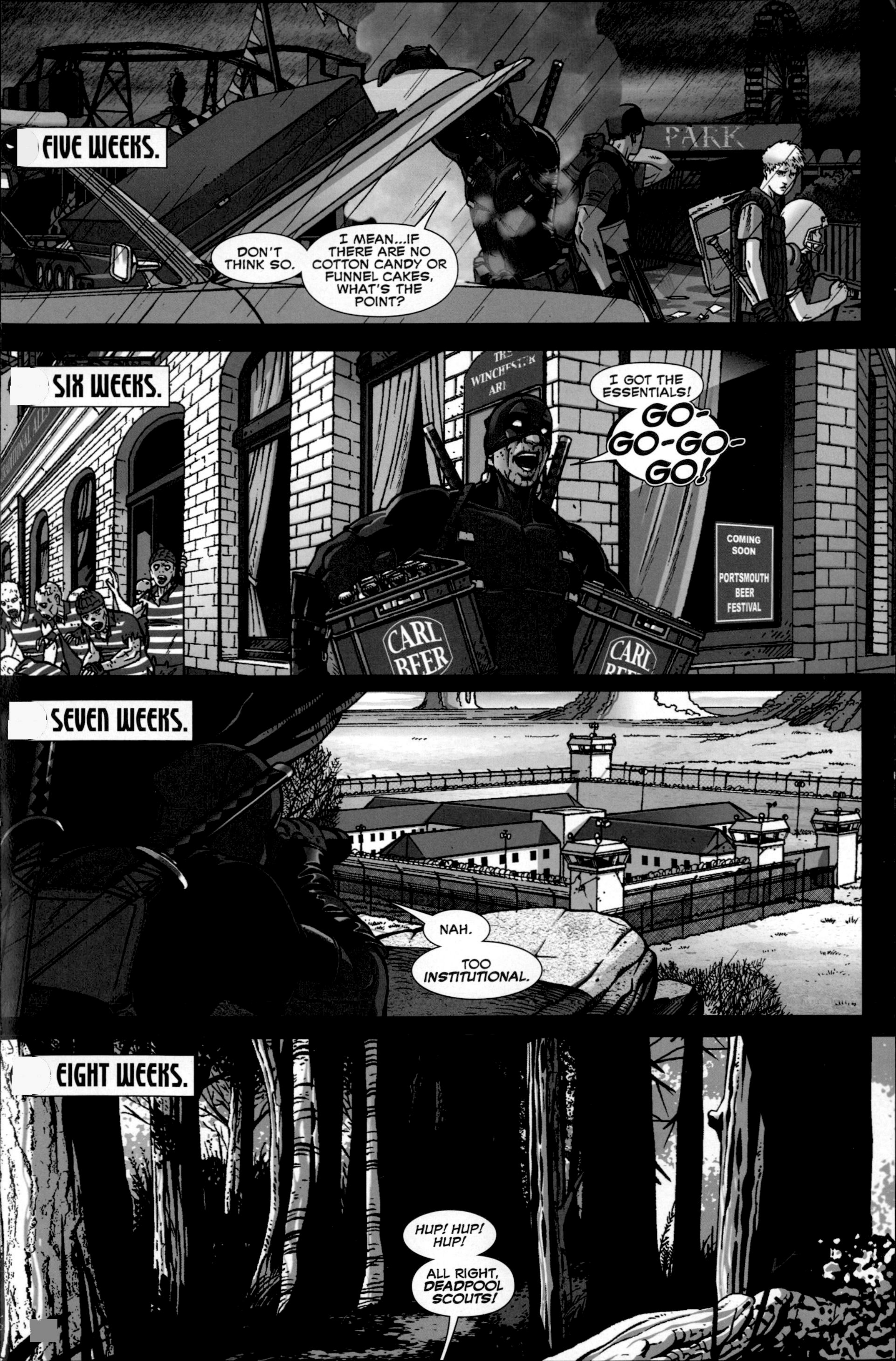
FIVE WEEKS.
PARK
DON'T THINK SO.
I MEAN...IF THERE ARE NO COTTON CANDY OR FUNNEL CAKES, WHAT'S THE POINT?
SIX WEEKS.
THE WINCHESTER ARI
I GOT THE ESSENTIALS!
GO-GO-GO-GO-GO!
COMING SOON PORTSMOUTH BEER FESTIVAL
CARL BEER
SEVEN WEEKS.
NAH.
TOO INSTITUTIONAL.
EIGHT WEEKS.
HUP! HUP! HUP!
ALL RIGHT, DEADPOOL SCOUTS!

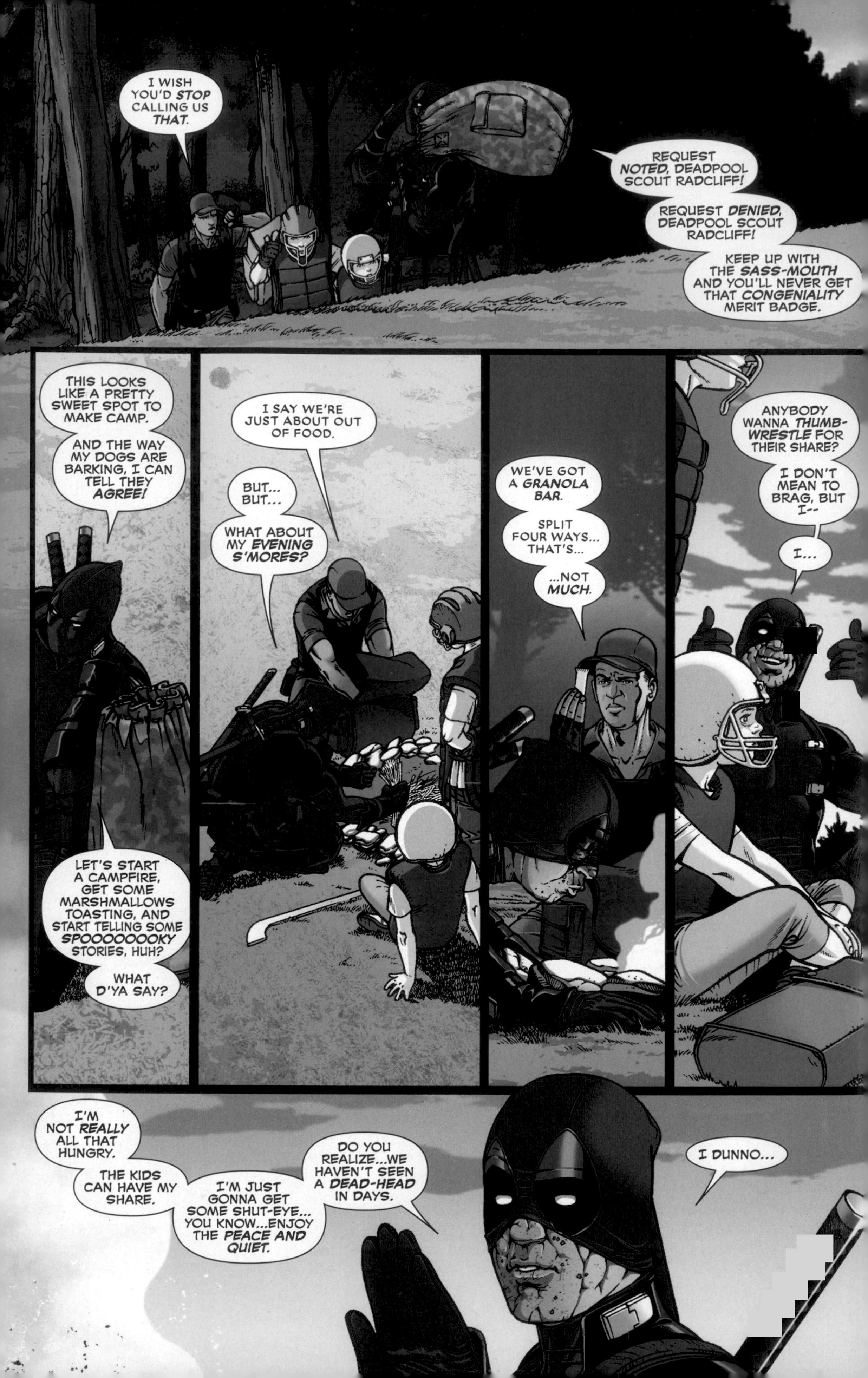
I WISH YOU'D STOP CALLING US THAT.
REQUEST NOTED, DEADPOOL SCOUT RADCLIFF!
REQUEST DENIED, DEADPOOL SCOUT RADCLIFF!
KEEP UP WITH THE SASS-MOUTH AND YOU'LL NEVER GET THAT CONGENIALITY MERIT BADGE.
THIS LOOKS LIKE A PRETTY SWEET SPOT TO MAKE CAMP.
AND THE WAY MY DOGS ARE BARKING, I CAN TELL THEY AGREE!
LET'S START A CAMPFIRE, GET SOME MARSHMALLOWS TOASTING, AND START TELLING SOME SPOOOOOOOKY STORIES, HUH?
WHAT D'YA SAY?
I SAY WE'RE JUST ABOUT OUT OF FOOD.
BUT... BUT...
WHAT ABOUT MY EVENING S'MORES?
WE'VE GOT A GRANOLA BAR.
SPLIT FOUR WAYS... THAT'S...
...NOT MUCH.
ANYBODY WANNA THUMB-WRESTLE FOR THEIR SHARE?
I DON'T MEAN TO BRAG, BUT I--
I...
I'M NOT REALLY ALL THAT HUNGRY.
THE KIDS CAN HAVE MY SHARE.
I'M JUST GONNA GET SOME SHUT-EYE... YOU KNOW...ENJOY THE PEACE AND QUIET.
DO YOU REALIZE...WE HAVEN'T SEEN A DEAD-HEAD IN DAYS.
I DUNNO...

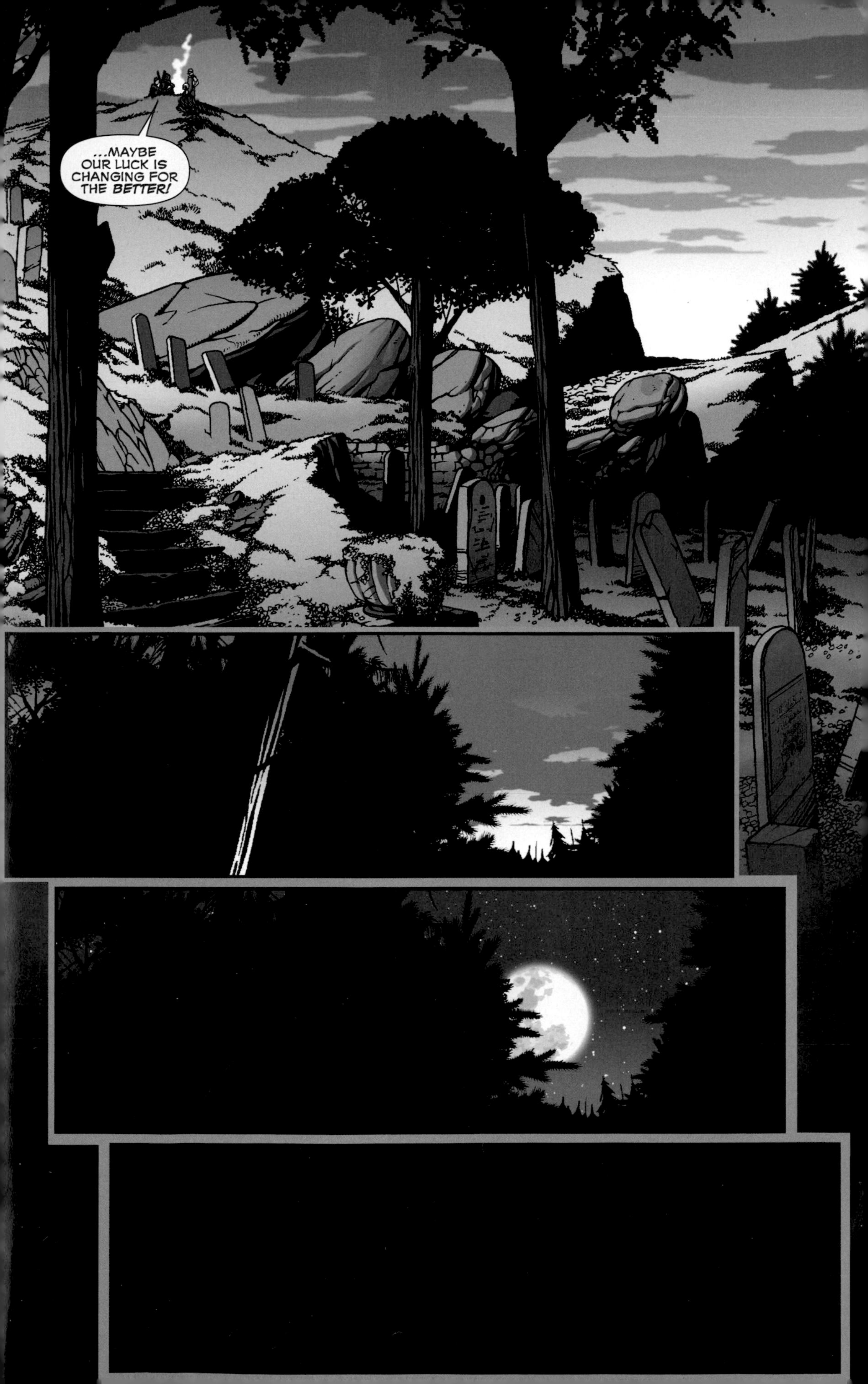
...MAYBE OUR LUCK IS CHANGING FOR THE BETTER!

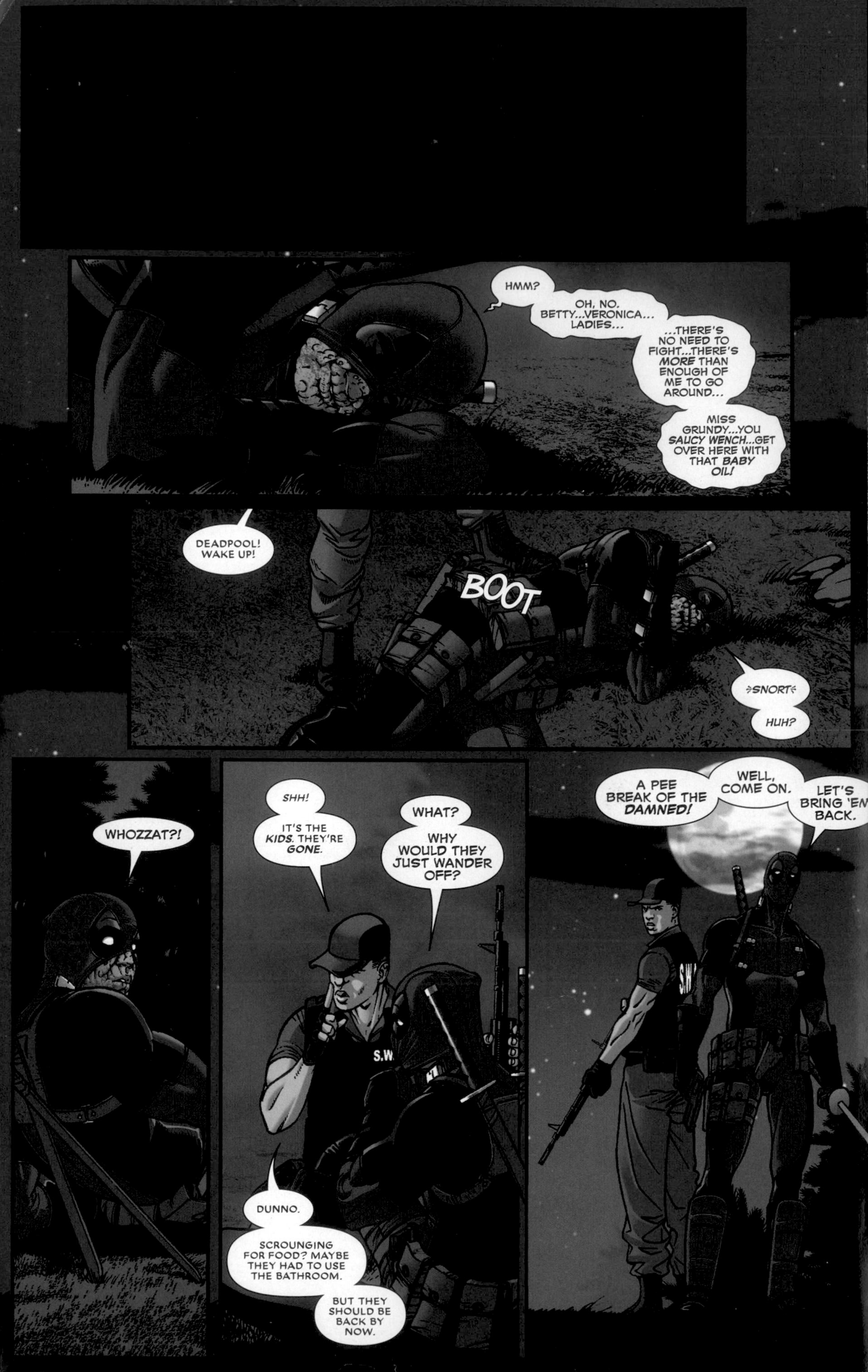
HMM?
OH, NO. BETTY...VERONICA... LADIES...
...THERE'S NO NEED TO FIGHT...THERE'S MORE THAN ENOUGH OF ME TO GO AROUND...
MISS GRUNDY...YOU SAUCY WENCH...GET OVER HERE WITH THAT BABY OIL!
DEADPOOL! WAKE UP!
BOOT
SNORT
HUH?
WHOZZAT?!
SHH!
IT'S THE KIDS. THEY'RE GONE.
WHAT?
WHY WOULD THEY JUST WANDER OFF?
DUNNO.
SCROUNGING FOR FOOD? MAYBE THEY HAD TO USE THE BATHROOM.
BUT THEY SHOULD BE BACK BY NOW.
A PEE BREAK OF THE DAMNED!
WELL, COME ON.
LET'S BRING 'EM BACK.

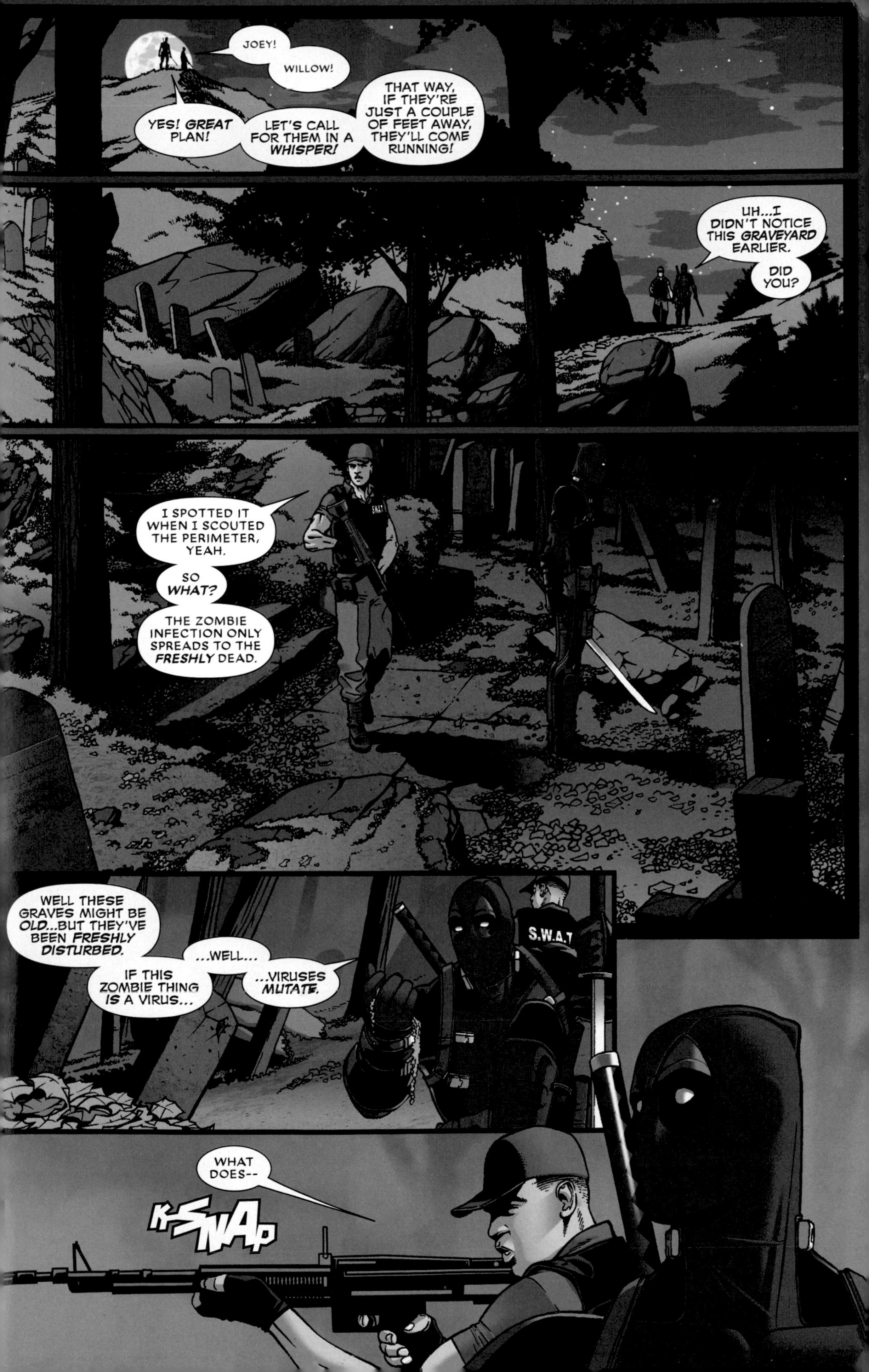
JOEY!
WILLOW!
YES! GREAT PLAN!
LET'S CALL FOR THEM IN A WHISPER!
THAT WAY, IF THEY'RE JUST A COUPLE OF FEET AWAY, THEY'LL COME RUNNING!
UH...I DIDN'T NOTICE THIS GRAVEYARD EARLIER.
DID YOU?
I SPOTTED IT WHEN I SCOUTED THE PERIMETER, YEAH.
SO WHAT?
THE ZOMBIE INFECTION ONLY SPREADS TO THE FRESHLY DEAD.
S.W.A.T
WELL THESE GRAVES MIGHT BE OLD...BUT THEY'VE BEEN FRESHLY DISTURBED.
...WELL...
IF THIS ZOMBIE THING IS A VIRUS...
...VIRUSES MUTATE.
S.W.A.T
WHAT DOES--
K-SNAP

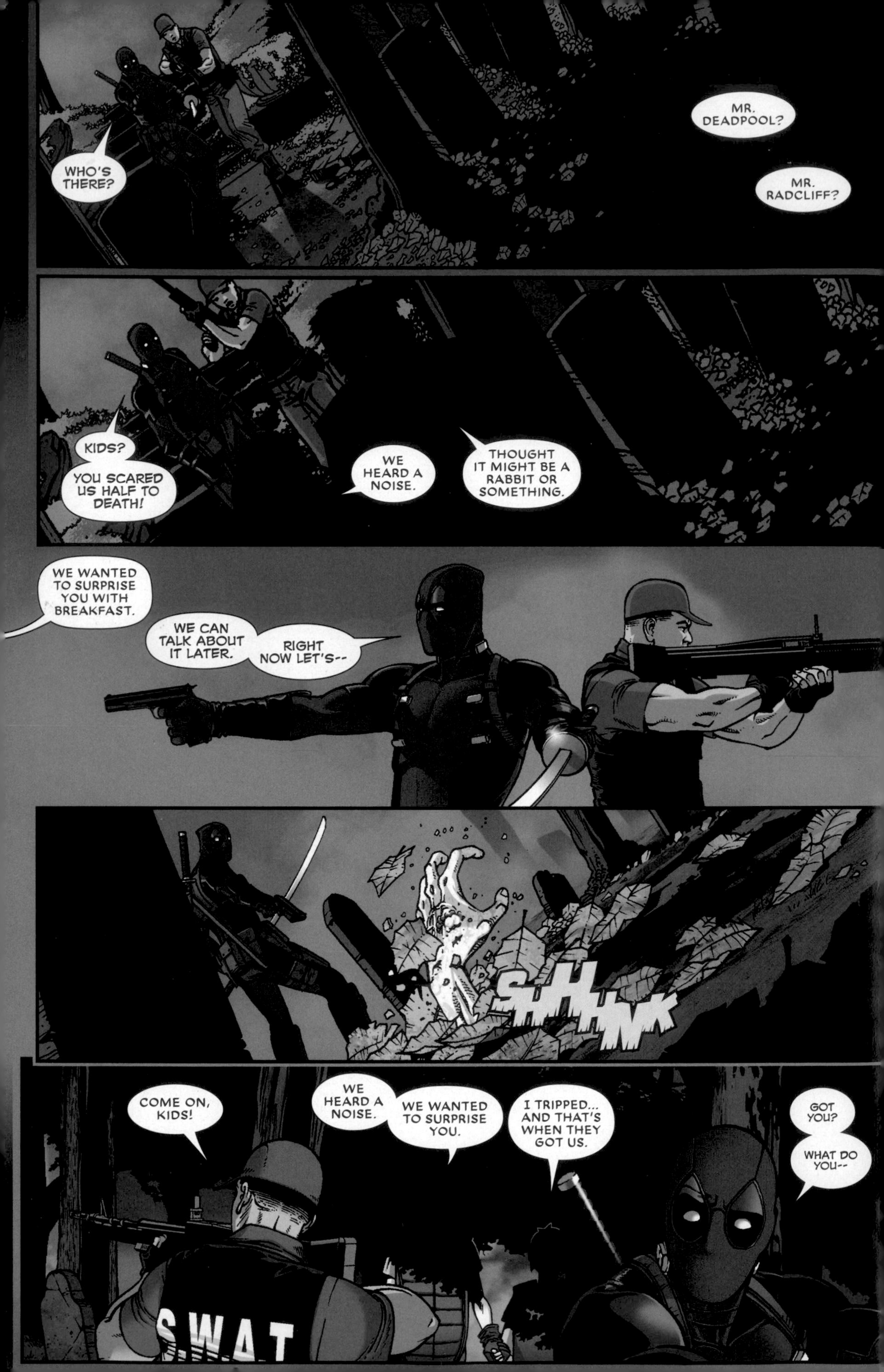

WHO'S THERE?
MR. DEADPOOL?
MR. RADCLIFF?
KIDS?
YOU SCARED US HALF TO DEATH!
WE HEARD A NOISE.
THOUGHT IT MIGHT BE A RABBIT OR SOMETHING.
WE WANTED TO SURPRISE YOU WITH BREAKFAST.
WE CAN TALK ABOUT IT LATER.
RIGHT NOW LET'S--
SHHHHNK
COME ON, KIDS!
WE HEARD A NOISE.
WE WANTED TO SURPRISE YOU.
I TRIPPED... AND THAT'S WHEN THEY GOT US.
GOT YOU?
WHAT DO YOU--
S.W.A.T

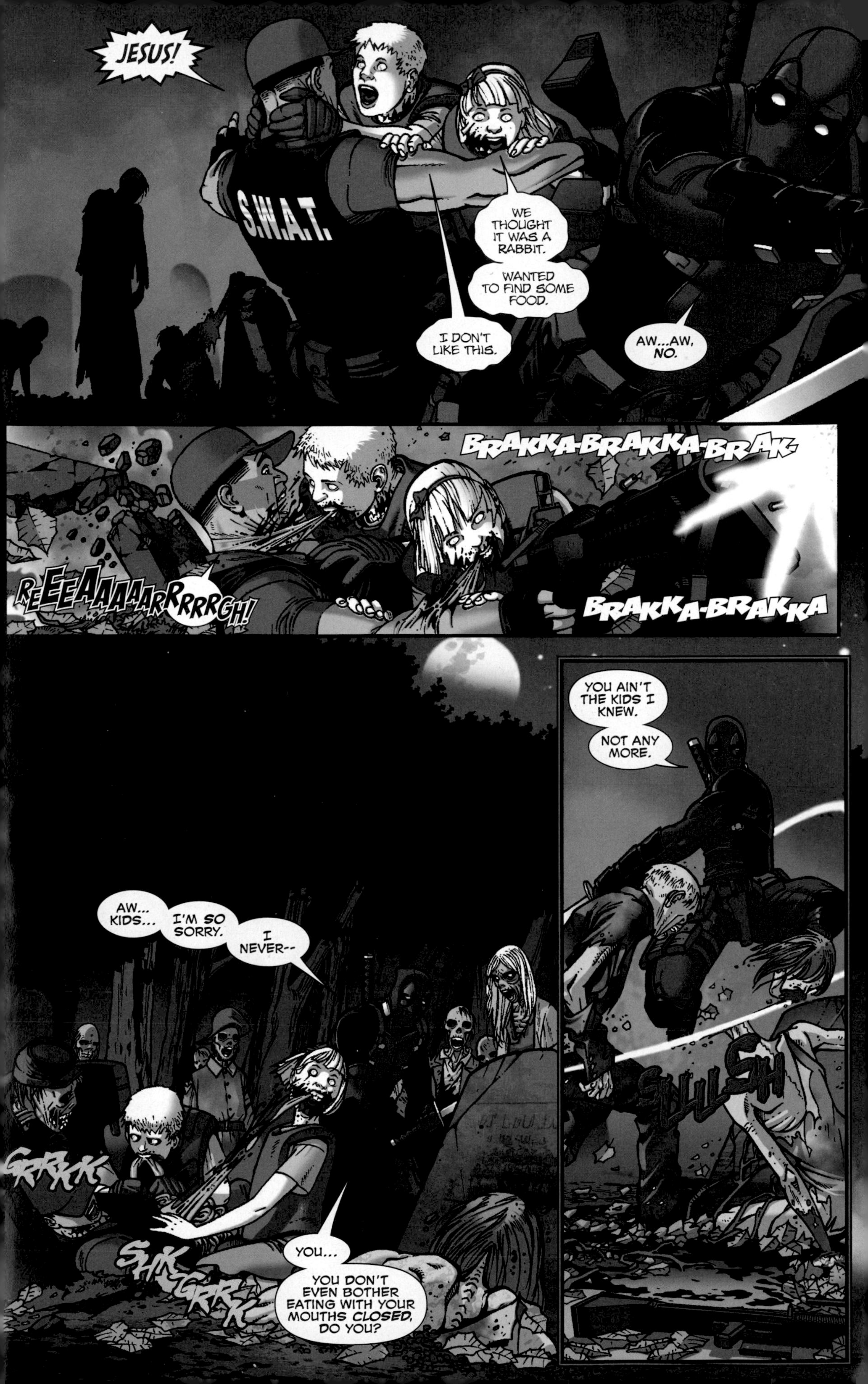

JESUS!
WE THOUGHT IT WAS A RABBIT.
WANTED TO FIND SOME FOOD.
I DON'T LIKE THIS.
AW...AW, NO.
BRAKKA-BRAKKA-BRAK-
REEEAAAAARRRRGH!
BRAKKA-BRAKKA
YOU AIN'T THE KIDS I KNEW.
NOT ANY MORE.
AW... KIDS...
I'M SO SORRY.
I NEVER--
SHLLSH
GRRKK
SHK GRRK
YOU...
YOU DON'T EVEN BOTHER EATING WITH YOUR MOUTHS CLOSED, DO YOU?

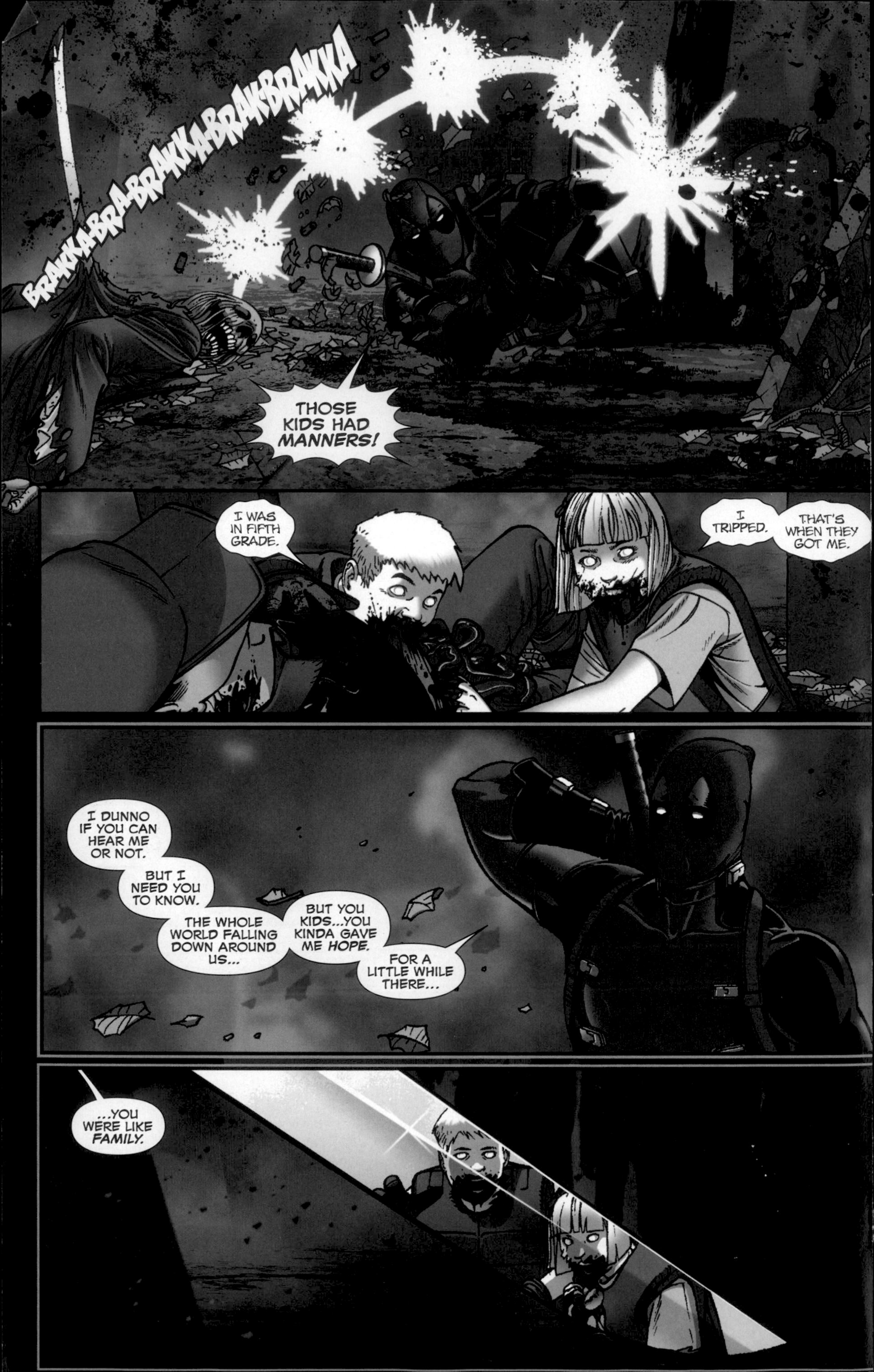
BRAKKA-BRA-BRAKKA-BRAK-BRAKKA
THOSE KIDS HAD MANNERS!
I WAS IN FIFTH GRADE.
I TRIPPED.
THAT'S WHEN THEY GOT ME.
I DUNNO IF YOU CAN HEAR ME OR NOT.
BUT I NEED YOU TO KNOW.
THE WHOLE WORLD FALLING DOWN AROUND US...
BUT YOU KIDS...YOU KINDA GAVE ME HOPE.
FOR A LITTLE WHILE THERE...
...YOU WERE LIKE FAMILY.

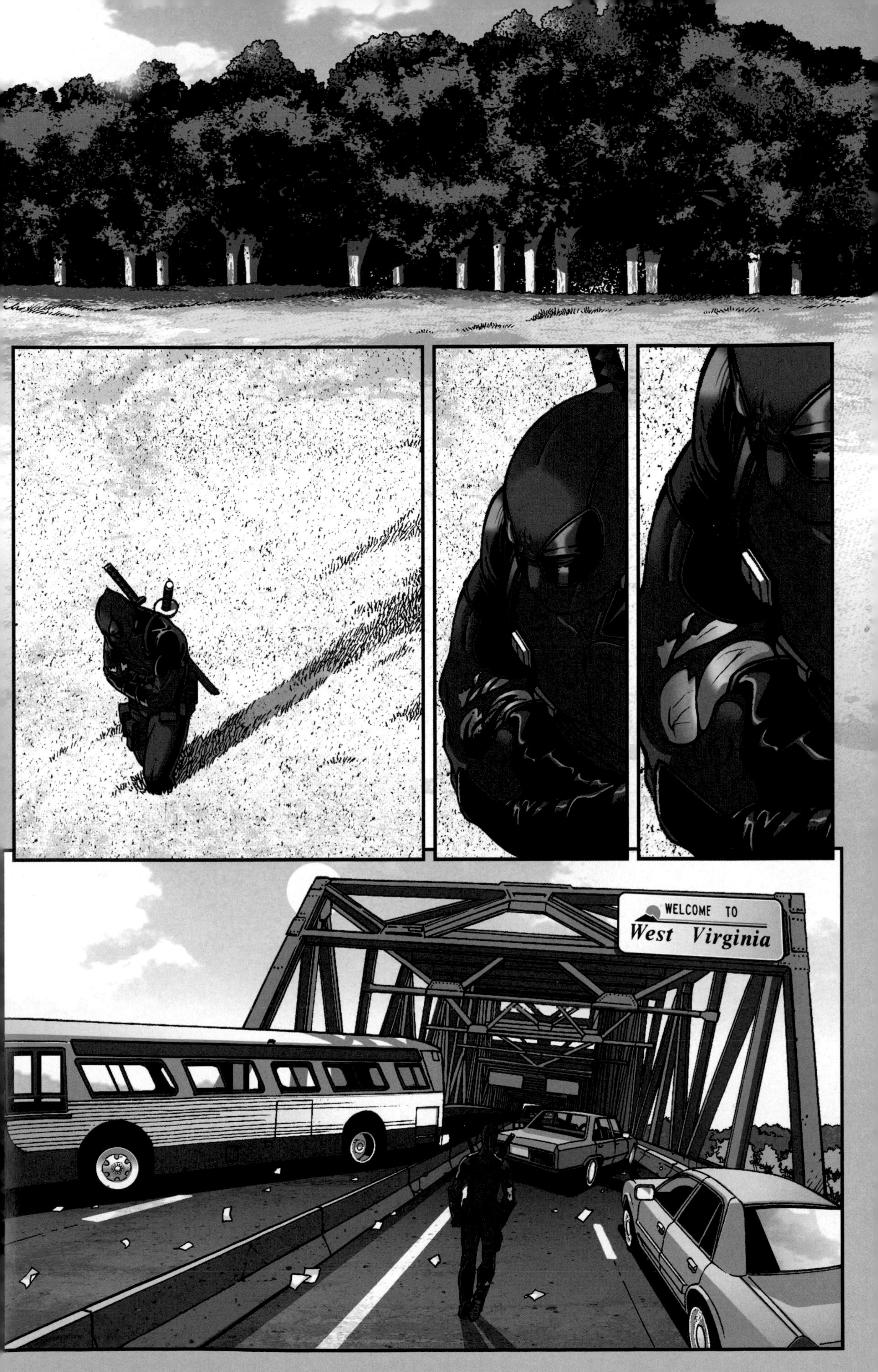
WELCOME TO
West Virginia

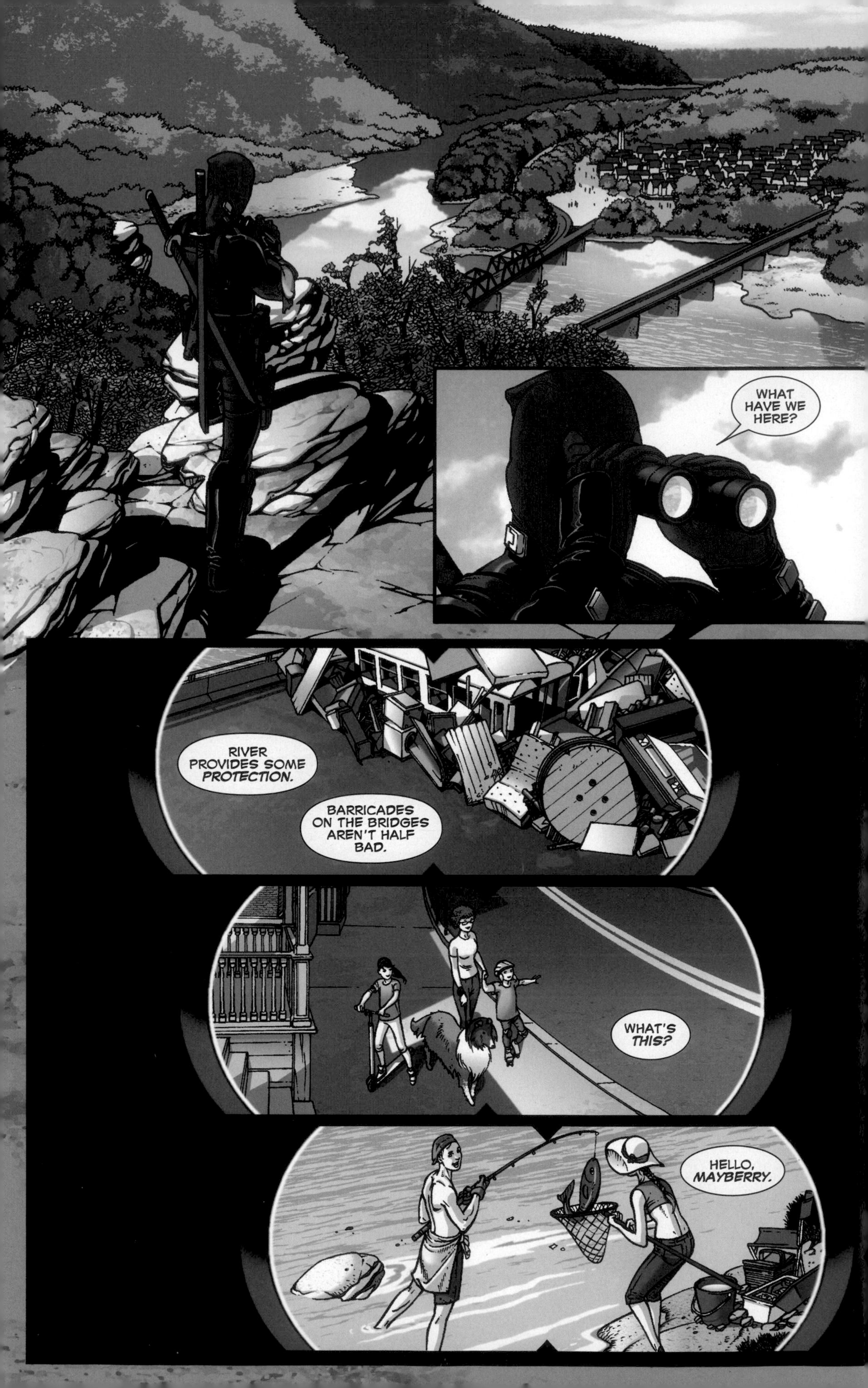
WHAT HAVE WE HERE?
RIVER PROVIDES SOME *PROTECTION.*
BARRICADES ON THE BRIDGES AREN'T HALF BAD.
WHAT'S *THIS?*
HELLO, *MAYBERRY.*

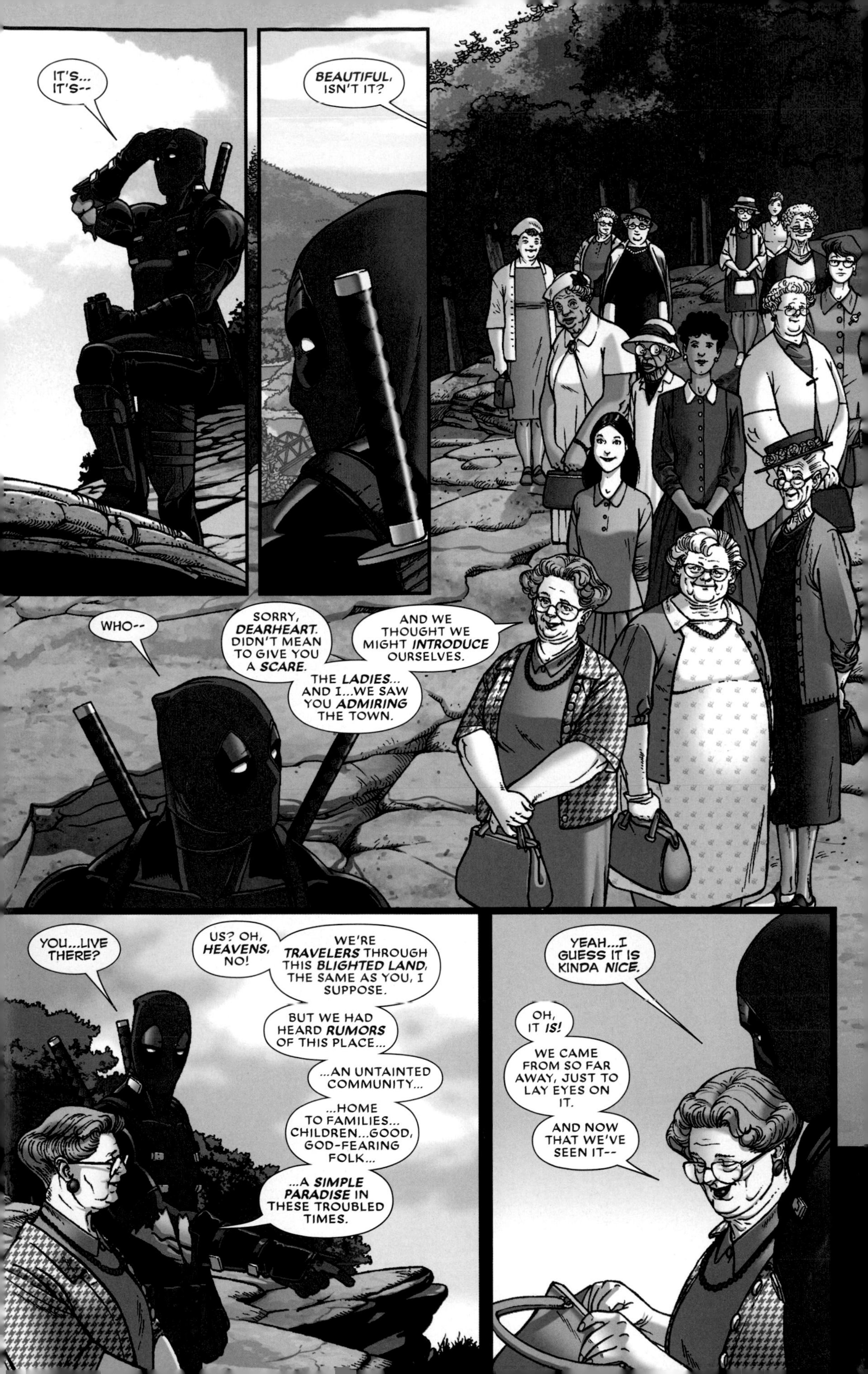
IT'S... IT'S--
BEAUTIFUL, ISN'T IT?
WHO--
SORRY, DEARHEART. DIDN'T MEAN TO GIVE YOU A SCARE.
AND WE THOUGHT WE MIGHT INTRODUCE OURSELVES.
THE LADIES... AND I...WE SAW YOU ADMIRING THE TOWN.
YOU...LIVE THERE?
US? OH, HEAVENS, NO!
WE'RE TRAVELERS THROUGH THIS BLIGHTED LAND, THE SAME AS YOU, I SUPPOSE.
BUT WE HAD HEARD RUMORS OF THIS PLACE...
...AN UNTAINTED COMMUNITY...
...HOME TO FAMILIES... CHILDREN...GOOD, GOD-FEARING FOLK...
...A SIMPLE PARADISE IN THESE TROUBLED TIMES.
YEAH...I GUESS IT IS KINDA NICE.
OH, IT IS!
WE CAME FROM SO FAR AWAY, JUST TO LAY EYES ON IT.
AND NOW THAT WE'VE SEEN IT--

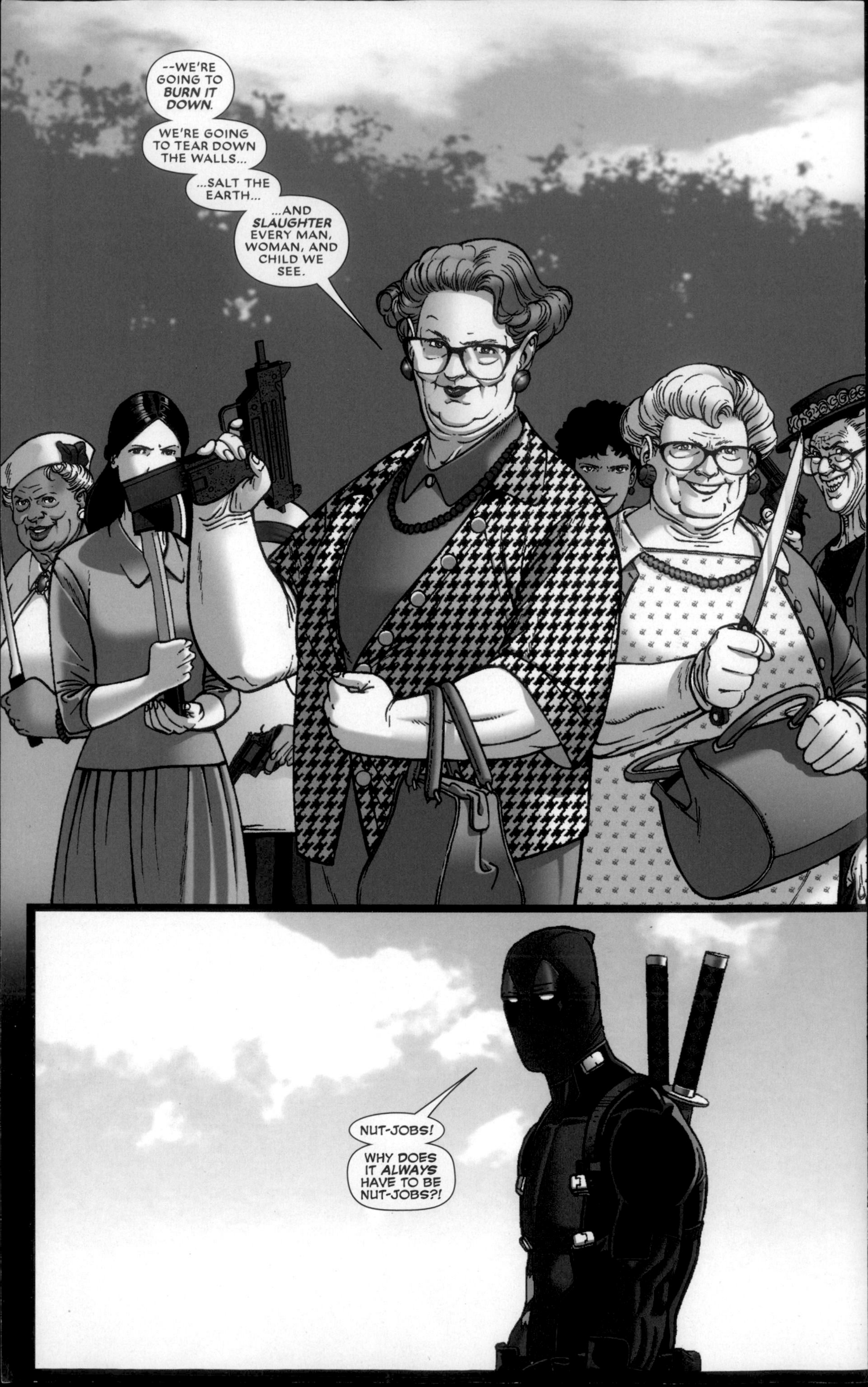
--WE'RE GOING TO *BURN IT DOWN*.
WE'RE GOING TO TEAR DOWN THE WALLS...
...SALT THE EARTH...
...AND *SLAUGHTER* EVERY MAN, WOMAN, AND CHILD WE SEE.
NUT-JOBS!
WHY *DOES* IT *ALWAYS* HAVE TO BE NUT-JOBS?!

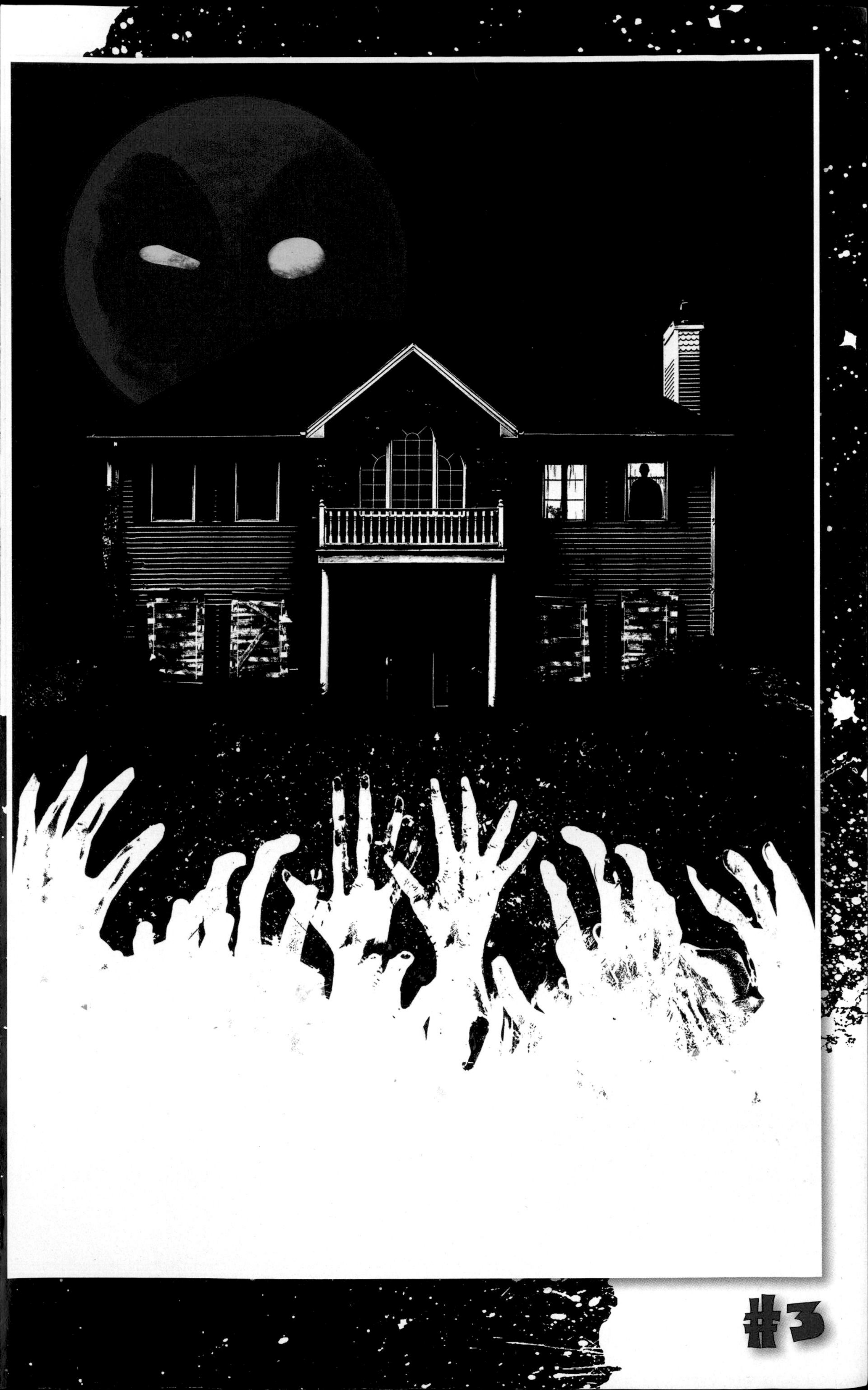
#3

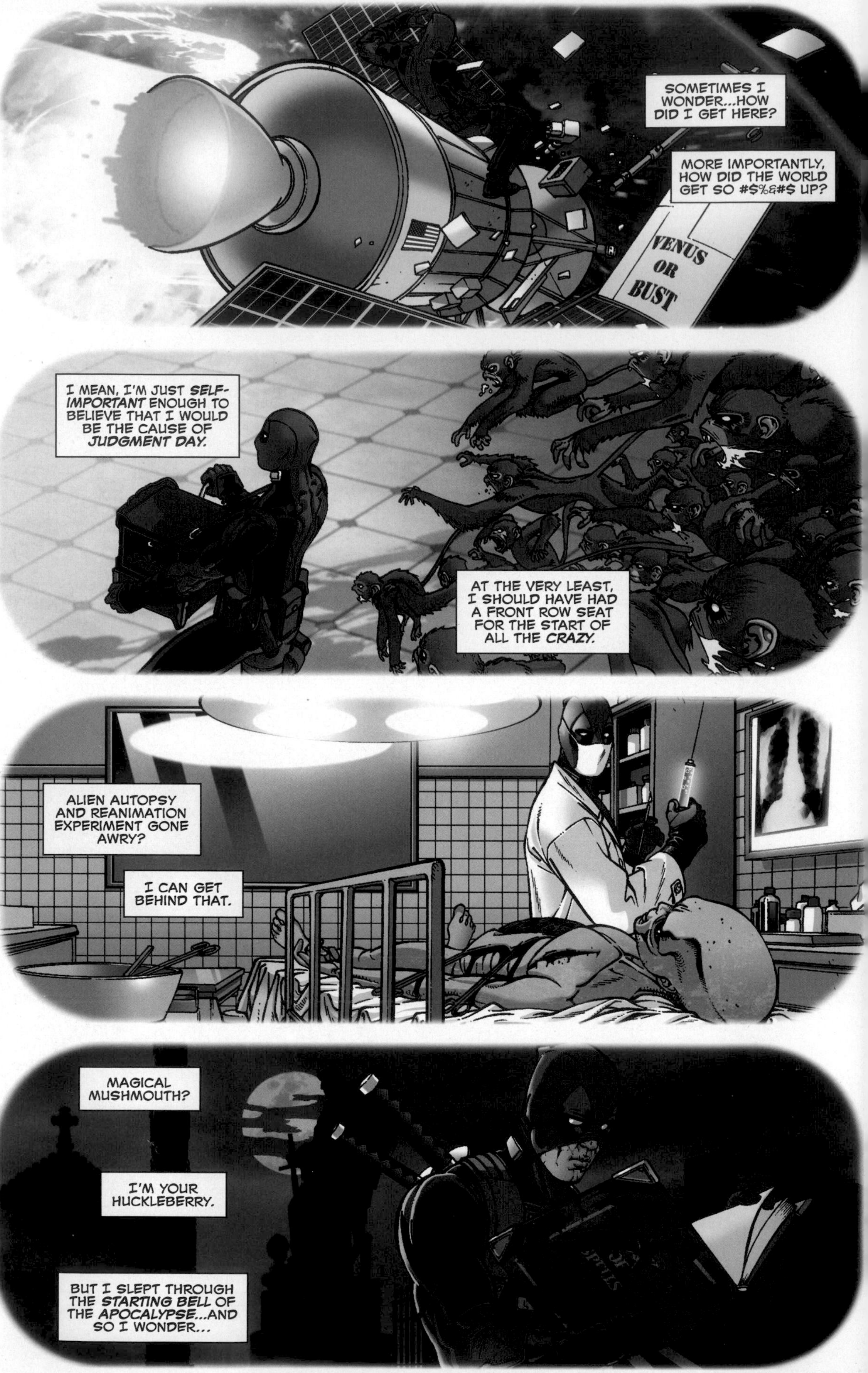
SOMETIMES I WONDER...HOW DID I GET HERE?
MORE IMPORTANTLY, HOW DID THE WORLD GET SO #$%&#$ UP?
VENUS OR BUST
I MEAN, I'M JUST *SELF-IMPORTANT* ENOUGH TO BELIEVE THAT I WOULD BE THE CAUSE OF *JUDGMENT DAY.*
AT THE VERY LEAST, I SHOULD HAVE HAD A FRONT ROW SEAT FOR THE START OF ALL THE *CRAZY.*
ALIEN AUTOPSY AND REANIMATION EXPERIMENT GONE AWRY?
I CAN GET BEHIND THAT.
MAGICAL MUSHMOUTH?
I'M YOUR HUCKLEBERRY.
BUT I SLEPT THROUGH THE *STARTING BELL* OF THE *APOCALYPSE*...AND SO I WONDER...

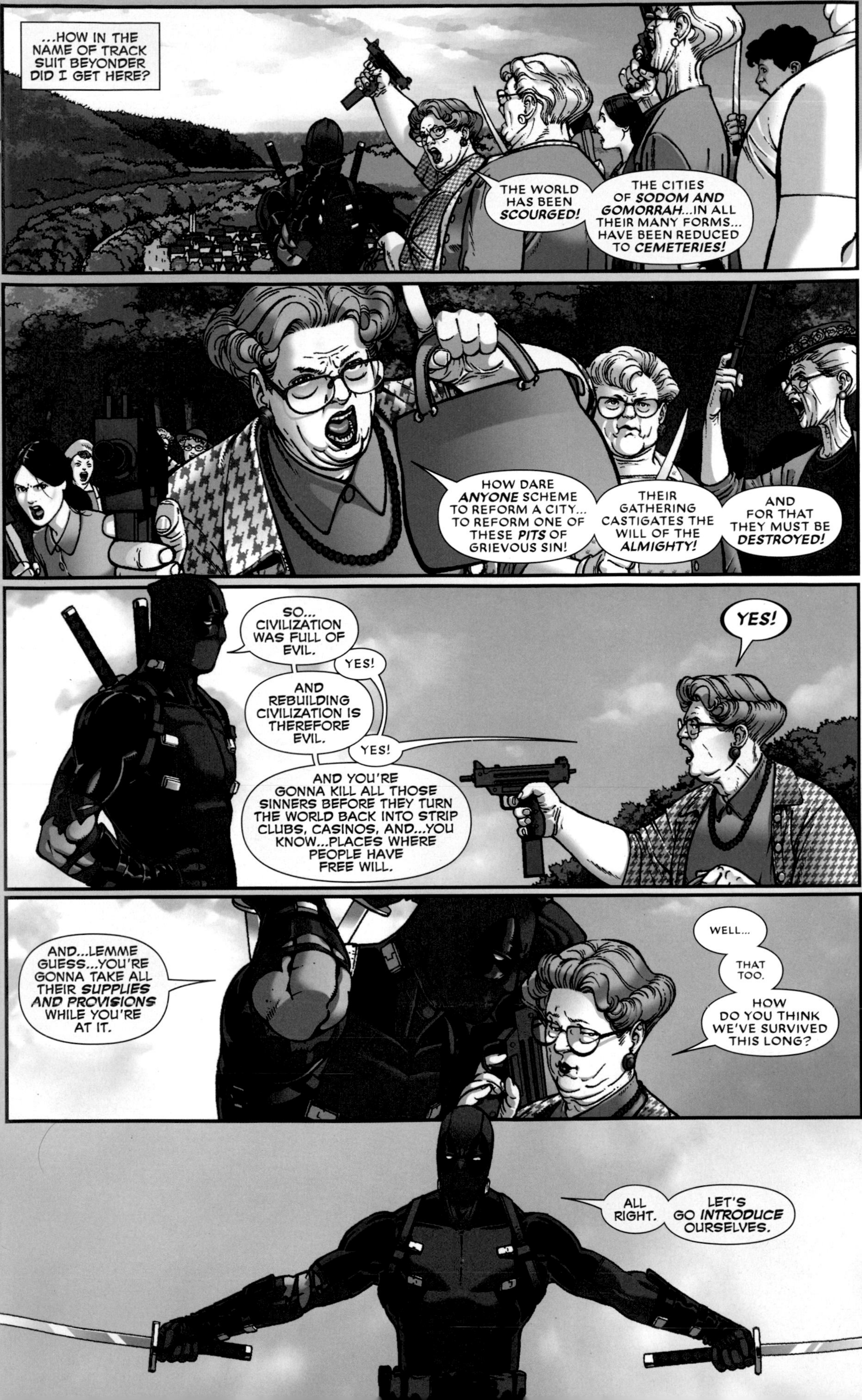
...HOW IN THE NAME OF TRACK SUIT BEYONDER DID I GET HERE?
THE WORLD HAS BEEN SCOURGED!
THE CITIES OF SODOM AND GOMORRAH...IN ALL THEIR MANY FORMS... HAVE BEEN REDUCED TO CEMETERIES!
HOW DARE ANYONE SCHEME TO REFORM A CITY... TO REFORM ONE OF THESE PITS OF GRIEVOUS SIN!
THEIR GATHERING CASTIGATES THE WILL OF THE ALMIGHTY!
AND FOR THAT THEY MUST BE DESTROYED!
SO... CIVILIZATION WAS FULL OF EVIL.
YES!
YES!
AND REBUILDING CIVILIZATION IS THEREFORE EVIL.
YES!
AND YOU'RE GONNA KILL ALL THOSE SINNERS BEFORE THEY TURN THE WORLD BACK INTO STRIP CLUBS, CASINOS, AND...YOU KNOW...PLACES WHERE PEOPLE HAVE FREE WILL.
AND...LEMME GUESS...YOU'RE GONNA TAKE ALL THEIR SUPPLIES AND PROVISIONS WHILE YOU'RE AT IT.
WELL...
THAT TOO.
HOW DO YOU THINK WE'VE SURVIVED THIS LONG?
ALL RIGHT.
LET'S GO INTRODUCE OURSELVES.

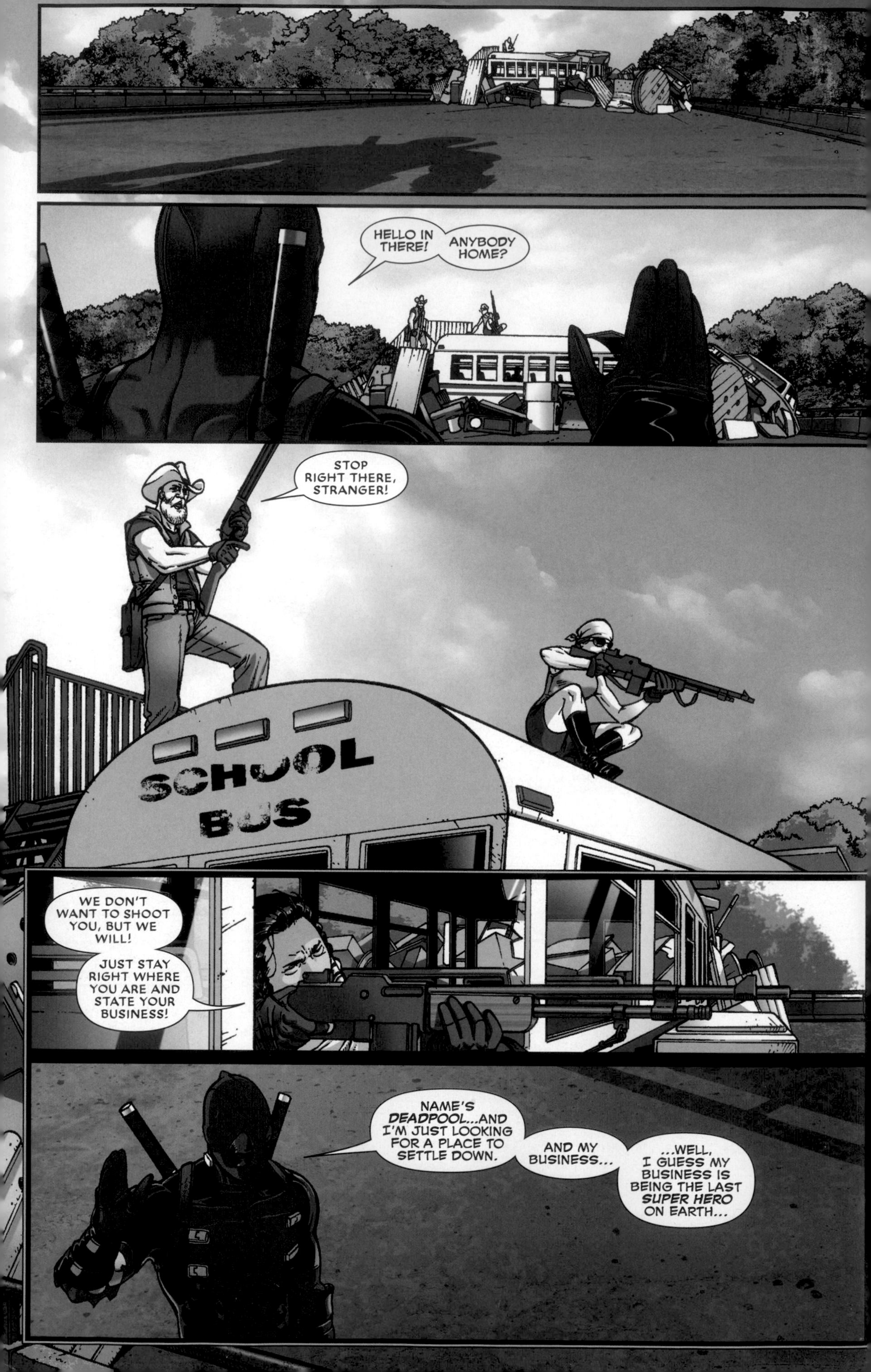
HELLO IN THERE!
ANYBODY HOME?
STOP RIGHT THERE, STRANGER!
SCHOOL BUS
WE DON'T WANT TO SHOOT YOU, BUT WE WILL!
JUST STAY RIGHT WHERE YOU ARE AND STATE YOUR BUSINESS!
NAME'S *DEADPOOL*...AND I'M JUST LOOKING FOR A PLACE TO SETTLE DOWN.
AND MY BUSINESS...
...WELL, I GUESS MY BUSINESS IS BEING THE LAST *SUPER HERO* ON EARTH...

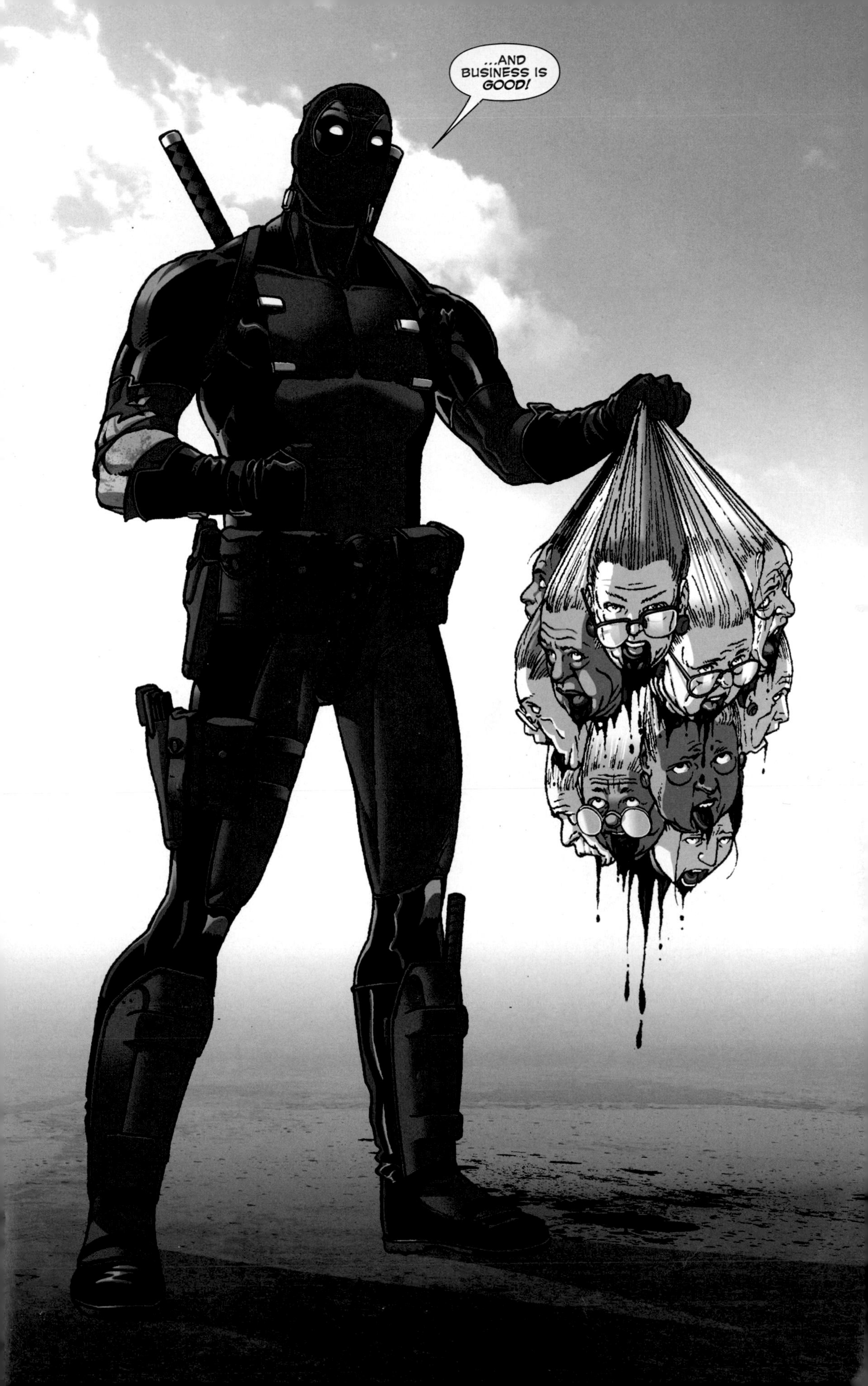
...AND BUSINESS IS GOOD!

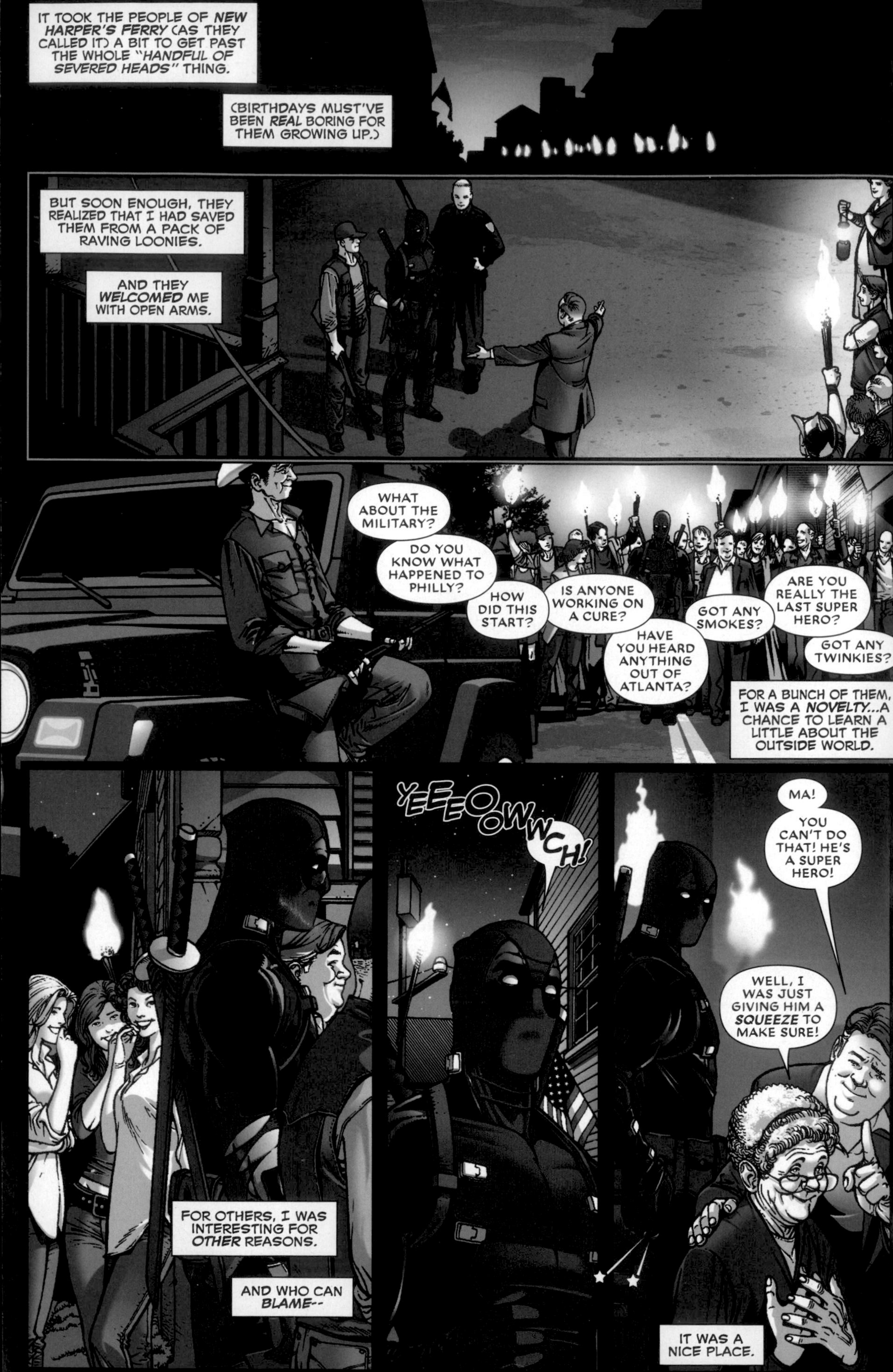
IT TOOK THE PEOPLE OF NEW HARPER'S FERRY (AS THEY CALLED IT) A BIT TO GET PAST THE WHOLE "HANDFUL OF SEVERED HEADS" THING.
(BIRTHDAYS MUST'VE BEEN REAL BORING FOR THEM GROWING UP.)
BUT SOON ENOUGH, THEY REALIZED THAT I HAD SAVED THEM FROM A PACK OF RAVING LOONIES.
AND THEY WELCOMED ME WITH OPEN ARMS.
WHAT ABOUT THE MILITARY?
DO YOU KNOW WHAT HAPPENED TO PHILLY?
HOW DID THIS START?
IS ANYONE WORKING ON A CURE?
HAVE YOU HEARD ANYTHING OUT OF ATLANTA?
GOT ANY SMOKES?
ARE YOU REALLY THE LAST SUPER HERO?
GOT ANY TWINKIES?
FOR A BUNCH OF THEM, I WAS A NOVELTY...A CHANCE TO LEARN A LITTLE ABOUT THE OUTSIDE WORLD.
FOR OTHERS, I WAS INTERESTING FOR OTHER REASONS.
AND WHO CAN BLAME--
YEEEOOWWCH!
MA!
YOU CAN'T DO THAT! HE'S A SUPER HERO!
WELL, I WAS JUST GIVING HIM A SQUEEZE TO MAKE SURE!
IT WAS A NICE PLACE.

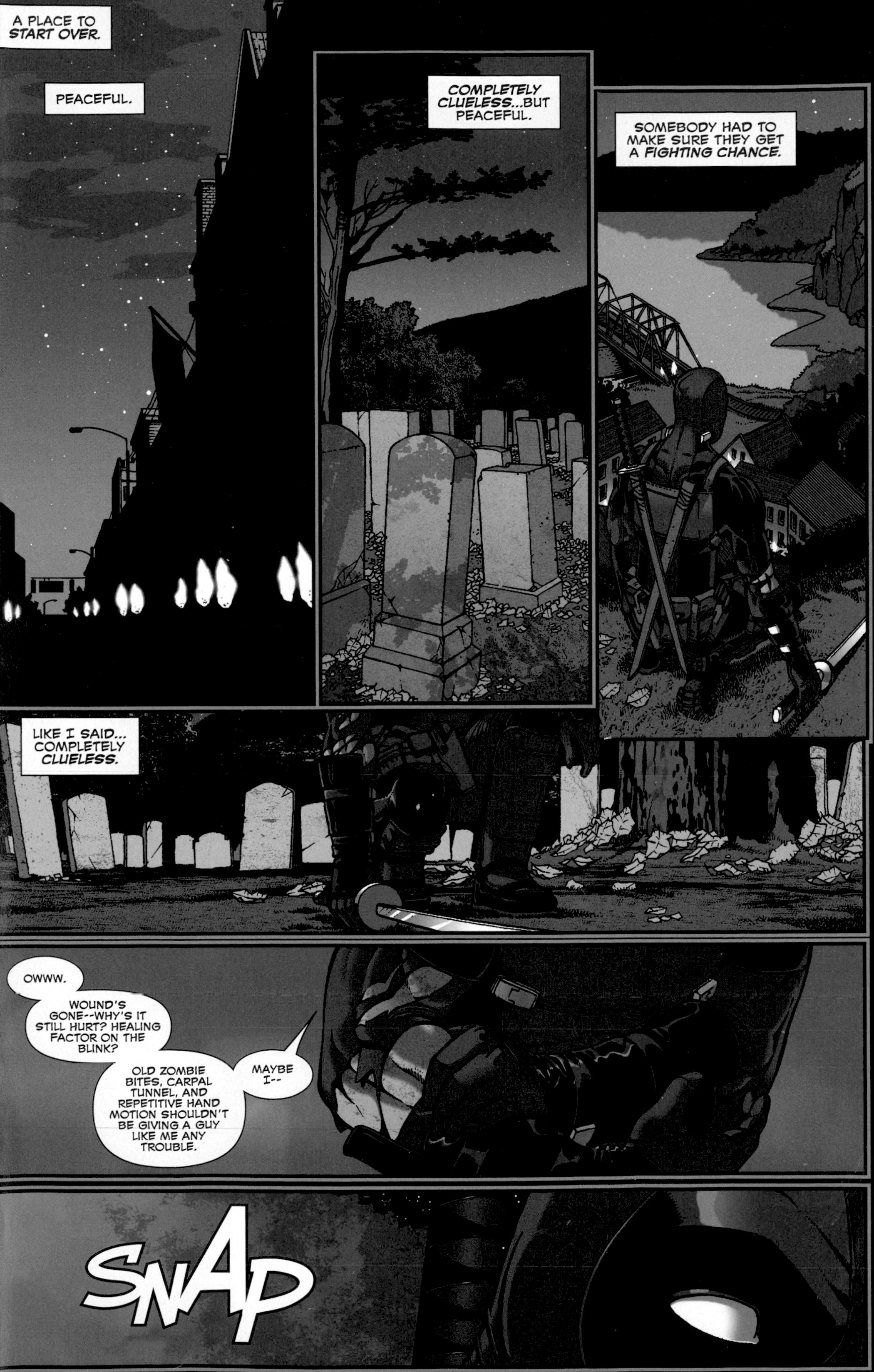
A PLACE TO START OVER.
PEACEFUL.
COMPLETELY CLUELESS...BUT PEACEFUL.
SOMEBODY HAD TO MAKE SURE THEY GET A FIGHTING CHANCE.
LIKE I SAID... COMPLETELY CLUELESS.
OWWW.
WOUND'S GONE--WHY'S IT STILL HURT? HEALING FACTOR ON THE BLINK?
OLD ZOMBIE BITES, CARPAL TUNNEL, AND REPETITIVE HAND MOTION SHOULDN'T BE GIVING A GUY LIKE ME ANY TROUBLE.
MAYBE I--
SNAP

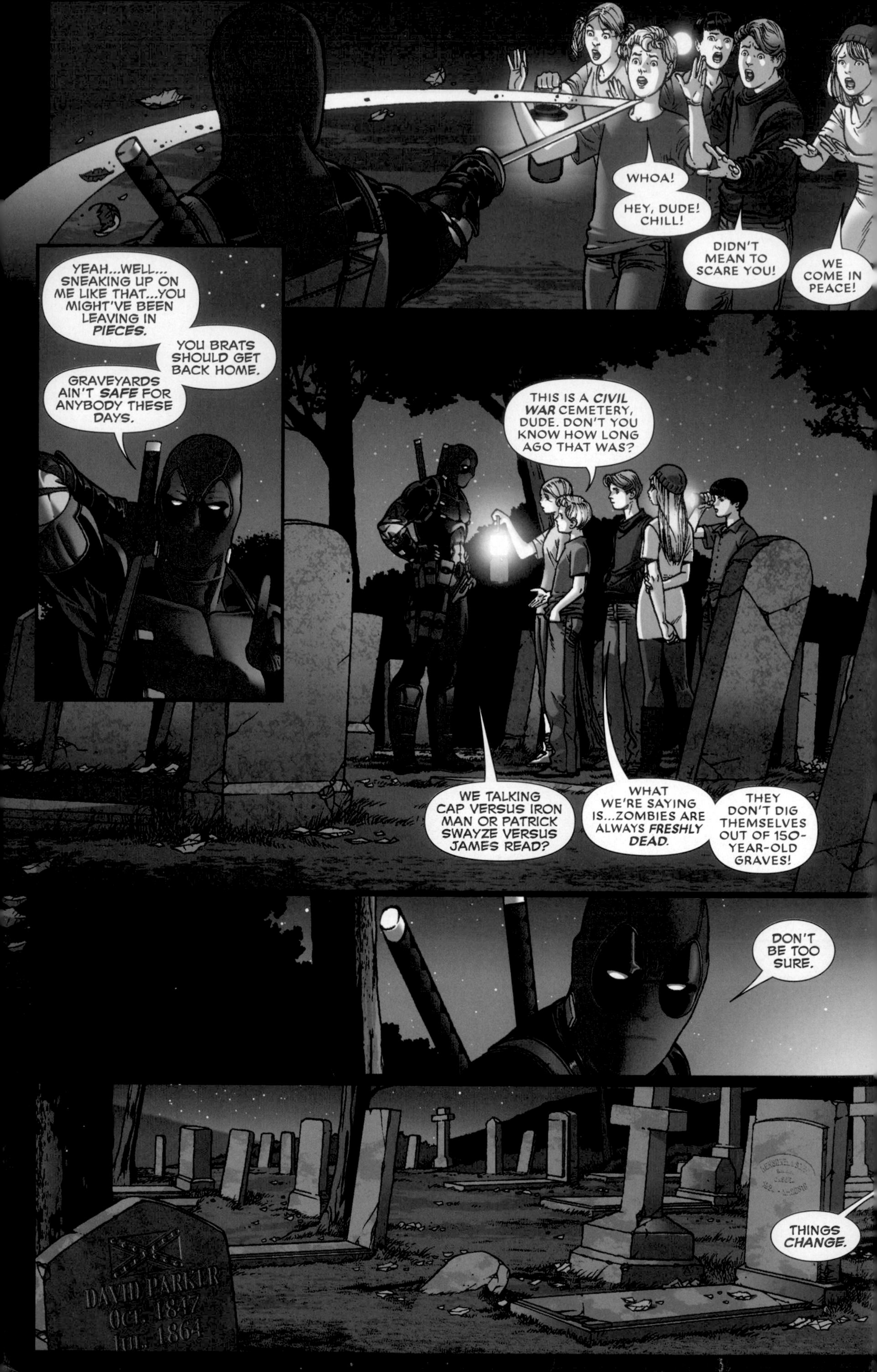
WHOA!
HEY, DUDE! CHILL!
DIDN'T MEAN TO SCARE YOU!
WE COME IN PEACE!
YEAH...WELL... SNEAKING UP ON ME LIKE THAT...YOU MIGHT'VE BEEN LEAVING IN *PIECES.*
YOU BRATS SHOULD GET BACK HOME.
GRAVEYARDS AIN'T *SAFE* FOR ANYBODY THESE DAYS.
THIS IS A *CIVIL WAR* CEMETERY, DUDE. DON'T YOU KNOW HOW LONG AGO THAT WAS?
WE TALKING CAP VERSUS IRON MAN OR PATRICK SWAYZE VERSUS JAMES READ?
WHAT WE'RE SAYING IS...ZOMBIES ARE ALWAYS *FRESHLY DEAD.*
THEY DON'T DIG THEMSELVES OUT OF 150-YEAR-OLD GRAVES!
DON'T BE TOO SURE.
DAVID PARKER
Oct. 1847
Jul. 1864
THINGS *CHANGE.*

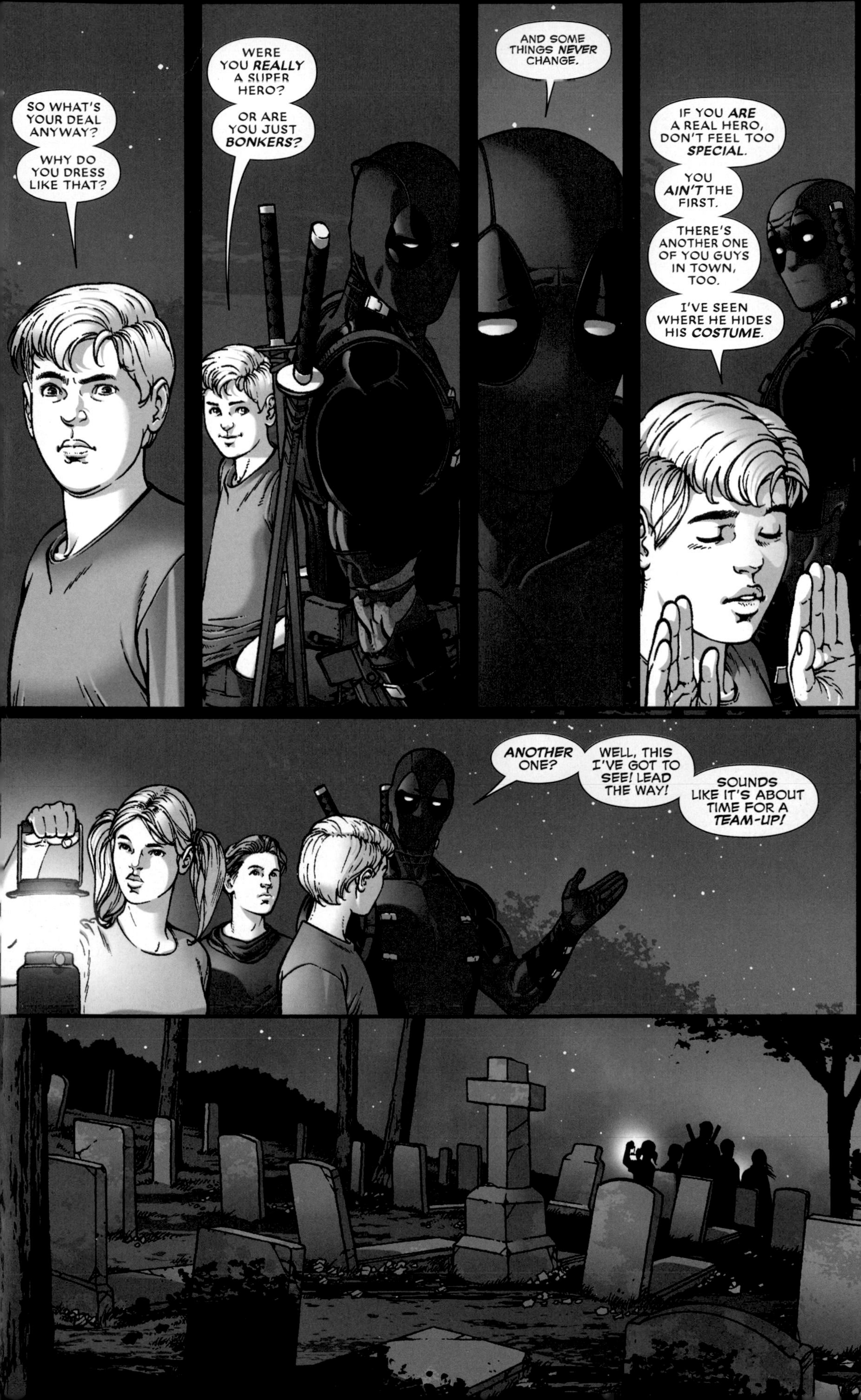
SO WHAT'S YOUR DEAL ANYWAY?
WHY DO YOU DRESS LIKE THAT?
WERE YOU REALLY A SUPER HERO?
OR ARE YOU JUST BONKERS?
AND SOME THINGS NEVER CHANGE.
IF YOU ARE A REAL HERO, DON'T FEEL TOO SPECIAL.
YOU AIN'T THE FIRST.
THERE'S ANOTHER ONE OF YOU GUYS IN TOWN, TOO.
I'VE SEEN WHERE HE HIDES HIS COSTUME.
ANOTHER ONE?
WELL, THIS I'VE GOT TO SEE! LEAD THE WAY!
SOUNDS LIKE IT'S ABOUT TIME FOR A TEAM-UP!

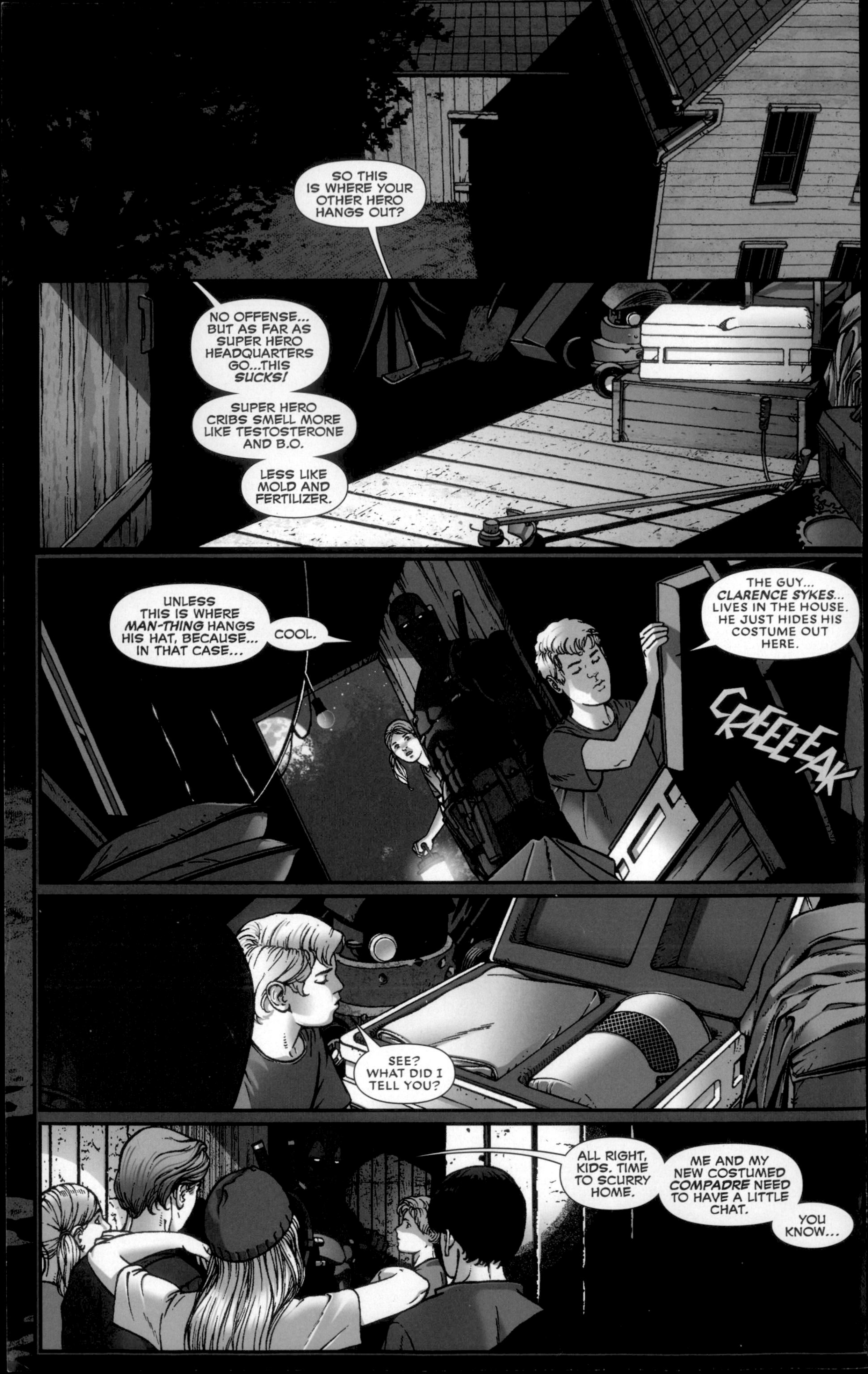

SO THIS IS WHERE YOUR OTHER HERO HANGS OUT?
NO OFFENSE... BUT AS FAR AS SUPER HERO HEADQUARTERS GO...THIS SUCKS!
SUPER HERO CRIBS SMELL MORE LIKE TESTOSTERONE AND B.O.
LESS LIKE MOLD AND FERTILIZER.
UNLESS THIS IS WHERE MAN-THING HANGS HIS HAT, BECAUSE... IN THAT CASE...
COOL.
THE GUY... CLARENCE SYKES... LIVES IN THE HOUSE. HE JUST HIDES HIS COSTUME OUT HERE.
CREEEEAK
SEE? WHAT DID I TELL YOU?
ALL RIGHT, KIDS. TIME TO SCURRY HOME.
ME AND MY NEW COSTUMED COMPADRE NEED TO HAVE A LITTLE CHAT.
YOU KNOW...

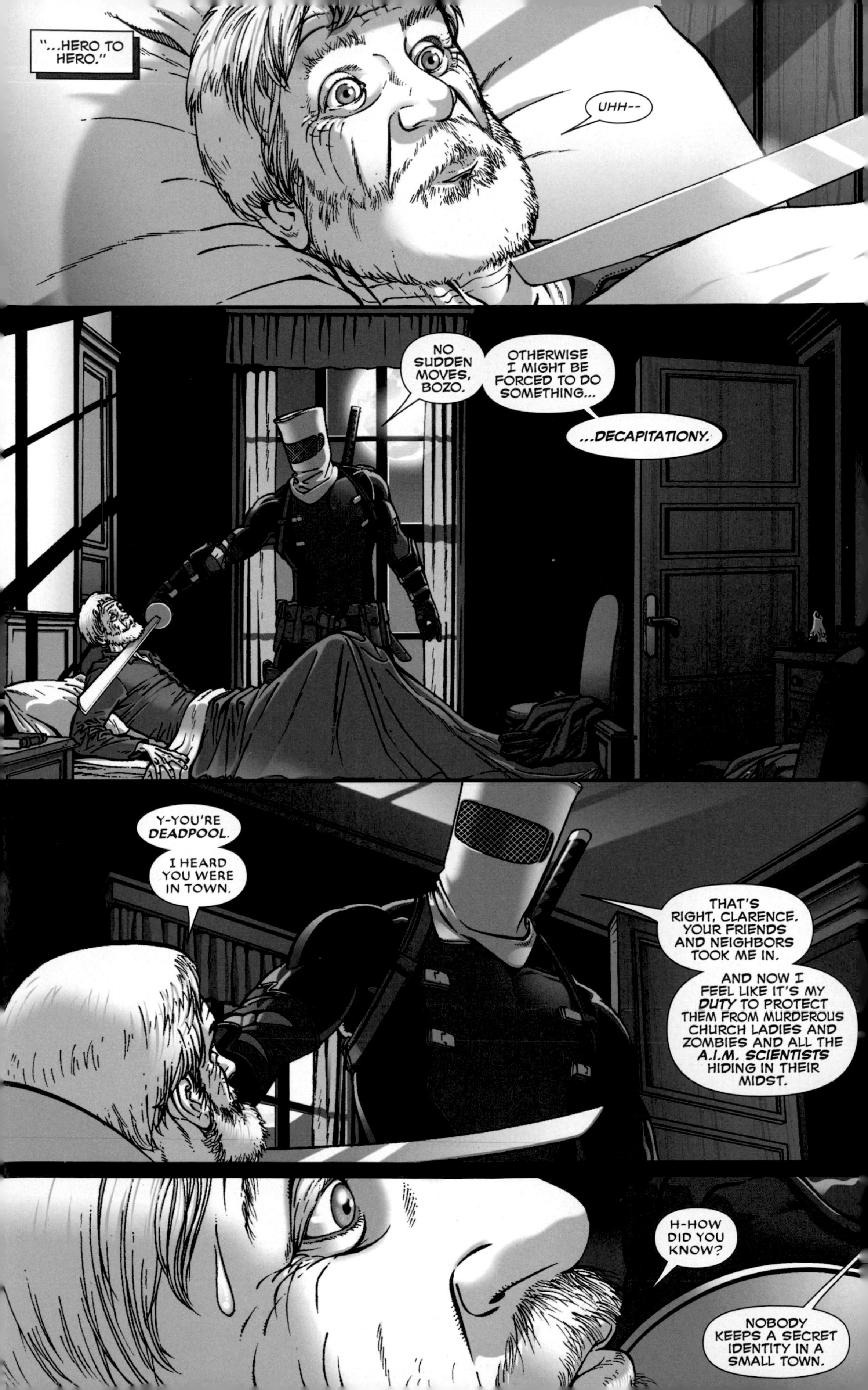
"...HERO TO HERO."
UHH--
NO SUDDEN MOVES, BOZO.
OTHERWISE I MIGHT BE FORCED TO DO SOMETHING...
...DECAPITATIONY.
Y-YOU'RE DEADPOOL.
I HEARD YOU WERE IN TOWN.
THAT'S RIGHT, CLARENCE. YOUR FRIENDS AND NEIGHBORS TOOK ME IN.
AND NOW I FEEL LIKE IT'S MY DUTY TO PROTECT THEM FROM MURDEROUS CHURCH LADIES AND ZOMBIES AND ALL THE A.I.M. SCIENTISTS HIDING IN THEIR MIDST.
H-HOW DID YOU KNOW?
NOBODY KEEPS A SECRET IDENTITY IN A SMALL TOWN.

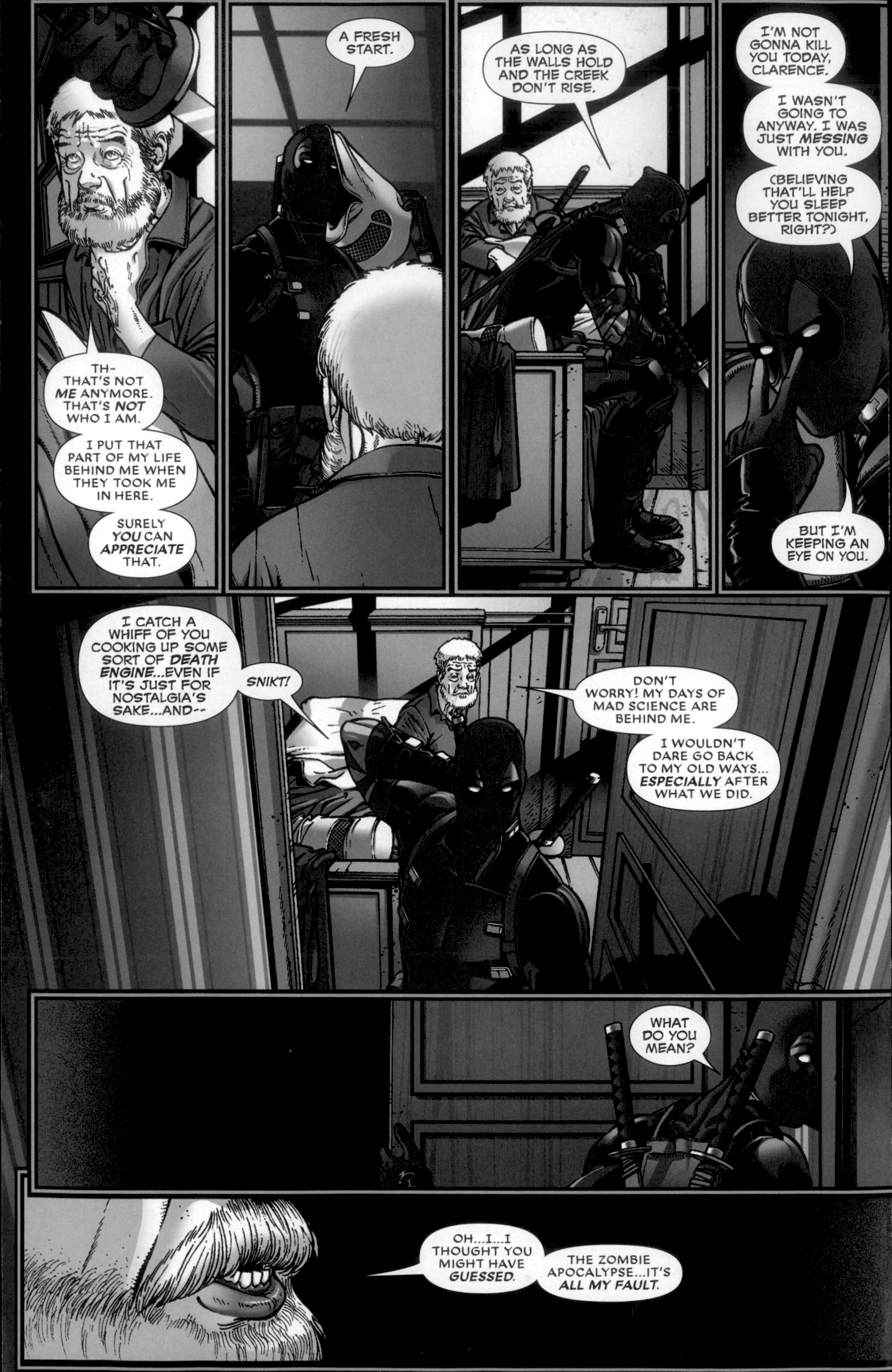
TH- THAT'S NOT ME ANYMORE. THAT'S NOT WHO I AM.
I PUT THAT PART OF MY LIFE BEHIND ME WHEN THEY TOOK ME IN HERE.
SURELY YOU CAN APPRECIATE THAT.
A FRESH START.
AS LONG AS THE WALLS HOLD AND THE CREEK DON'T RISE.
I'M NOT GONNA KILL YOU TODAY, CLARENCE.
I WASN'T GOING TO ANYWAY. I WAS JUST MESSING WITH YOU.
(BELIEVING THAT'LL HELP YOU SLEEP BETTER TONIGHT, RIGHT?)
BUT I'M KEEPING AN EYE ON YOU.
I CATCH A WHIFF OF YOU COOKING UP SOME SORT OF DEATH ENGINE...EVEN IF IT'S JUST FOR NOSTALGIA'S SAKE...AND--
SNIKT!
DON'T WORRY! MY DAYS OF MAD SCIENCE ARE BEHIND ME.
I WOULDN'T DARE GO BACK TO MY OLD WAYS... ESPECIALLY AFTER WHAT WE DID.
WHAT DO YOU MEAN?
OH...I...I THOUGHT YOU MIGHT HAVE GUESSED.
THE ZOMBIE APOCALYPSE...IT'S ALL MY FAULT.

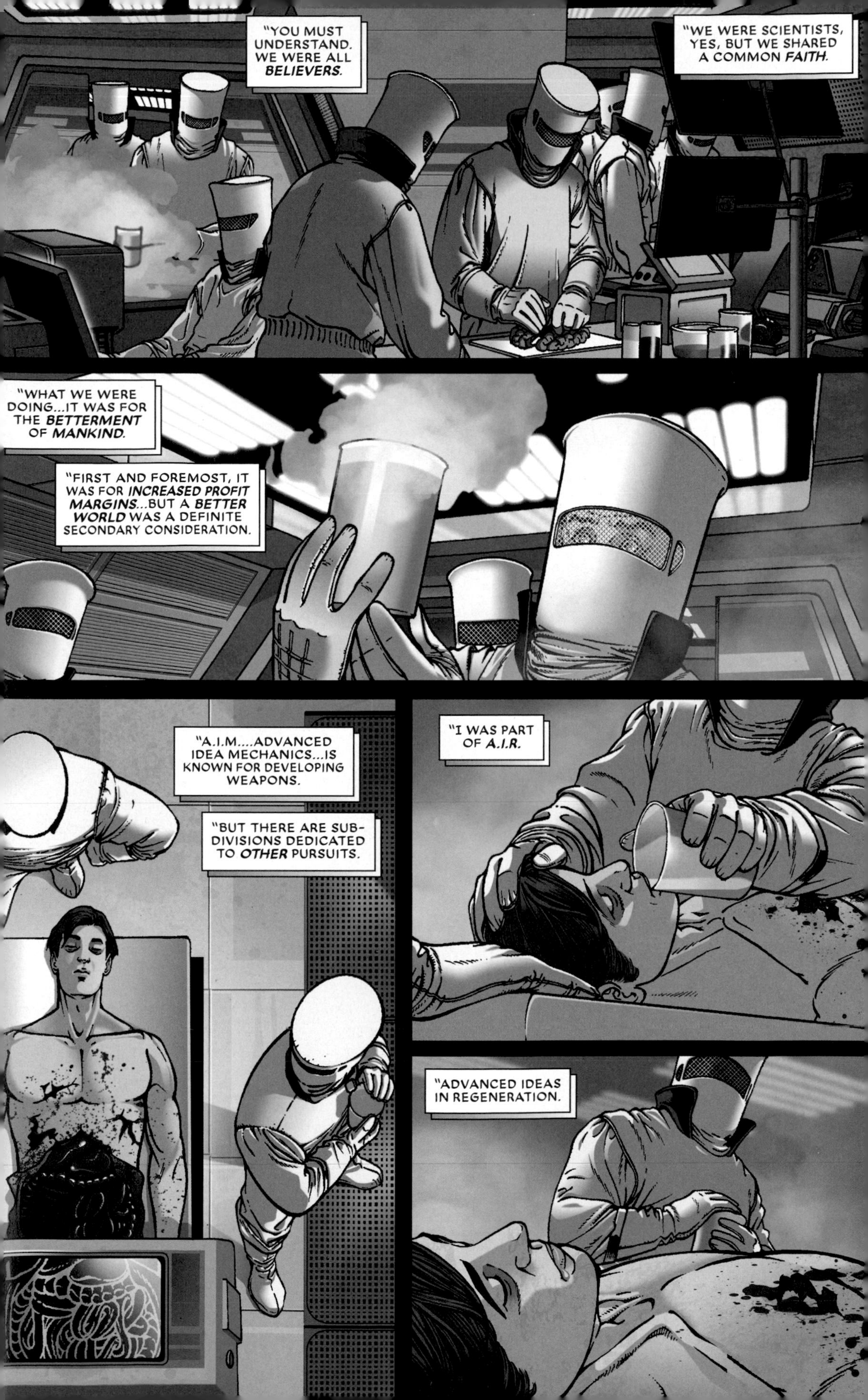
"YOU MUST UNDERSTAND. WE WERE ALL BELIEVERS.
"WE WERE SCIENTISTS, YES, BUT WE SHARED A COMMON FAITH.
"WHAT WE WERE DOING...IT WAS FOR THE BETTERMENT OF MANKIND.
"FIRST AND FOREMOST, IT WAS FOR INCREASED PROFIT MARGINS...BUT A BETTER WORLD WAS A DEFINITE SECONDARY CONSIDERATION.
"A.I.M....ADVANCED IDEA MECHANICS...IS KNOWN FOR DEVELOPING WEAPONS.
"BUT THERE ARE SUB-DIVISIONS DEDICATED TO OTHER PURSUITS.
"I WAS PART OF A.I.R.
"ADVANCED IDEAS IN REGENERATION.

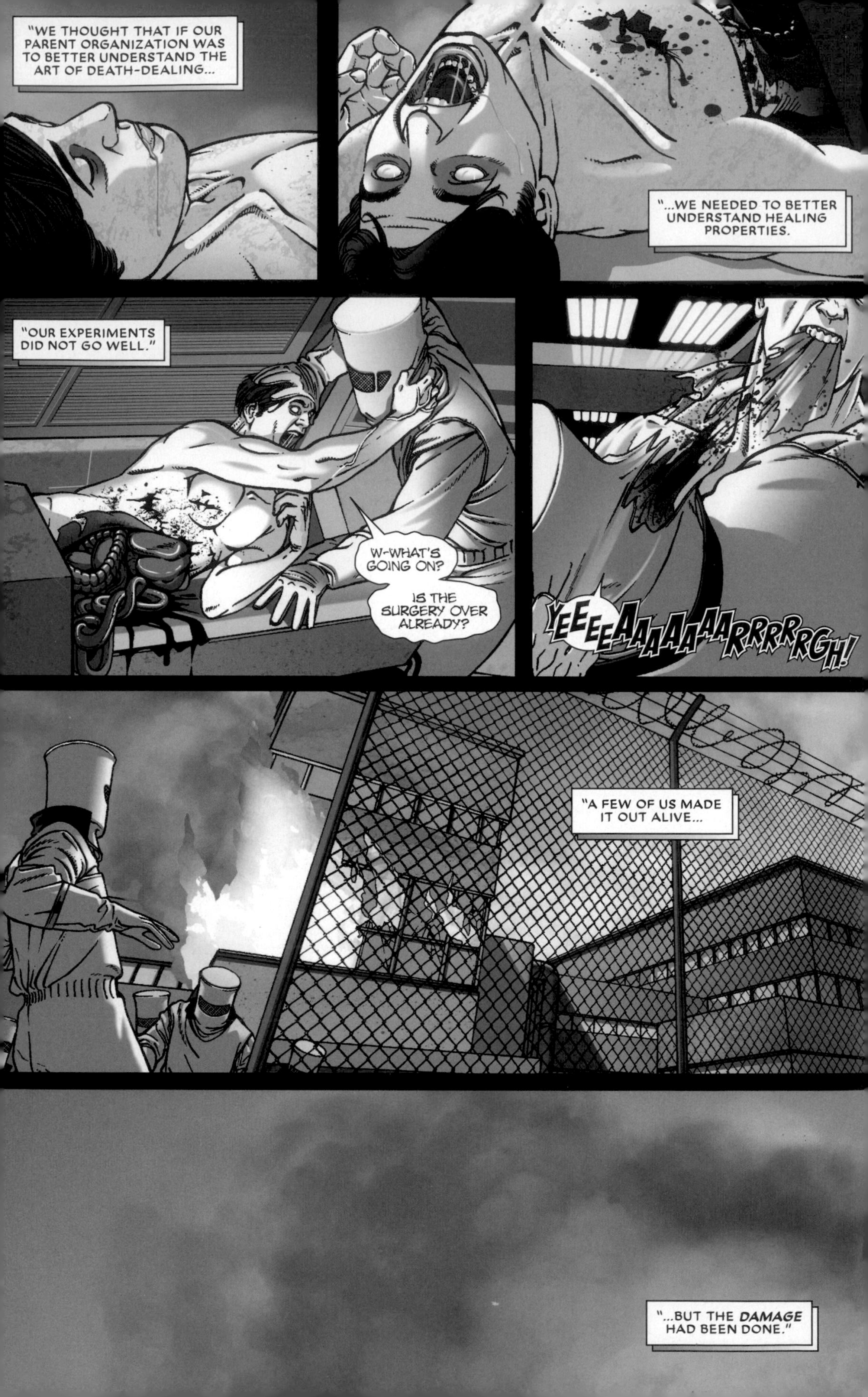
"WE THOUGHT THAT IF OUR PARENT ORGANIZATION WAS TO BETTER UNDERSTAND THE ART OF DEATH-DEALING...
"...WE NEEDED TO BETTER UNDERSTAND HEALING PROPERTIES.
"OUR EXPERIMENTS DID NOT GO WELL."
W-WHAT'S GOING ON?
IS THE SURGERY OVER ALREADY?
YEEEEAAAAAAARRRRRGH!
"A FEW OF US MADE IT OUT ALIVE...
"...BUT THE *DAMAGE* HAD BEEN DONE."

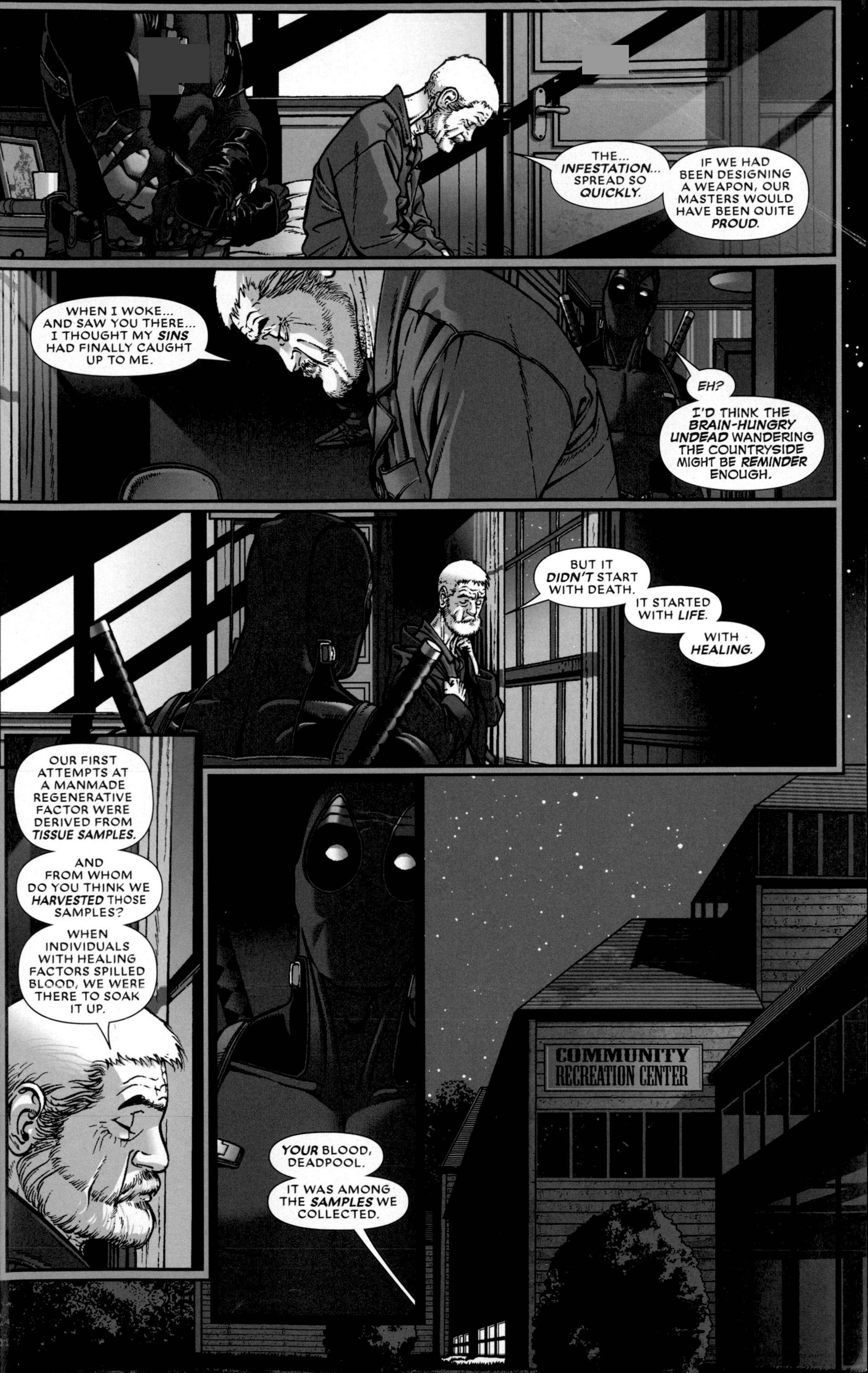
THE... INFESTATION... SPREAD SO QUICKLY.
IF WE HAD BEEN DESIGNING A WEAPON, OUR MASTERS WOULD HAVE BEEN QUITE PROUD.
WHEN I WOKE... AND SAW YOU THERE... I THOUGHT MY SINS HAD FINALLY CAUGHT UP TO ME.
EH?
I'D THINK THE BRAIN-HUNGRY UNDEAD WANDERING THE COUNTRYSIDE MIGHT BE REMINDER ENOUGH.
BUT IT DIDN'T START WITH DEATH.
IT STARTED WITH LIFE.
WITH HEALING.
OUR FIRST ATTEMPTS AT A MANMADE REGENERATIVE FACTOR WERE DERIVED FROM TISSUE SAMPLES.
AND FROM WHOM DO YOU THINK WE HARVESTED THOSE SAMPLES?
WHEN INDIVIDUALS WITH HEALING FACTORS SPILLED BLOOD, WE WERE THERE TO SOAK IT UP.
COMMUNITY RECREATION CENTER
YOUR BLOOD, DEADPOOL.
IT WAS AMONG THE SAMPLES WE COLLECTED.

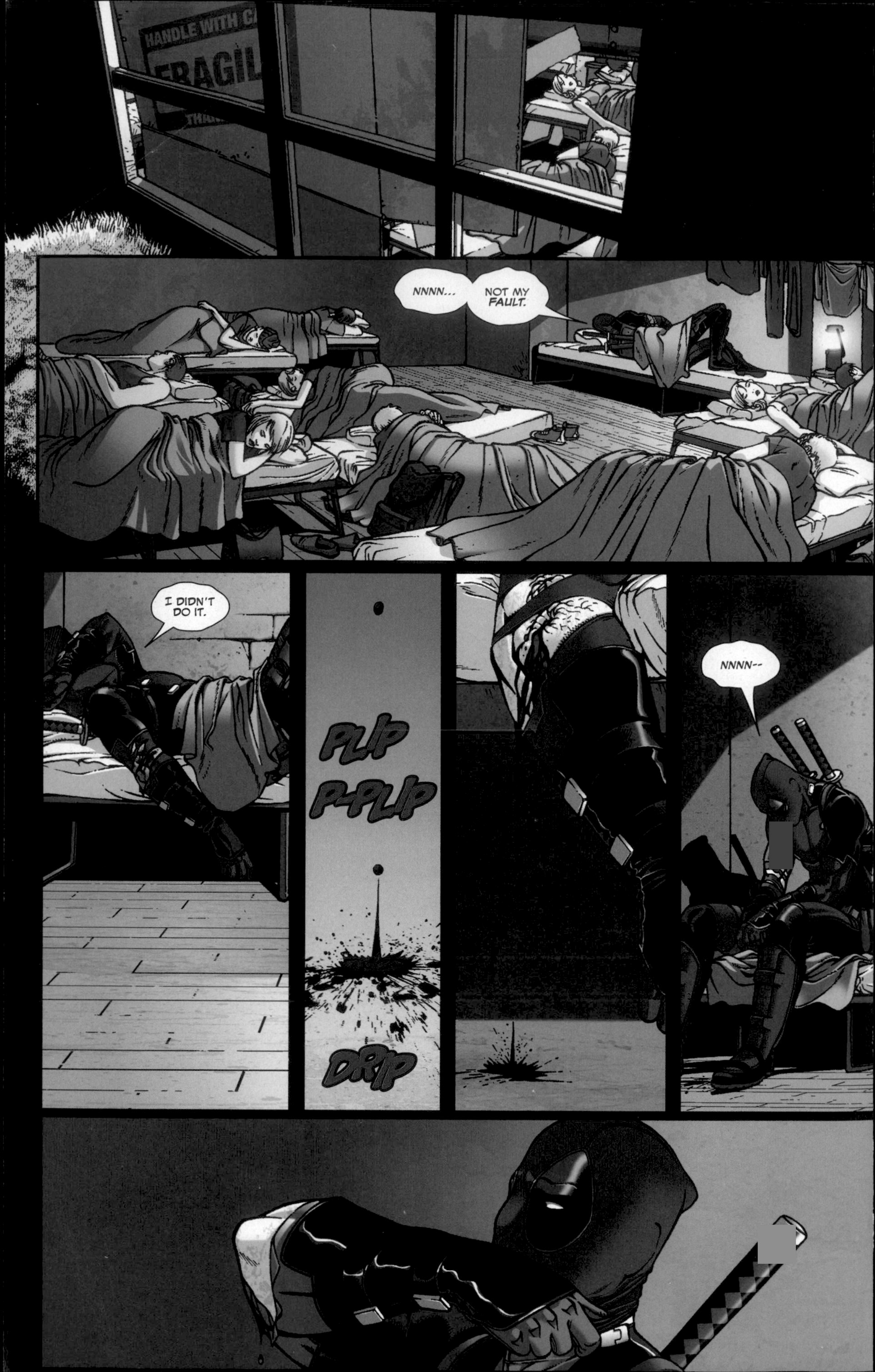
HANDLE WITH CA
FRAGIL
NNNN...
NOT MY FAULT.
I DIDN'T DO IT.
PLIP
P-PLIP
DRIP
NNNN--

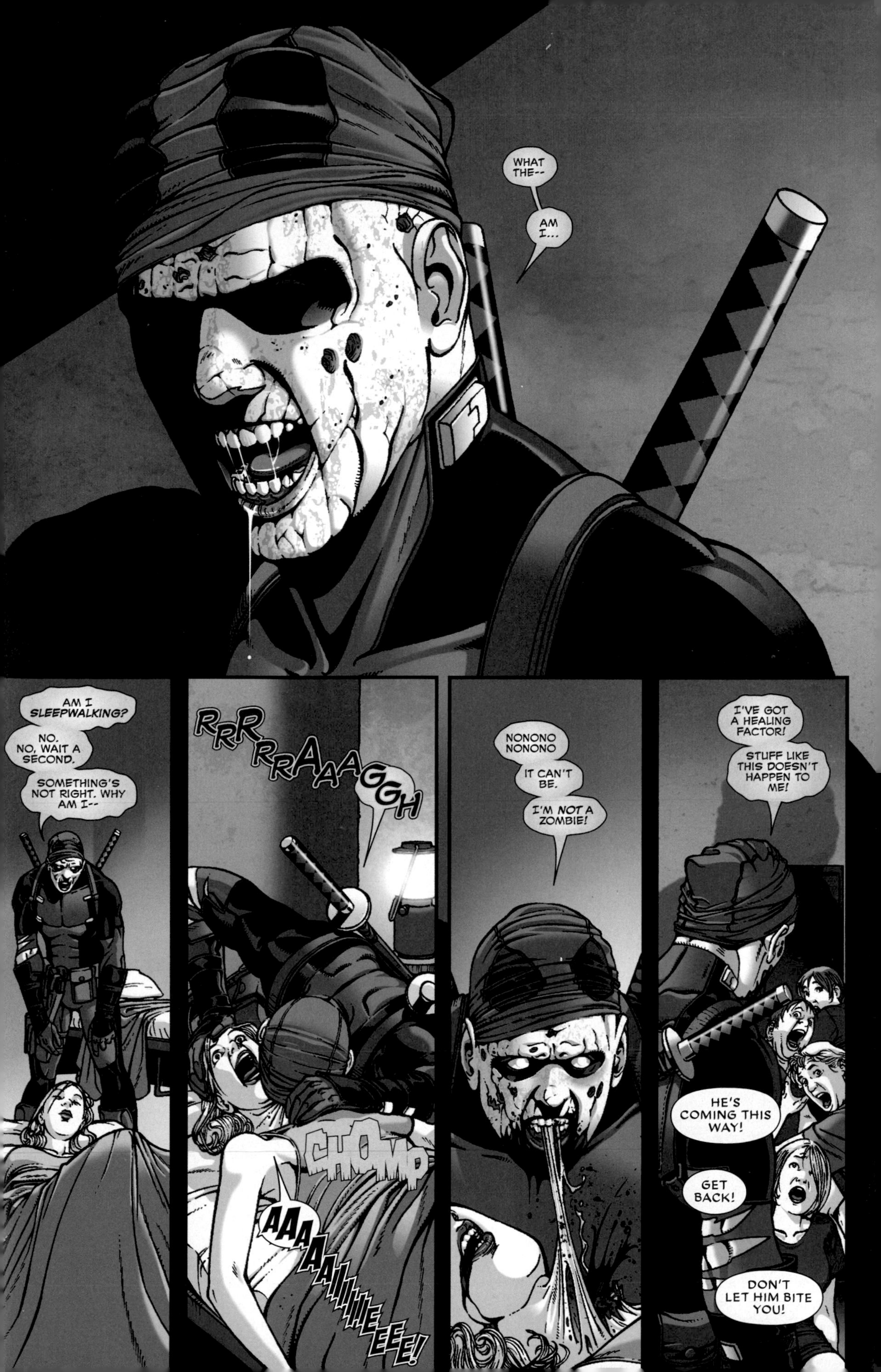
WHAT THE--
AM I...
AM I SLEEPWALKING?
NO. NO, WAIT A SECOND.
SOMETHING'S NOT RIGHT. WHY AM I--
RRRRRRAAAAGGH
CHOMP
AAAAAIIIIIEEEEE!
NONONO NONONO
IT CAN'T BE.
I'M NOT A ZOMBIE!
I'VE GOT A HEALING FACTOR!
STUFF LIKE THIS DOESN'T HAPPEN TO ME!
HE'S COMING THIS WAY!
GET BACK!
DON'T LET HIM BITE YOU!

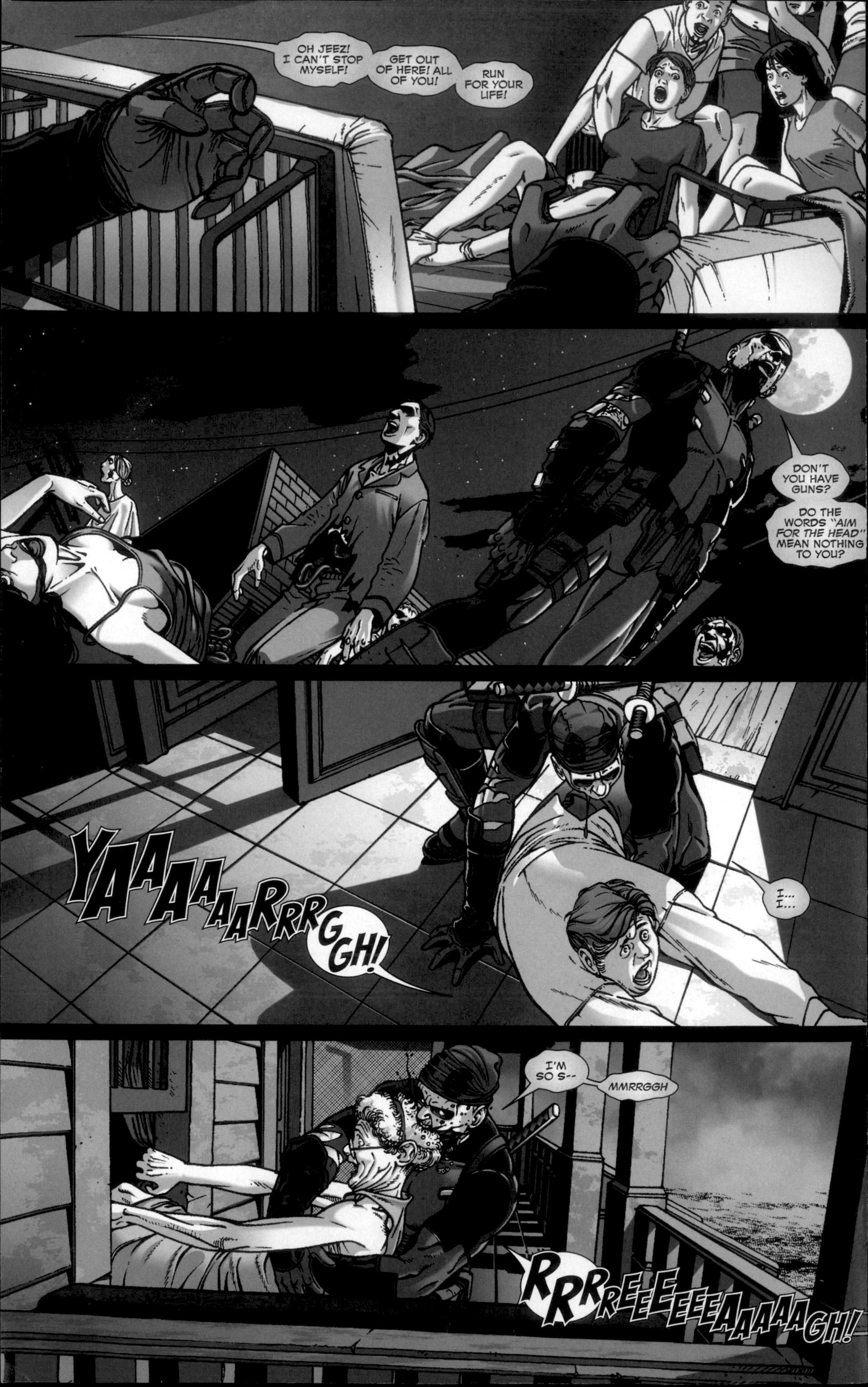
OH JEEZ! I CAN'T STOP MYSELF!
GET OUT OF HERE! ALL OF YOU!
RUN FOR YOUR LIFE!
DON'T YOU HAVE GUNS?
DO THE WORDS "AIM FOR THE HEAD" MEAN NOTHING TO YOU?
YAAAAARRRGGH!
I... I...
I'M SO S--
MMRRGGH
RRRREEEEEEAAAAAGH!

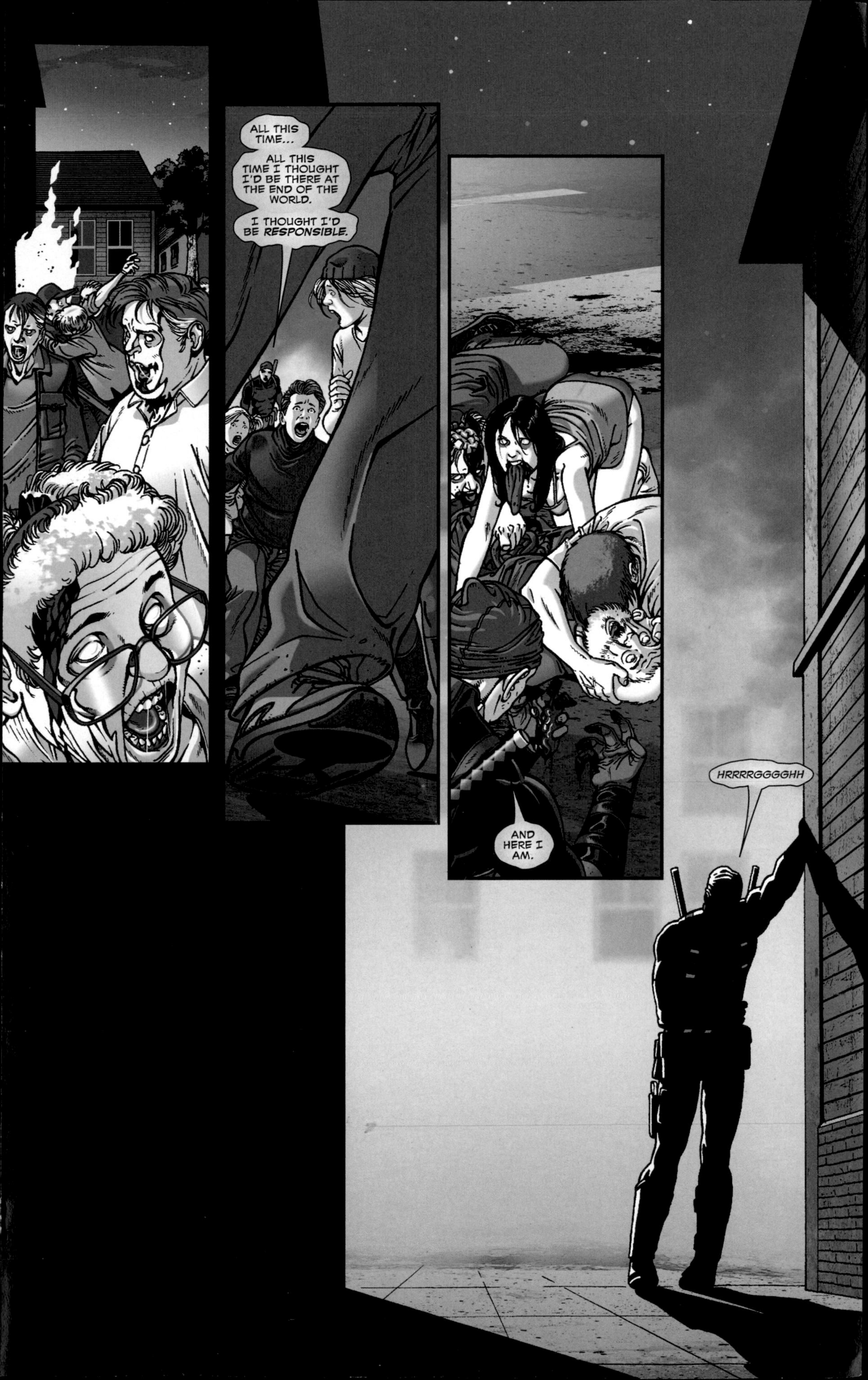
ALL THIS TIME...
ALL THIS TIME I THOUGHT I'D BE THERE AT THE END OF THE WORLD.
I THOUGHT I'D BE *RESPONSIBLE.*
AND HERE I AM.
HRRRRGGGGHH

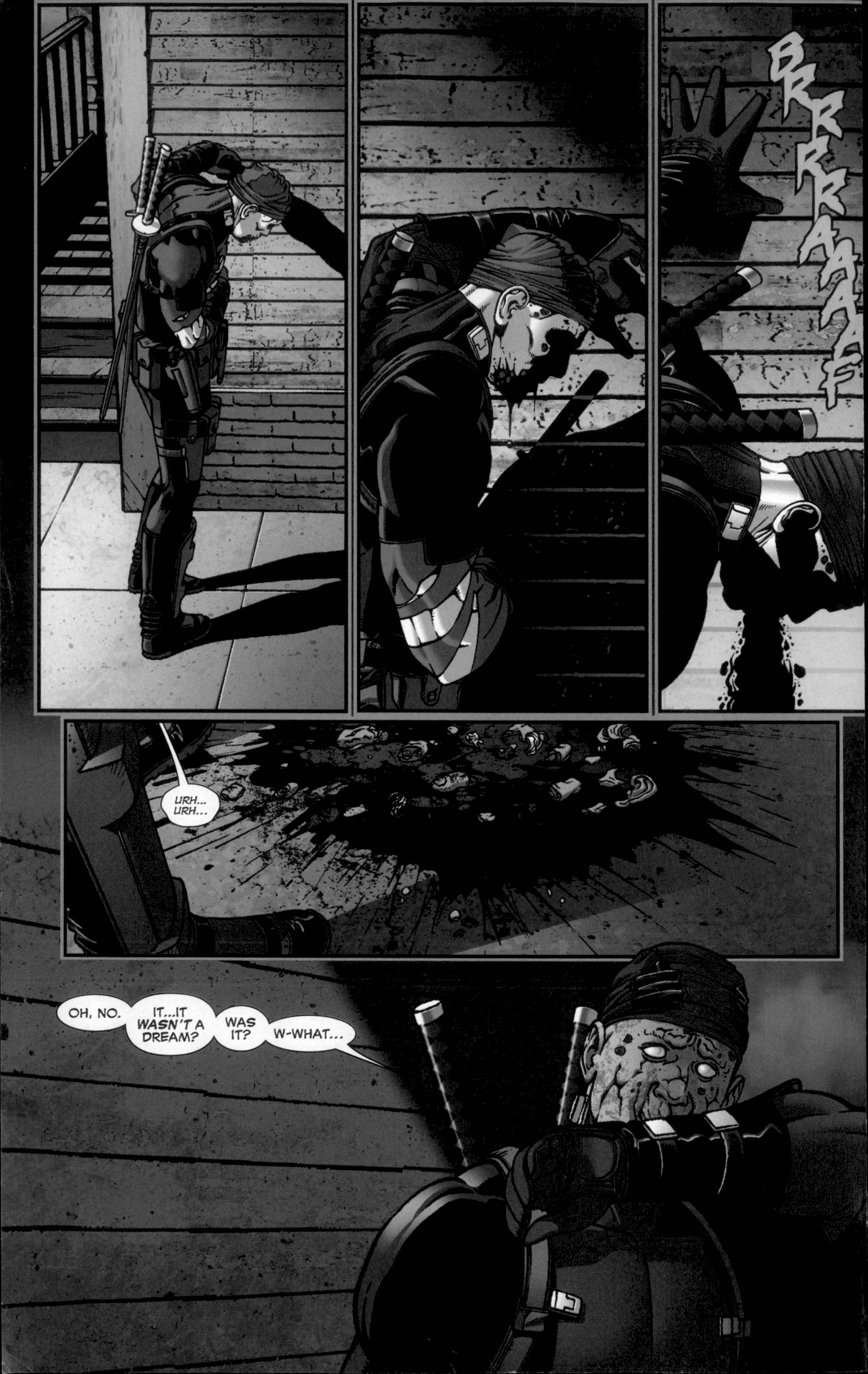
BRRRAAAAAF
URH... URH...
OH, NO.
IT...IT WASN'T A DREAM?
WAS IT?
W-WHAT...

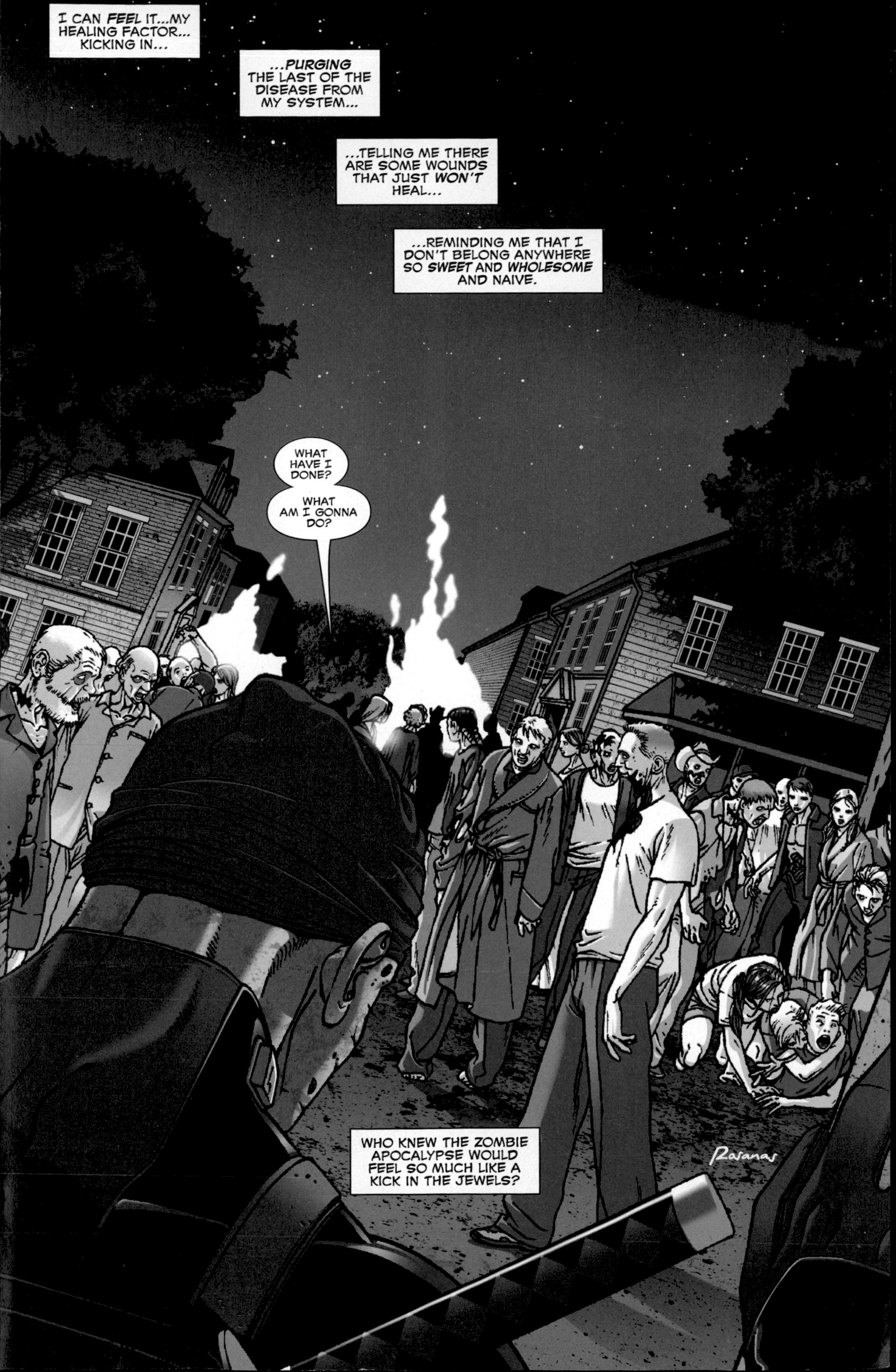
I CAN FEEL IT...MY HEALING FACTOR... KICKING IN...
...PURGING THE LAST OF THE DISEASE FROM MY SYSTEM...
...TELLING ME THERE ARE SOME WOUNDS THAT JUST WON'T HEAL...
...REMINDING ME THAT I DON'T BELONG ANYWHERE SO SWEET AND WHOLESOME AND NAIVE.
WHAT HAVE I DONE?
WHAT AM I GONNA DO?
WHO KNEW THE ZOMBIE APOCALYPSE WOULD FEEL SO MUCH LIKE A KICK IN THE JEWELS?
Rosanas

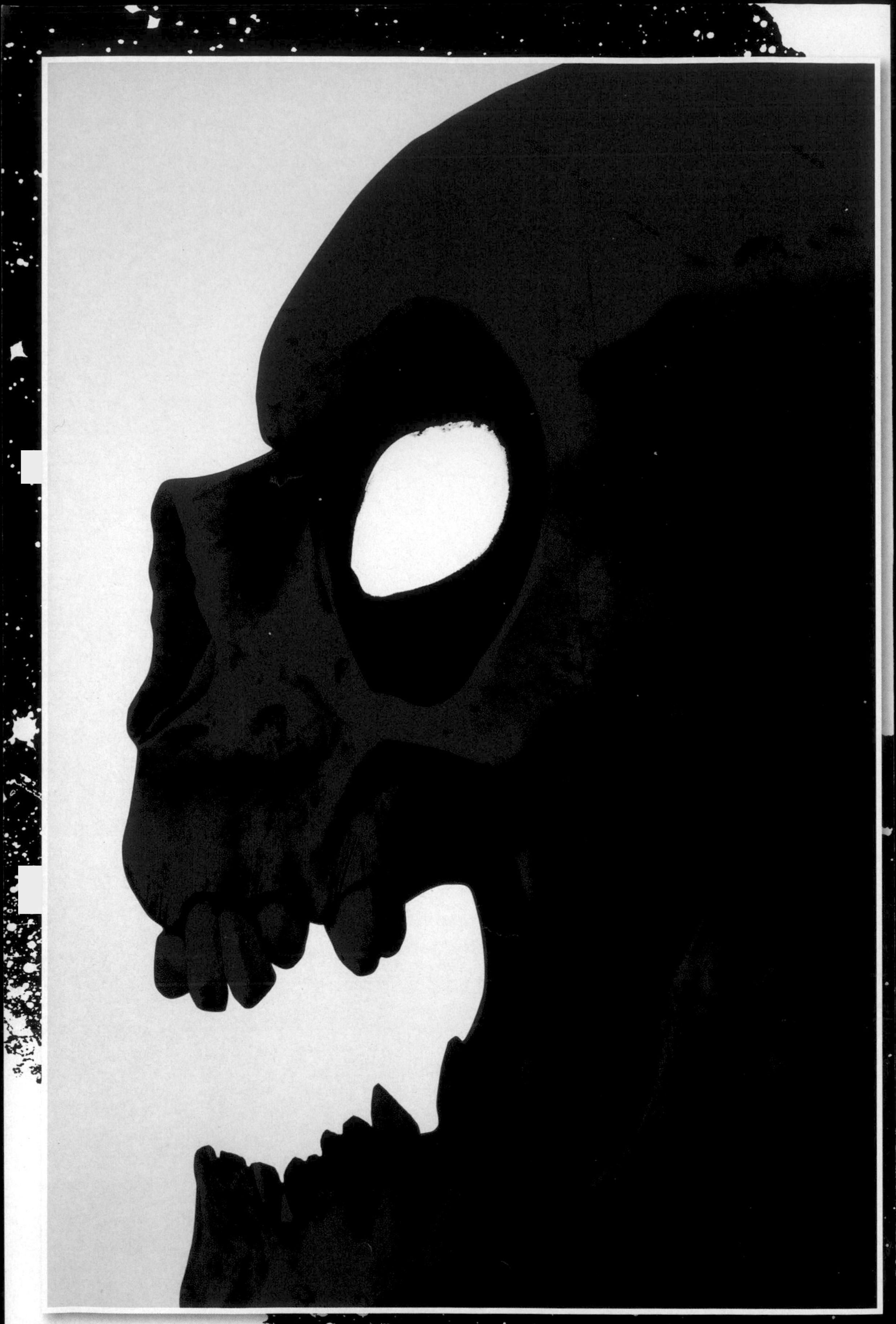

#4

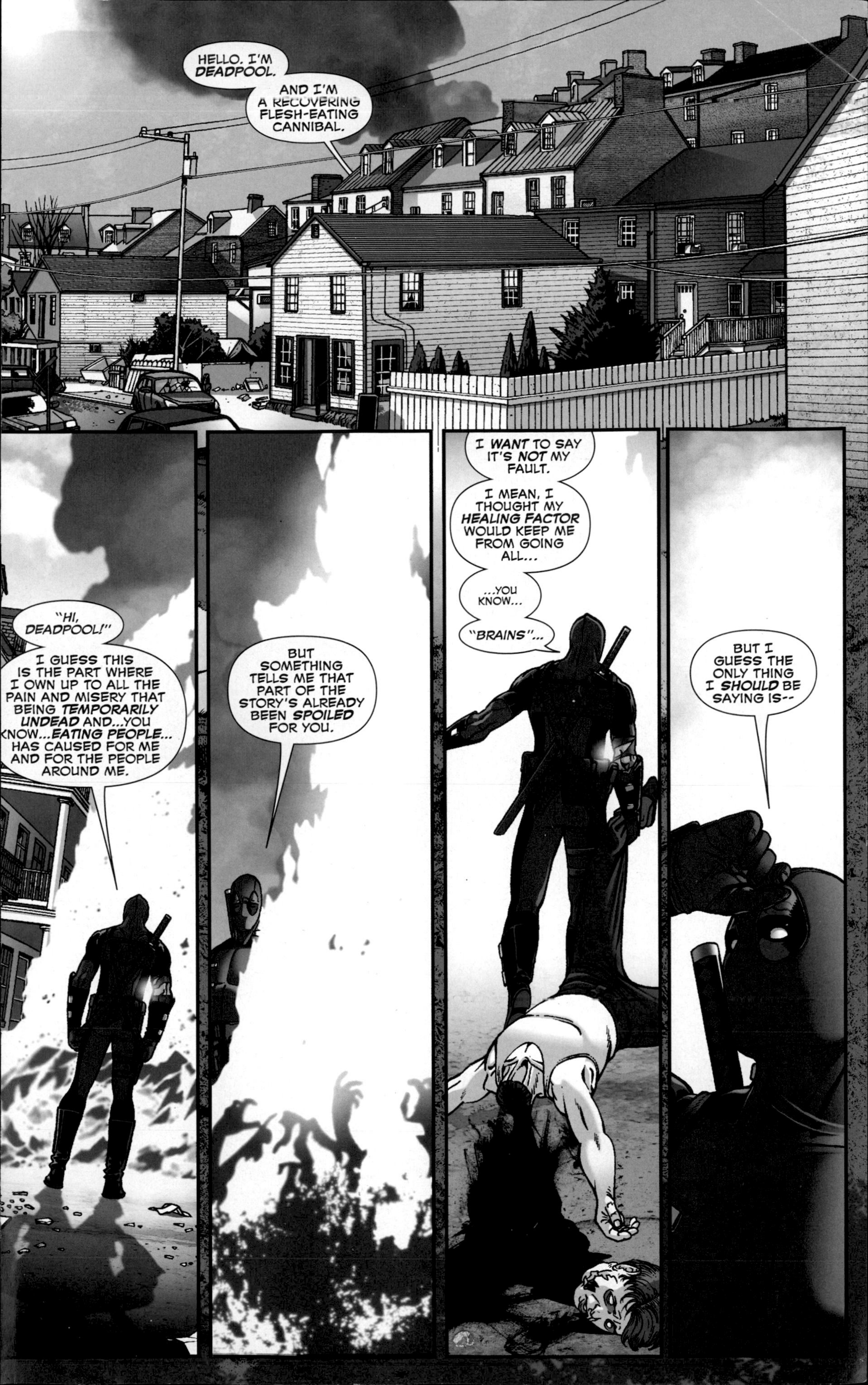

HELLO. I'M DEADPOOL.
AND I'M A RECOVERING FLESH-EATING CANNIBAL.
"HI, DEADPOOL!"
I GUESS THIS IS THE PART WHERE I OWN UP TO ALL THE PAIN AND MISERY THAT BEING TEMPORARILY UNDEAD AND...YOU KNOW...EATING PEOPLE... HAS CAUSED FOR ME AND FOR THE PEOPLE AROUND ME.
BUT SOMETHING TELLS ME THAT PART OF THE STORY'S ALREADY BEEN SPOILED FOR YOU.
I WANT TO SAY IT'S NOT MY FAULT.
I MEAN, I THOUGHT MY HEALING FACTOR WOULD KEEP ME FROM GOING ALL...
...YOU KNOW...
"BRAINS"...
BUT I GUESS THE ONLY THING I SHOULD BE SAYING IS--

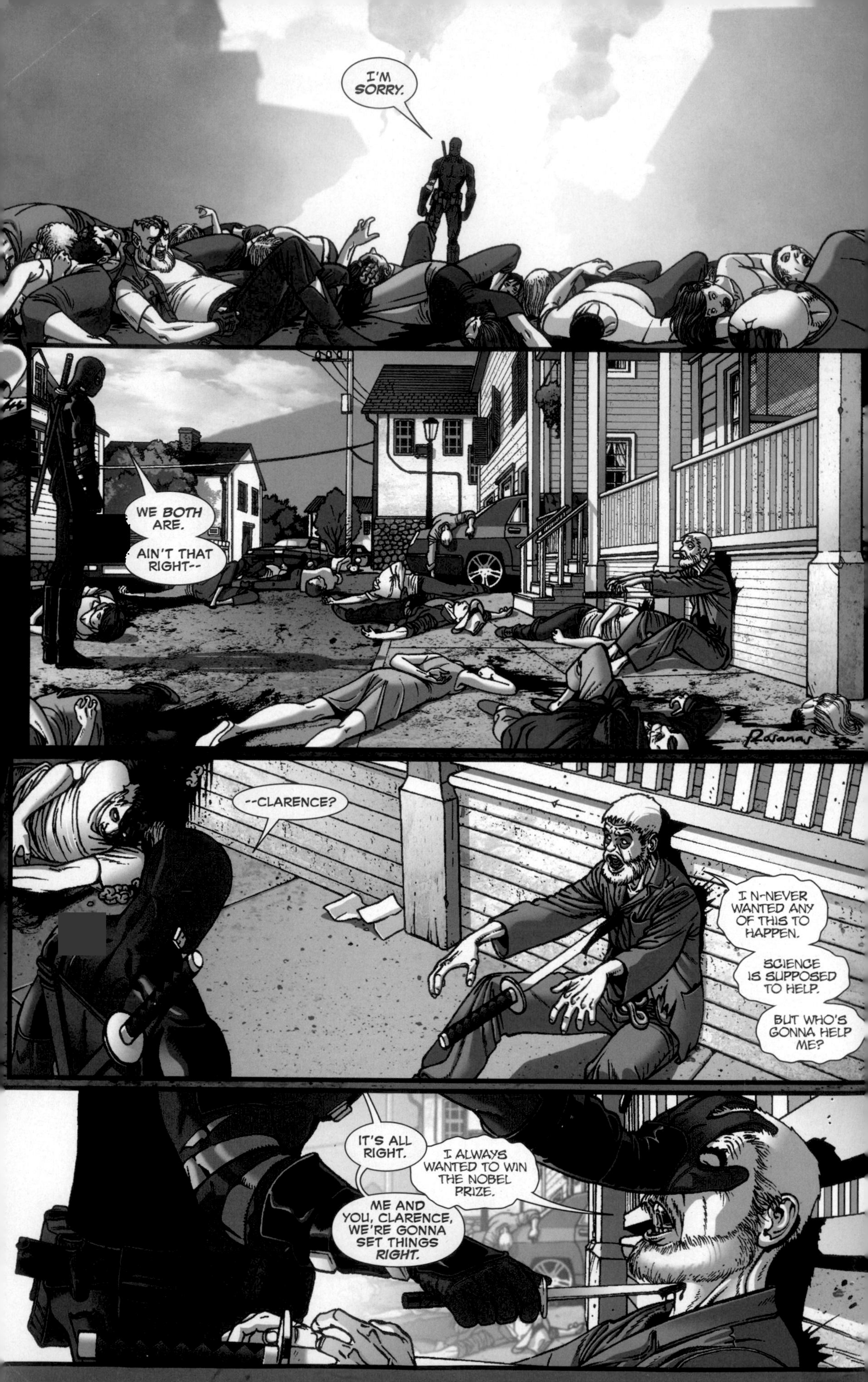
I'M SORRY.
WE BOTH ARE.
AIN'T THAT RIGHT--
--CLARENCE?
I N-NEVER WANTED ANY OF THIS TO HAPPEN.
SCIENCE IS SUPPOSED TO HELP.
BUT WHO'S GONNA HELP ME?
IT'S ALL RIGHT.
I ALWAYS WANTED TO WIN THE NOBEL PRIZE.
ME AND YOU, CLARENCE, WE'RE GONNA SET THINGS RIGHT.

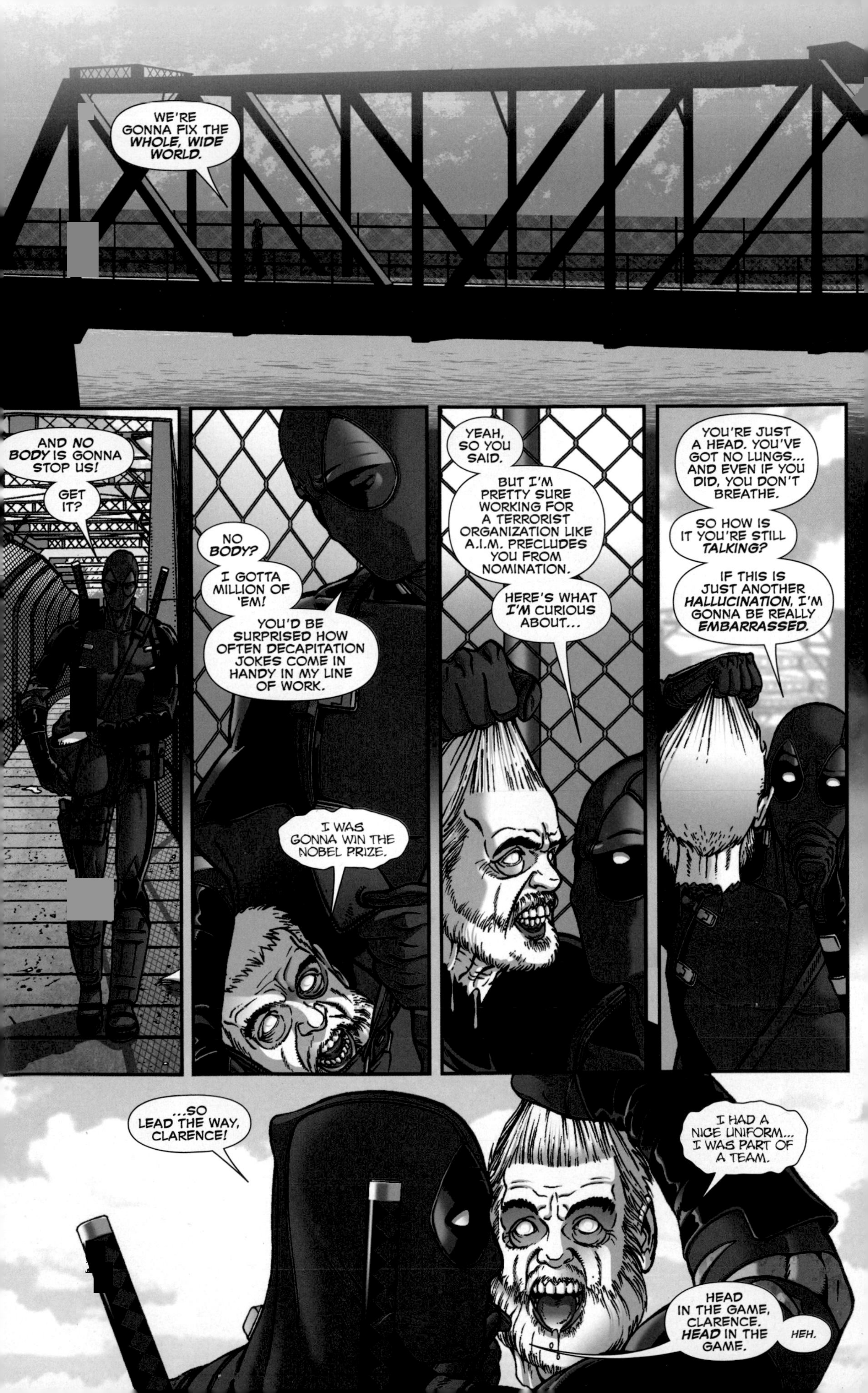
WE'RE GONNA FIX THE WHOLE, WIDE WORLD.
AND NO BODY IS GONNA STOP US!
GET IT?
NO BODY?
I GOTTA MILLION OF 'EM!
YOU'D BE SURPRISED HOW OFTEN DECAPITATION JOKES COME IN HANDY IN MY LINE OF WORK.
I WAS GONNA WIN THE NOBEL PRIZE.
YEAH, SO YOU SAID.
BUT I'M PRETTY SURE WORKING FOR A TERRORIST ORGANIZATION LIKE A.I.M. PRECLUDES YOU FROM NOMINATION.
HERE'S WHAT I'M CURIOUS ABOUT...
YOU'RE JUST A HEAD. YOU'VE GOT NO LUNGS... AND EVEN IF YOU DID, YOU DON'T BREATHE.
SO HOW IS IT YOU'RE STILL TALKING?
IF THIS IS JUST ANOTHER HALLUCINATION, I'M GONNA BE REALLY EMBARRASSED.
...SO LEAD THE WAY, CLARENCE!
I HAD A NICE UNIFORM... I WAS PART OF A TEAM.
HEAD IN THE GAME, CLARENCE. HEAD IN THE GAME.
HEH.

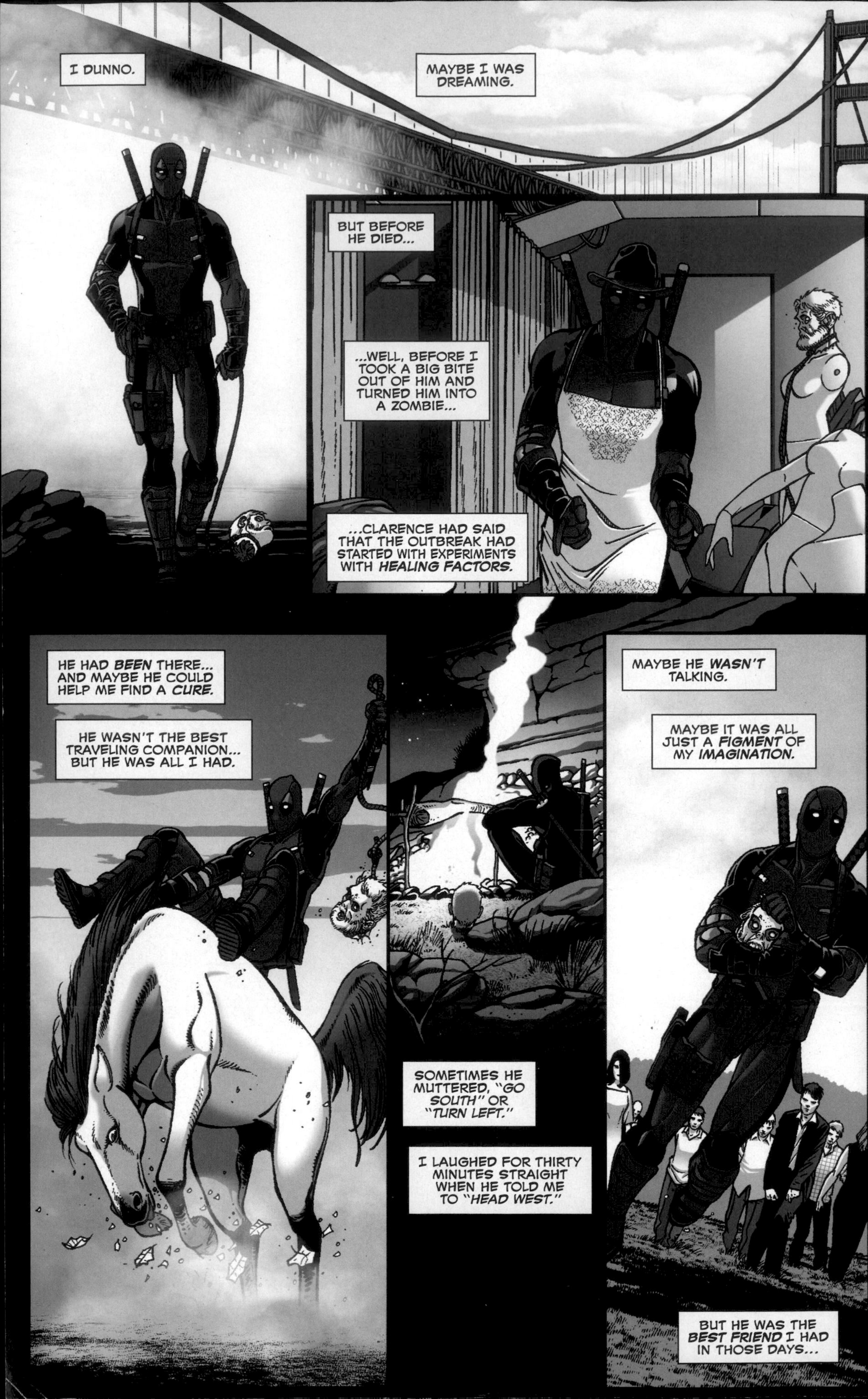
I DUNNO.
MAYBE I WAS DREAMING.
BUT BEFORE HE DIED...
...WELL, BEFORE I TOOK A BIG BITE OUT OF HIM AND TURNED HIM INTO A ZOMBIE...
...CLARENCE HAD SAID THAT THE OUTBREAK HAD STARTED WITH EXPERIMENTS WITH *HEALING FACTORS.*
HE HAD *BEEN* THERE... AND MAYBE HE COULD HELP ME FIND A *CURE.*
HE WASN'T THE BEST TRAVELING COMPANION... BUT HE WAS ALL I HAD.
SOMETIMES HE MUTTERED, "*GO SOUTH*" OR "*TURN LEFT.*"
I LAUGHED FOR THIRTY MINUTES STRAIGHT WHEN HE TOLD ME TO "*HEAD WEST.*"
MAYBE HE *WASN'T* TALKING.
MAYBE IT WAS ALL JUST A *FIGMENT* OF MY *IMAGINATION.*
BUT HE WAS THE *BEST FRIEND* I HAD IN THOSE DAYS...

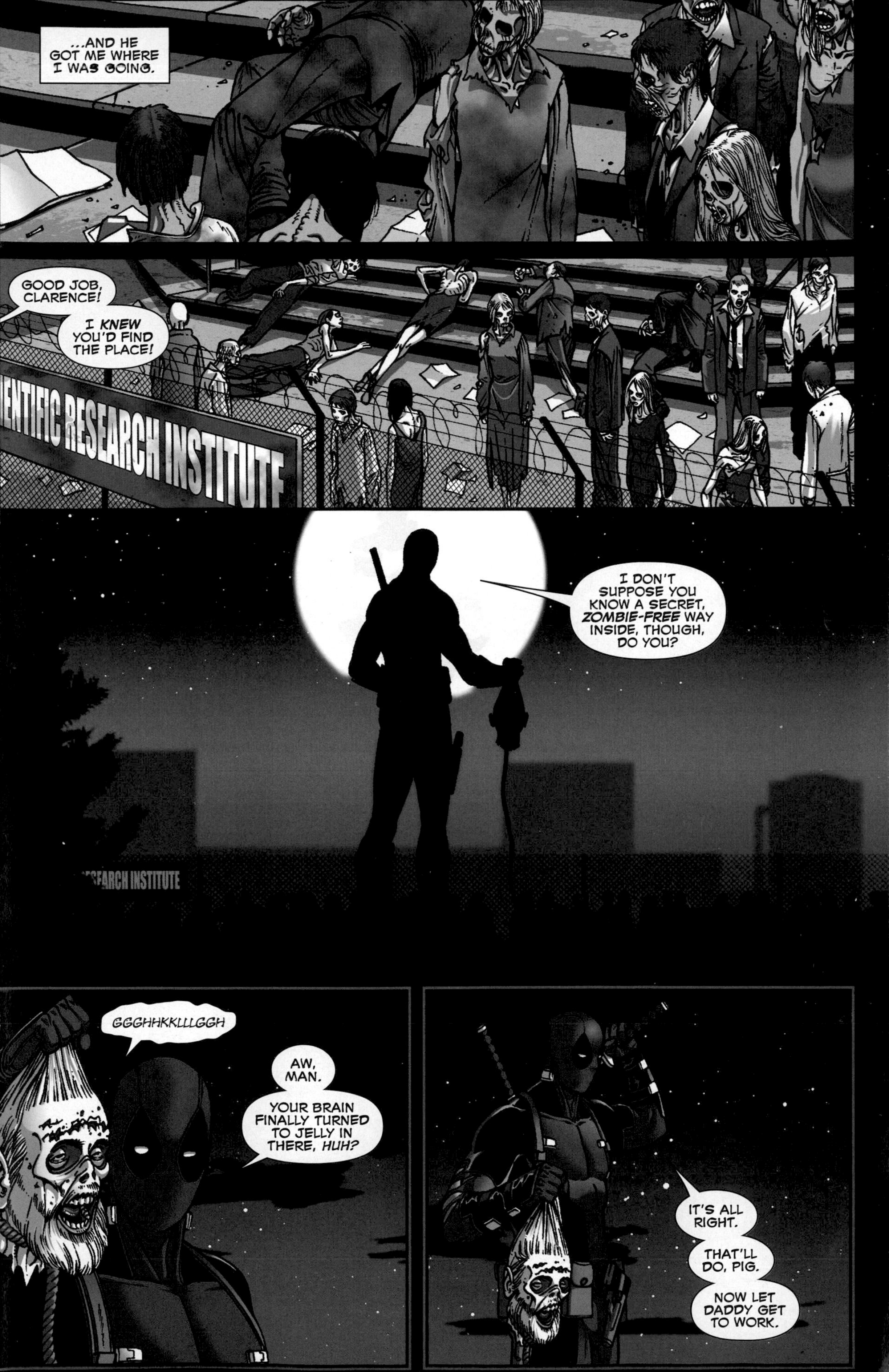

...AND HE GOT ME WHERE I WAS GOING.
GOOD JOB, CLARENCE!
I KNEW YOU'D FIND THE PLACE!
ENTIFIC RESEARCH INSTITUTE
I DON'T SUPPOSE YOU KNOW A SECRET, ZOMBIE-FREE WAY INSIDE, THOUGH, DO YOU?
RESEARCH INSTITUTE
GGGHHKKLLLGGH
AW, MAN.
YOUR BRAIN FINALLY TURNED TO JELLY IN THERE, HUH?
IT'S ALL RIGHT.
THAT'LL DO, PIG.
NOW LET DADDY GET TO WORK.

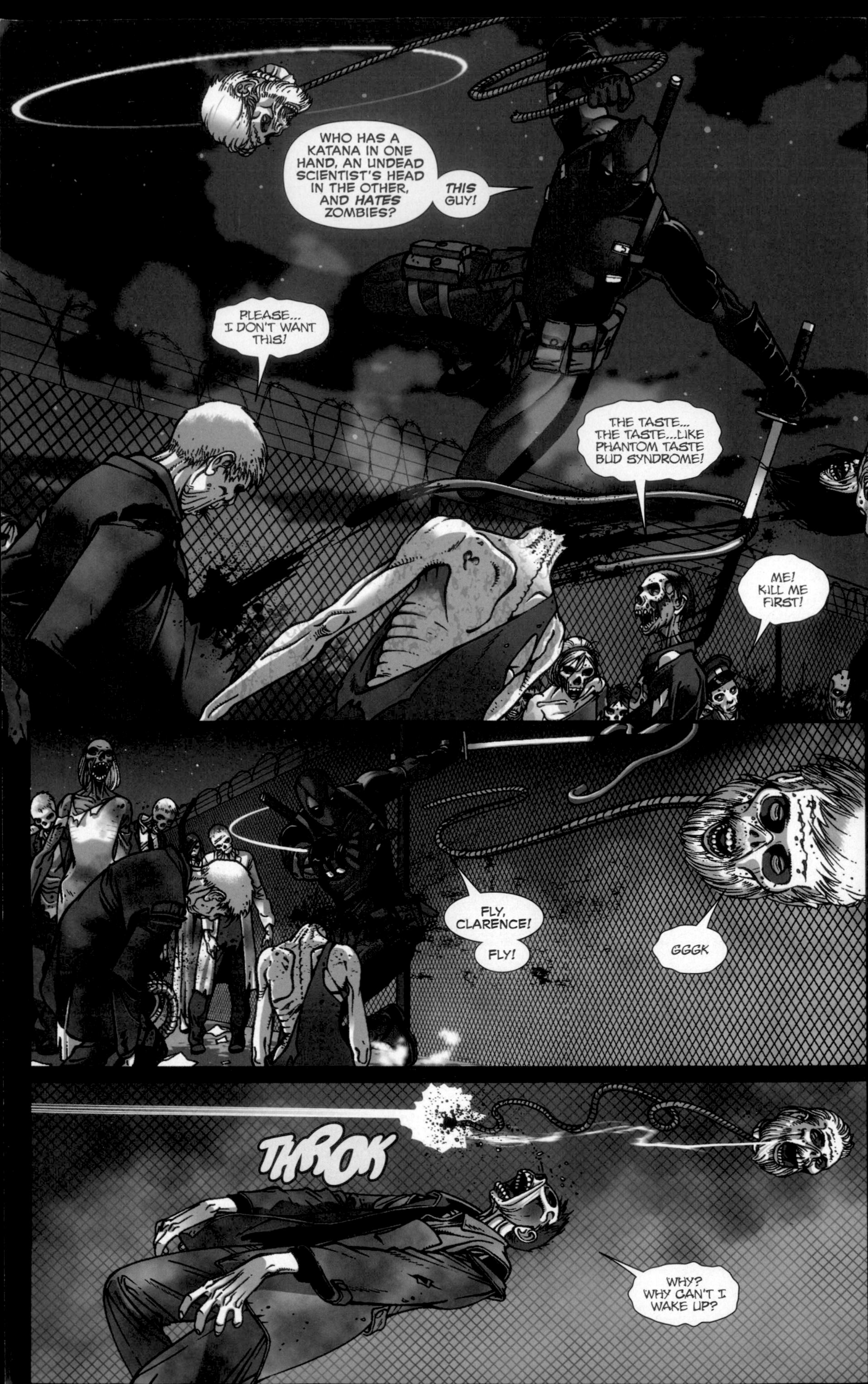
WHO HAS A KATANA IN ONE HAND, AN UNDEAD SCIENTIST'S HEAD IN THE OTHER, AND HATES ZOMBIES?
THIS GUY!
PLEASE... I DON'T WANT THIS!
THE TASTE... THE TASTE...LIKE PHANTOM TASTE BUD SYNDROME!
ME! KILL ME FIRST!
FLY, CLARENCE!
FLY!
GGGK
THROK
WHY? WHY CAN'T I WAKE UP?

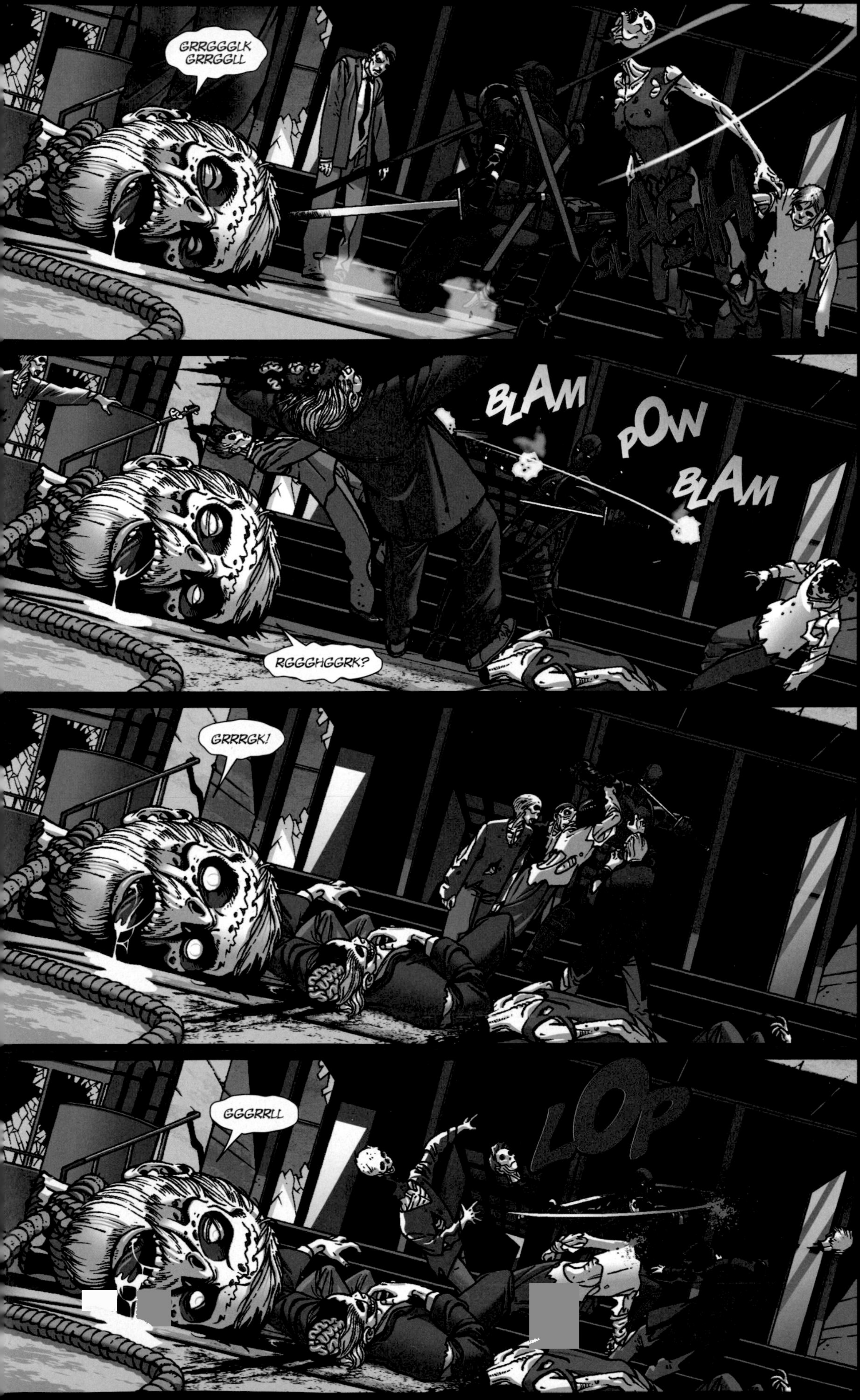
GRRGGGLK GRRGGLL
SLASH
BLAM
POW
BLAM
RGGGHGGRK?
GRRRGK!
GGGRRLL
LOP

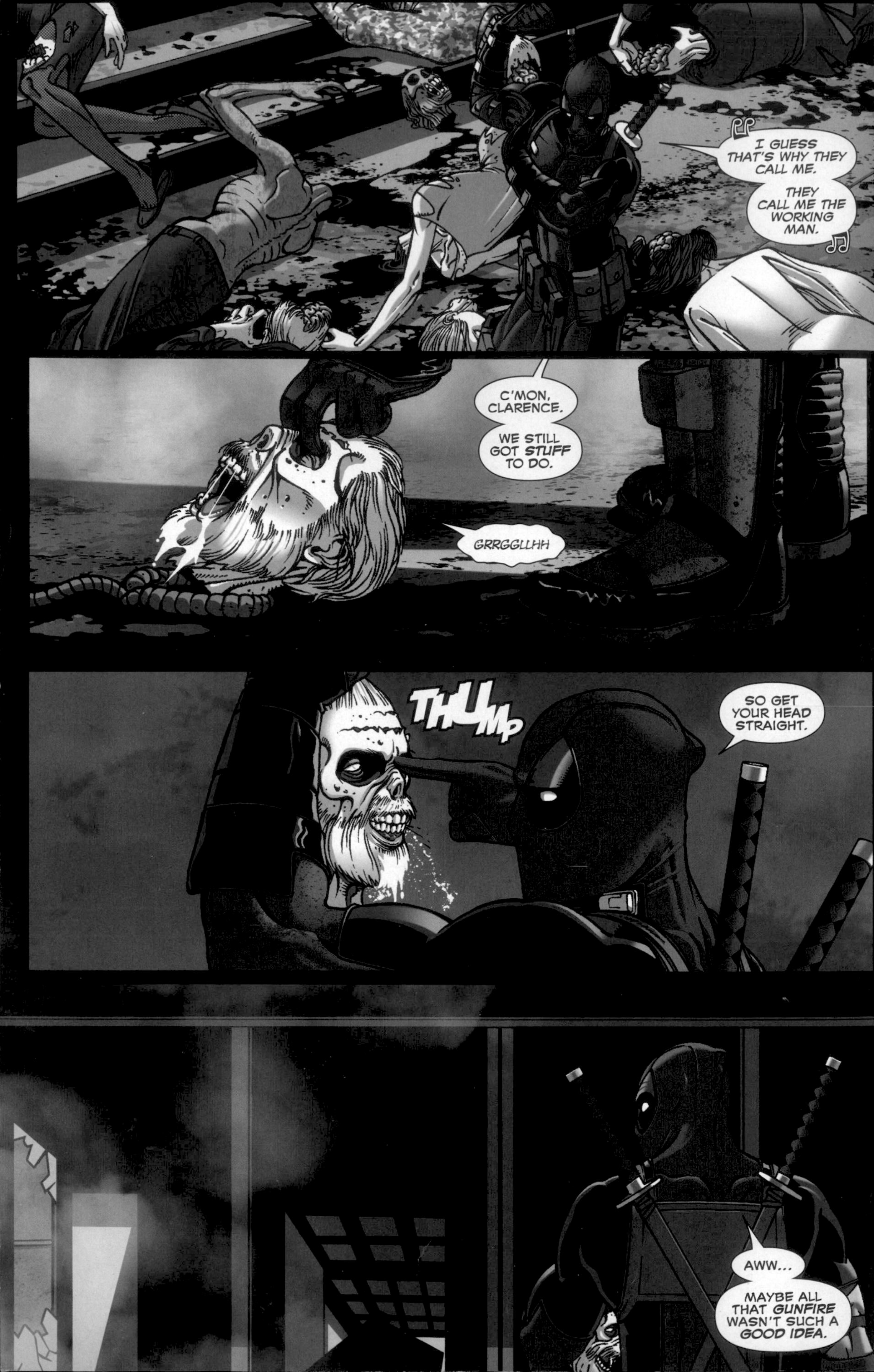
I GUESS THAT'S WHY THEY CALL ME.
THEY CALL ME THE WORKING MAN.
C'MON, CLARENCE.
WE STILL GOT STUFF TO DO.
GRRGGLLHH
THUMP
SO GET YOUR HEAD STRAIGHT.
AWW...
MAYBE ALL THAT GUNFIRE WASN'T SUCH A GOOD IDEA.

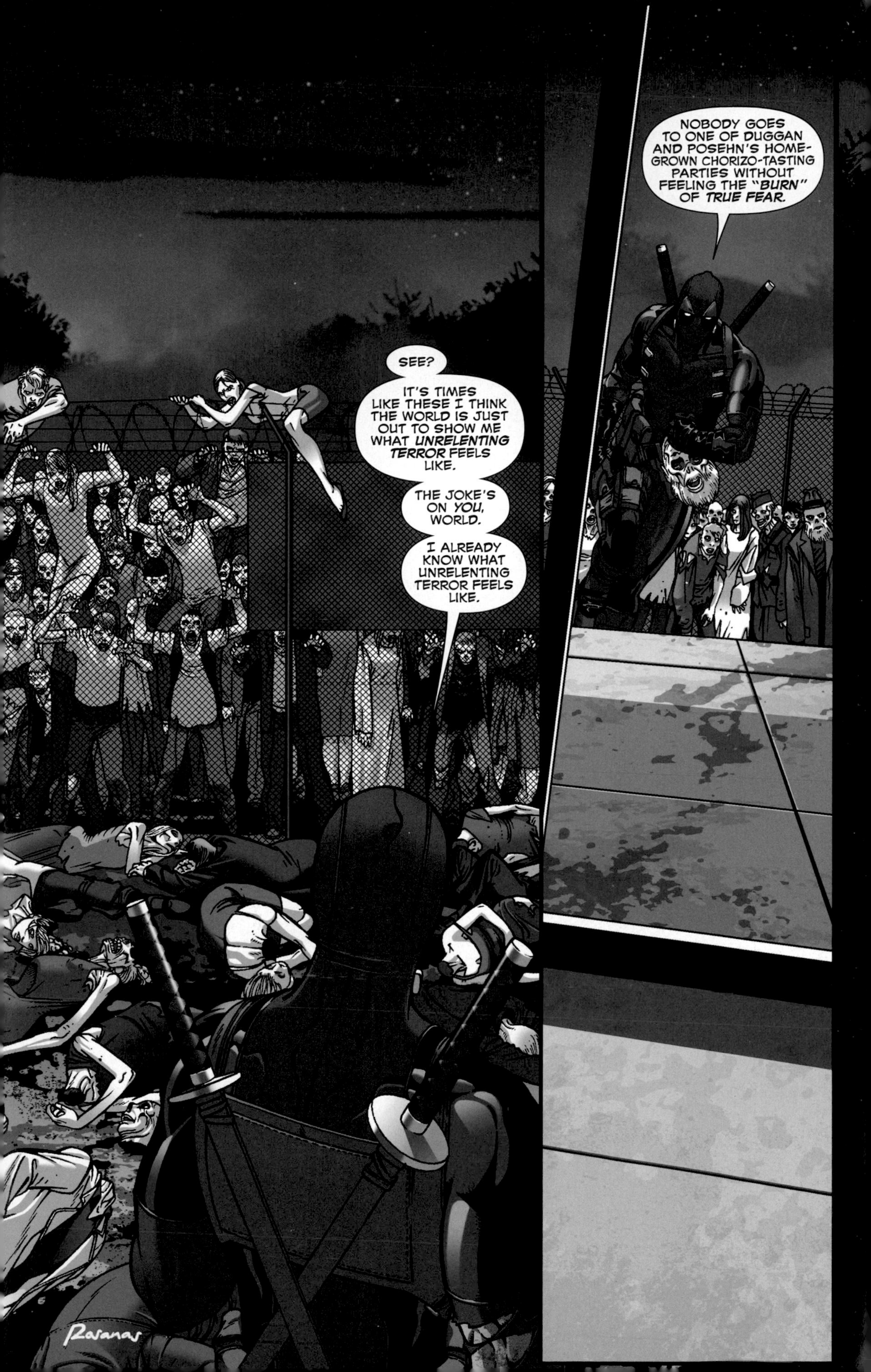
SEE?
IT'S TIMES LIKE THESE I THINK THE WORLD IS JUST OUT TO SHOW ME WHAT UNRELENTING TERROR FEELS LIKE.
THE JOKE'S ON YOU, WORLD.
I ALREADY KNOW WHAT UNRELENTING TERROR FEELS LIKE.
NOBODY GOES TO ONE OF DUGGAN AND POSEHN'S HOME-GROWN CHORIZO-TASTING PARTIES WITHOUT FEELING THE "BURN" OF TRUE FEAR.
Rosanas

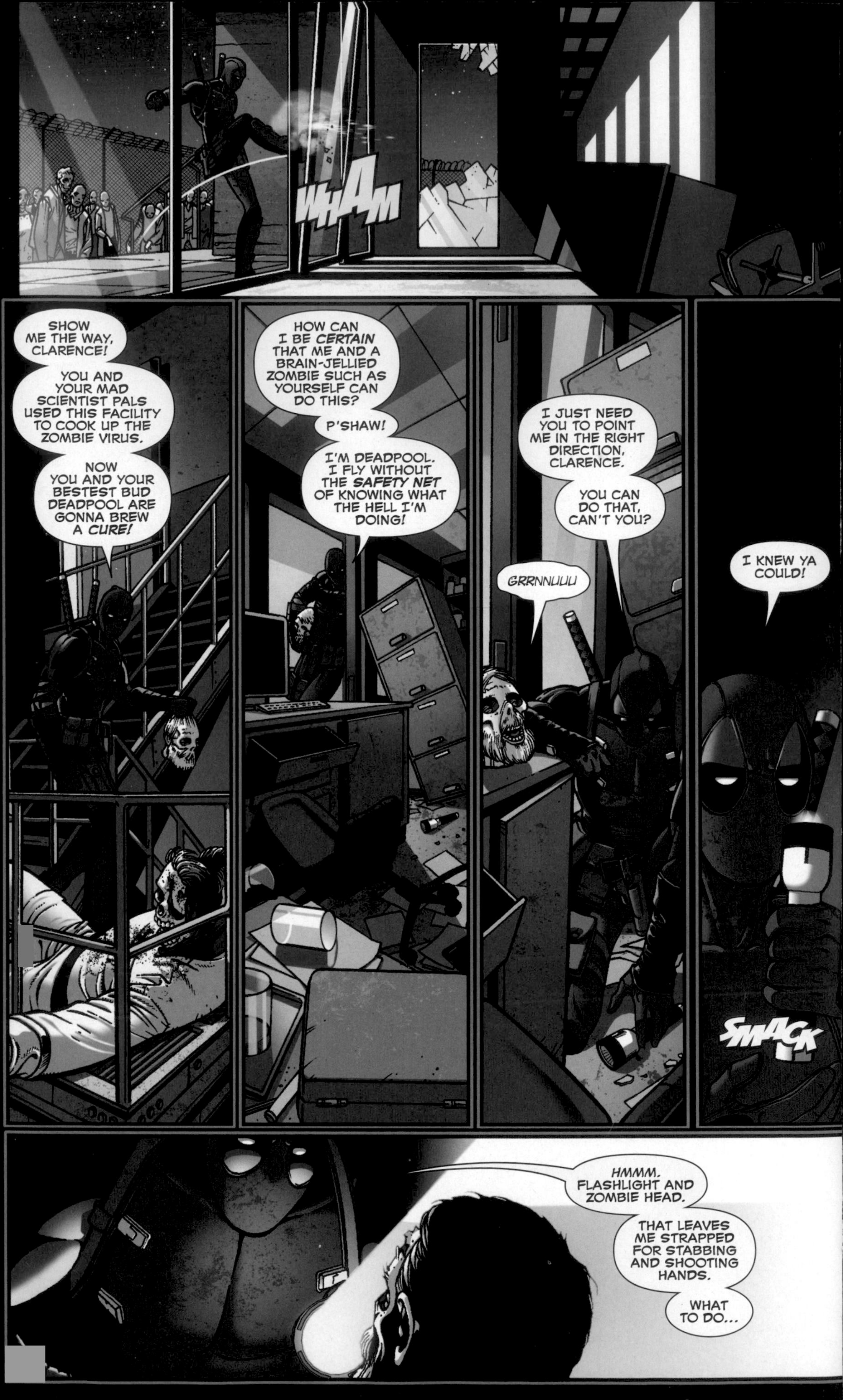
WHAM
SHOW ME THE WAY, CLARENCE!
YOU AND YOUR MAD SCIENTIST PALS USED THIS FACILITY TO COOK UP THE ZOMBIE VIRUS.
NOW YOU AND YOUR BESTEST BUD DEADPOOL ARE GONNA BREW A *CURE!*
HOW CAN I BE *CERTAIN* THAT ME AND A BRAIN-JELLIED ZOMBIE SUCH AS YOURSELF CAN DO THIS?
P'SHAW!
I'M DEADPOOL. I FLY WITHOUT THE *SAFETY NET* OF KNOWING WHAT THE HELL I'M DOING!
I JUST NEED YOU TO POINT ME IN THE RIGHT DIRECTION, CLARENCE.
YOU CAN DO THAT, CAN'T YOU?
GRRNNUUU
I KNEW YA COULD!
SMACK
HMMM. FLASHLIGHT AND ZOMBIE HEAD.
THAT LEAVES ME STRAPPED FOR STABBING AND SHOOTING HANDS.
WHAT TO DO...

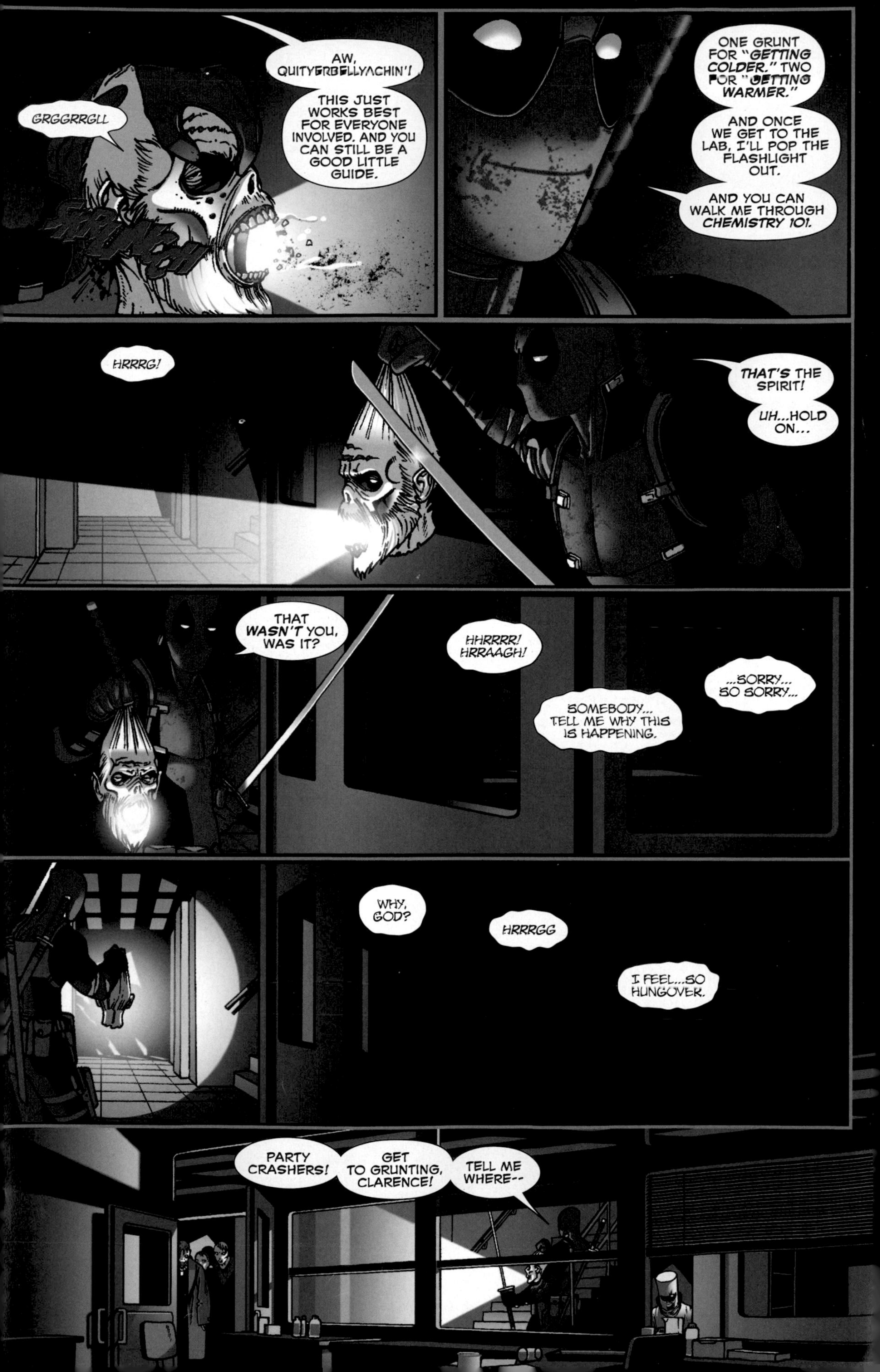
GRGGRRGLL
AW, QUITYERBELLYACHIN'!
THIS JUST WORKS BEST FOR EVERYONE INVOLVED. AND YOU CAN STILL BE A GOOD LITTLE GUIDE.
SKRUNCH
ONE GRUNT FOR "GETTING COLDER." TWO FOR "GETTING WARMER."
AND ONCE WE GET TO THE LAB, I'LL POP THE FLASHLIGHT OUT.
AND YOU CAN WALK ME THROUGH CHEMISTRY 101.
HRRRG!
THAT'S THE SPIRIT!
UH...HOLD ON...
THAT WASN'T YOU, WAS IT?
HHRRRR! HRRAAGH!
SOMEBODY... TELL ME WHY THIS IS HAPPENING.
...SORRY... SO SORRY...
WHY, GOD?
HRRRGG
I FEEL...SO HUNGOVER.
PARTY CRASHERS!
GET TO GRUNTING, CLARENCE!
TELL ME WHERE--

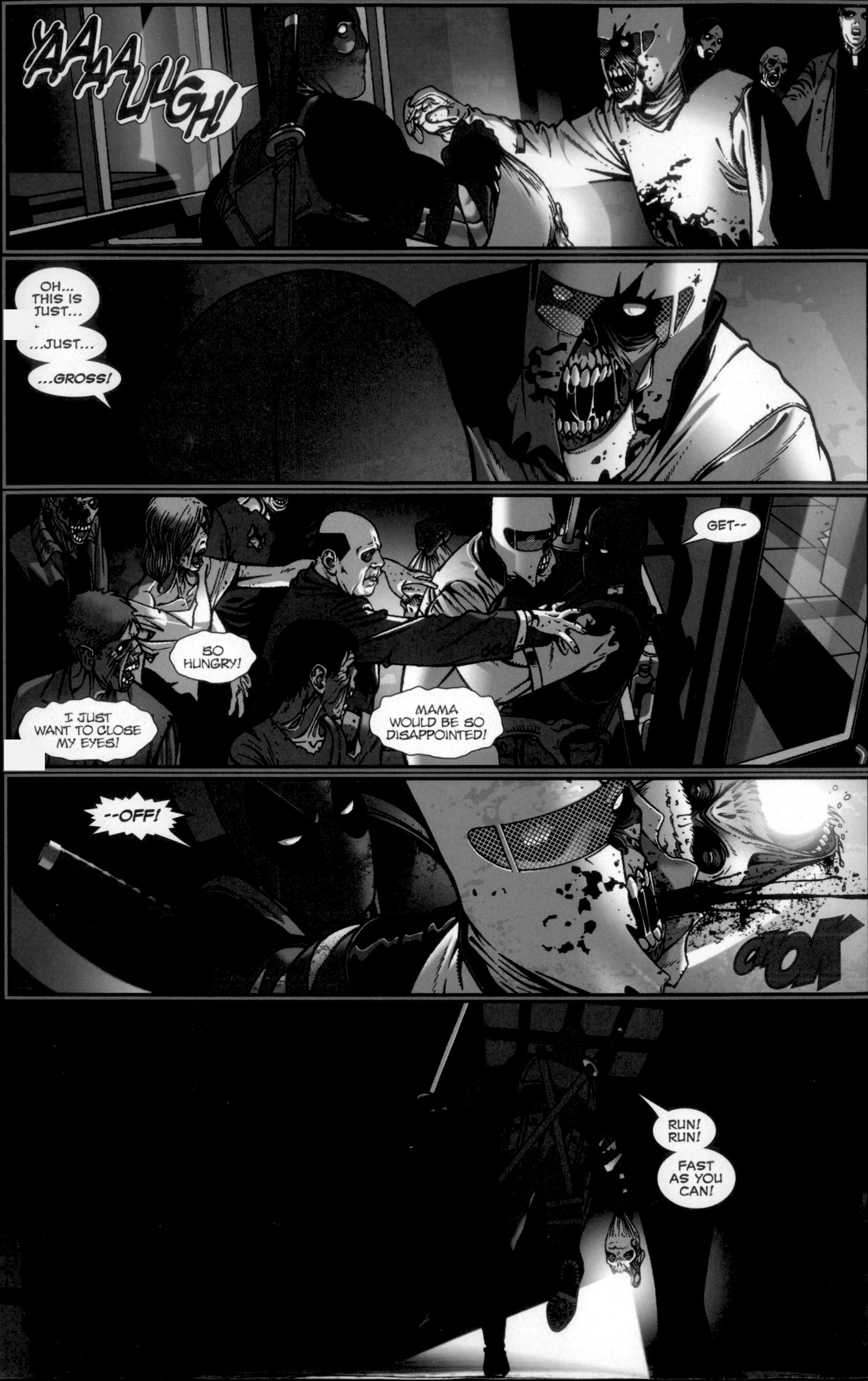
YAAAAUUGH!
OH... THIS IS JUST...
...JUST...
...GROSS!
GET--
SO HUNGRY!
I JUST WANT TO CLOSE MY EYES!
MAMA WOULD BE SO DISAPPOINTED!
--OFF!
CHOK
RUN! RUN!
FAST AS YOU CAN!

OR...YOU KNOW...

SHAMBLE! SHAMBLE!

AS CLUMSY AS YOU CAN!

EITHER WAY.

YOU CAN'T CATCH ME!

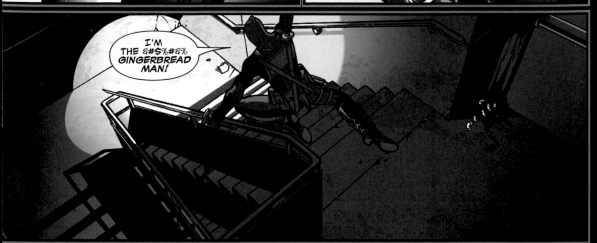

I'M THE a#$%#a% GINGERBREAD MAN!

A LOT OF YOUR SCIENTIST BUDDIES DIDN'T MAKE IT OUT ALIVE, CLARENCE.

AND FOR A SUPER-SCIENCY LAB, YOU MUST NOT HAVE HAD THE BEST VENTILATION SYSTEM!

PE-EEW!

THERE'S NO REGENERATING THE MEMORY OF THAT SMELL AWAY!

SNNRK SNNRK

WHAT'S THAT, CLARE-BEAR?

ARE WE GETTING--

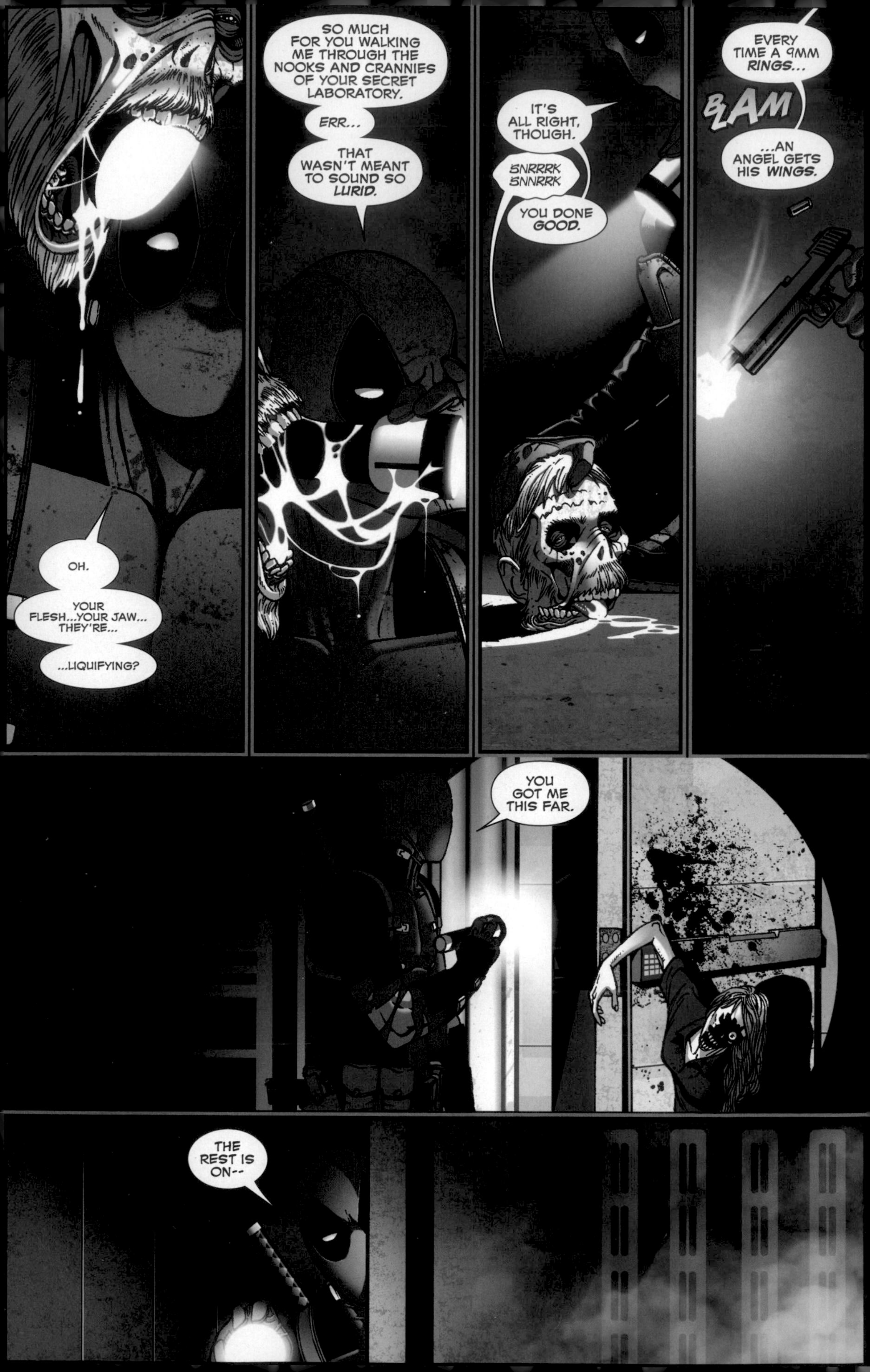
OH.
YOUR FLESH...YOUR JAW... THEY'RE...
...LIQUIFYING?
SO MUCH FOR YOU WALKING ME THROUGH THE NOOKS AND CRANNIES OF YOUR SECRET LABORATORY.
ERR...
THAT WASN'T MEANT TO SOUND SO LURID.
IT'S ALL RIGHT, THOUGH.
SNRRRK SNNRRK
YOU DONE GOOD.
EVERY TIME A 9MM RINGS...
BLAM
...AN ANGEL GETS HIS WINGS.
YOU GOT ME THIS FAR.
THE REST IS ON--

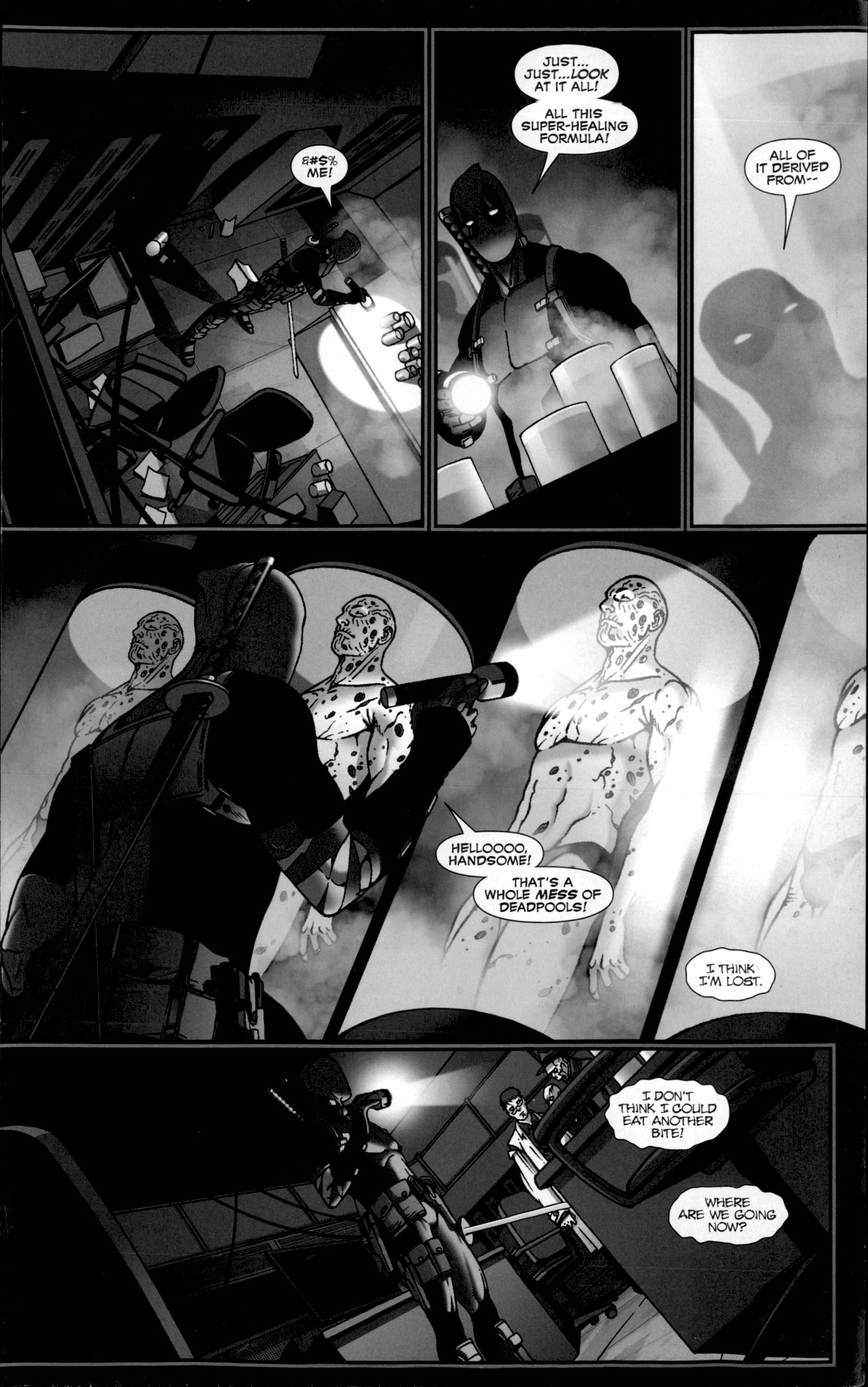
&#$% ME!
JUST... JUST...LOOK AT IT ALL!
ALL THIS SUPER-HEALING FORMULA!
ALL OF IT DERIVED FROM--
HELLOOOO, HANDSOME!
THAT'S A WHOLE MESS OF DEADPOOLS!
I THINK I'M LOST.
I DON'T THINK I COULD EAT ANOTHER BITE!
WHERE ARE WE GOING NOW?

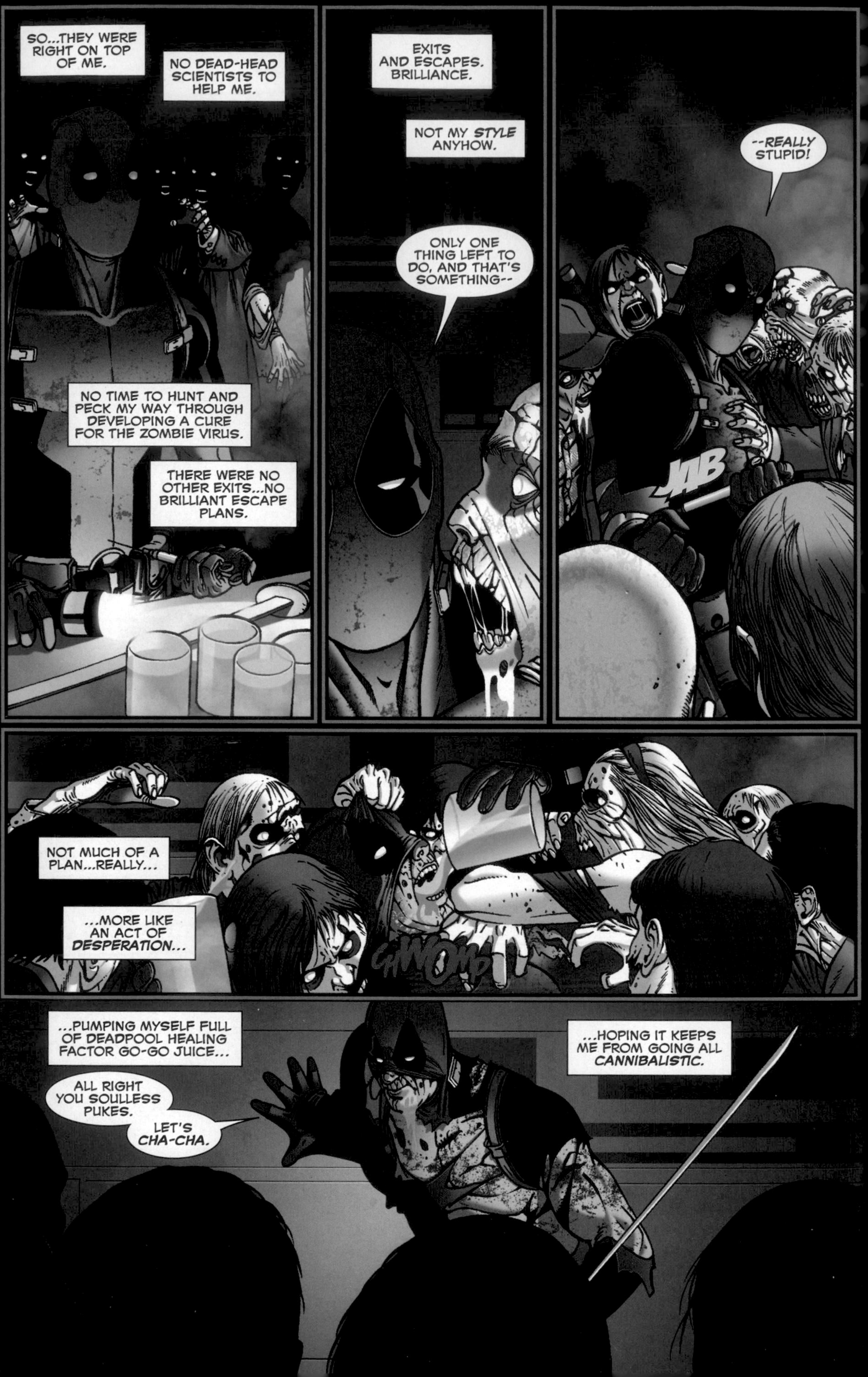
SO...THEY WERE RIGHT ON TOP OF ME.
NO DEAD-HEAD SCIENTISTS TO HELP ME.
NO TIME TO HUNT AND PECK MY WAY THROUGH DEVELOPING A CURE FOR THE ZOMBIE VIRUS.
THERE WERE NO OTHER EXITS...NO BRILLIANT ESCAPE PLANS.
EXITS AND ESCAPES. BRILLIANCE.
NOT MY STYLE ANYHOW.
ONLY ONE THING LEFT TO DO, AND THAT'S SOMETHING--
--REALLY STUPID!
JAB
NOT MUCH OF A PLAN...REALLY...
...MORE LIKE AN ACT OF DESPERATION...
GHWOMP
...PUMPING MYSELF FULL OF DEADPOOL HEALING FACTOR GO-GO JUICE...
...HOPING IT KEEPS ME FROM GOING ALL CANNIBALISTIC.
ALL RIGHT YOU SOULLESS PUKES.
LET'S CHA-CHA.

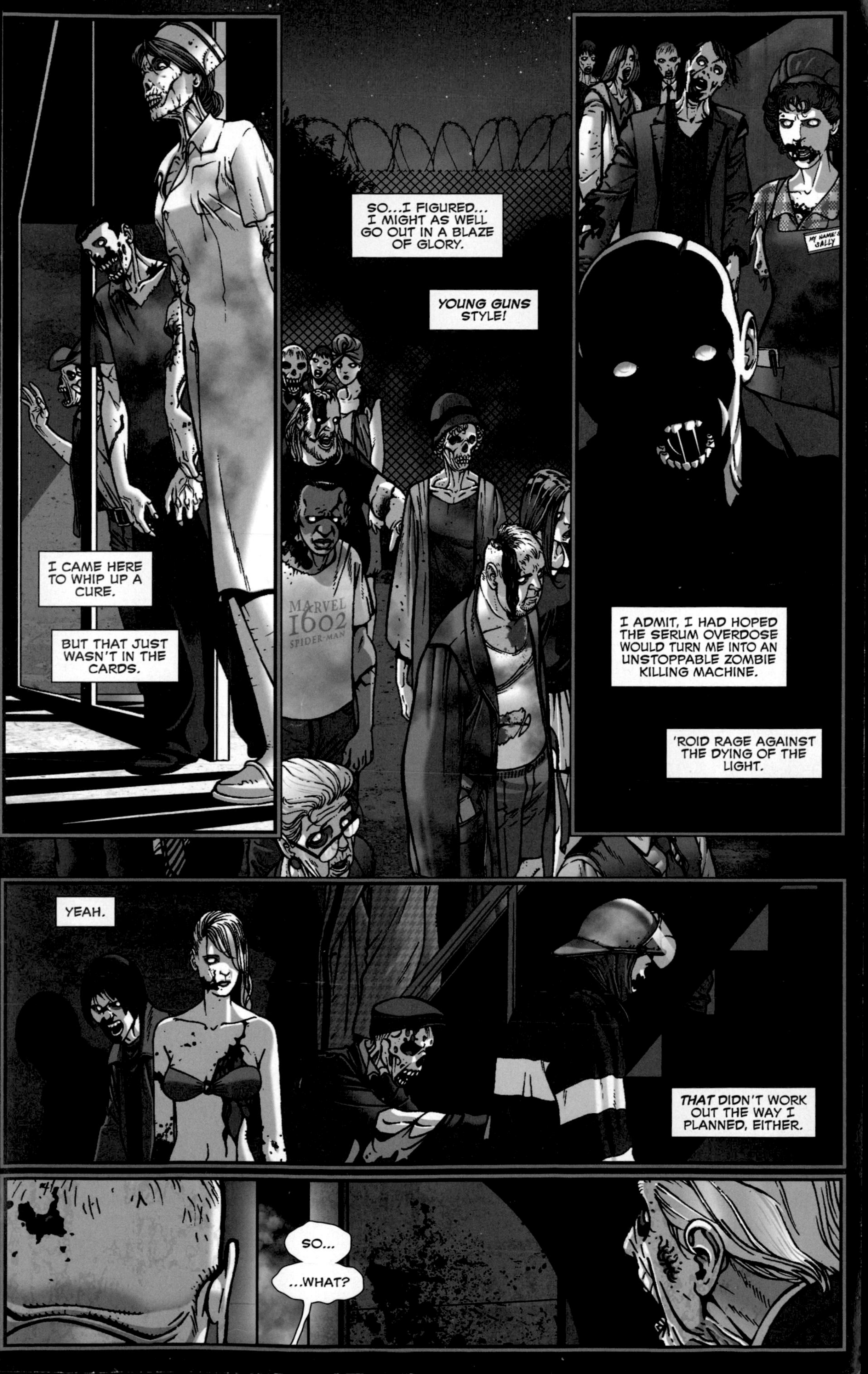
I CAME HERE TO WHIP UP A CURE.
BUT THAT JUST WASN'T IN THE CARDS.
SO...I FIGURED... I MIGHT AS WELL GO OUT IN A BLAZE OF GLORY.
YOUNG GUNS STYLE!
MARVEL 1602 SPIDER-MAN
MY NAME'S SALLY
I ADMIT, I HAD HOPED THE SERUM OVERDOSE WOULD TURN ME INTO AN UNSTOPPABLE ZOMBIE KILLING MACHINE.
'ROID RAGE AGAINST THE DYING OF THE LIGHT.
YEAH.
THAT DIDN'T WORK OUT THE WAY I PLANNED, EITHER.
SO...
...WHAT?

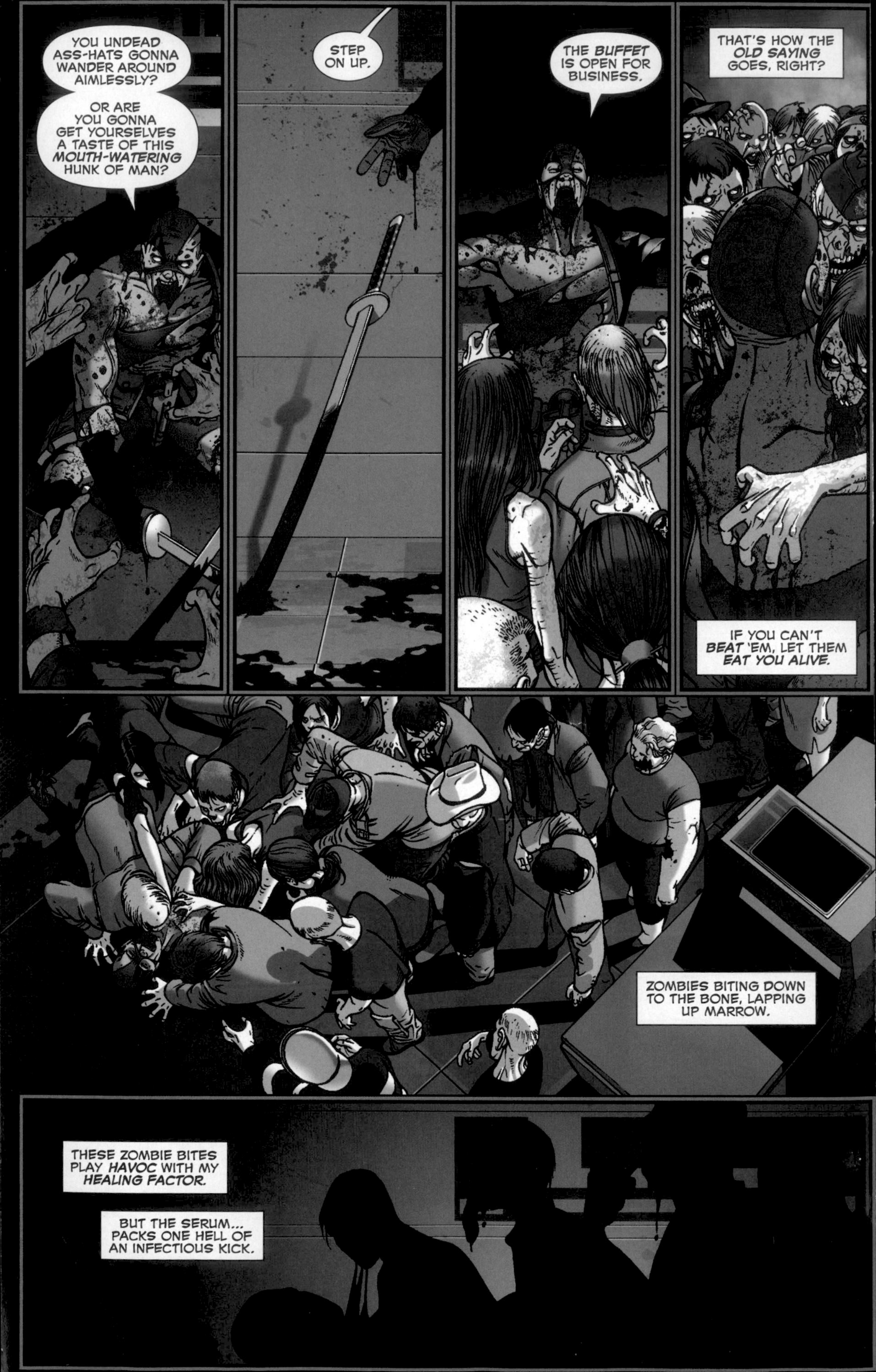
YOU UNDEAD ASS-HATS GONNA WANDER AROUND AIMLESSLY?
OR ARE YOU GONNA GET YOURSELVES A TASTE OF THIS *MOUTH-WATERING* HUNK OF MAN?
STEP ON UP.
THE *BUFFET* IS OPEN FOR BUSINESS.
THAT'S HOW THE *OLD SAYING* GOES, RIGHT?
IF YOU CAN'T *BEAT* 'EM, LET THEM *EAT YOU ALIVE.*
ZOMBIES BITING DOWN TO THE BONE, LAPPING UP MARROW.
THESE ZOMBIE BITES PLAY *HAVOC* WITH MY *HEALING FACTOR.*
BUT THE SERUM... PACKS ONE HELL OF AN INFECTIOUS KICK.

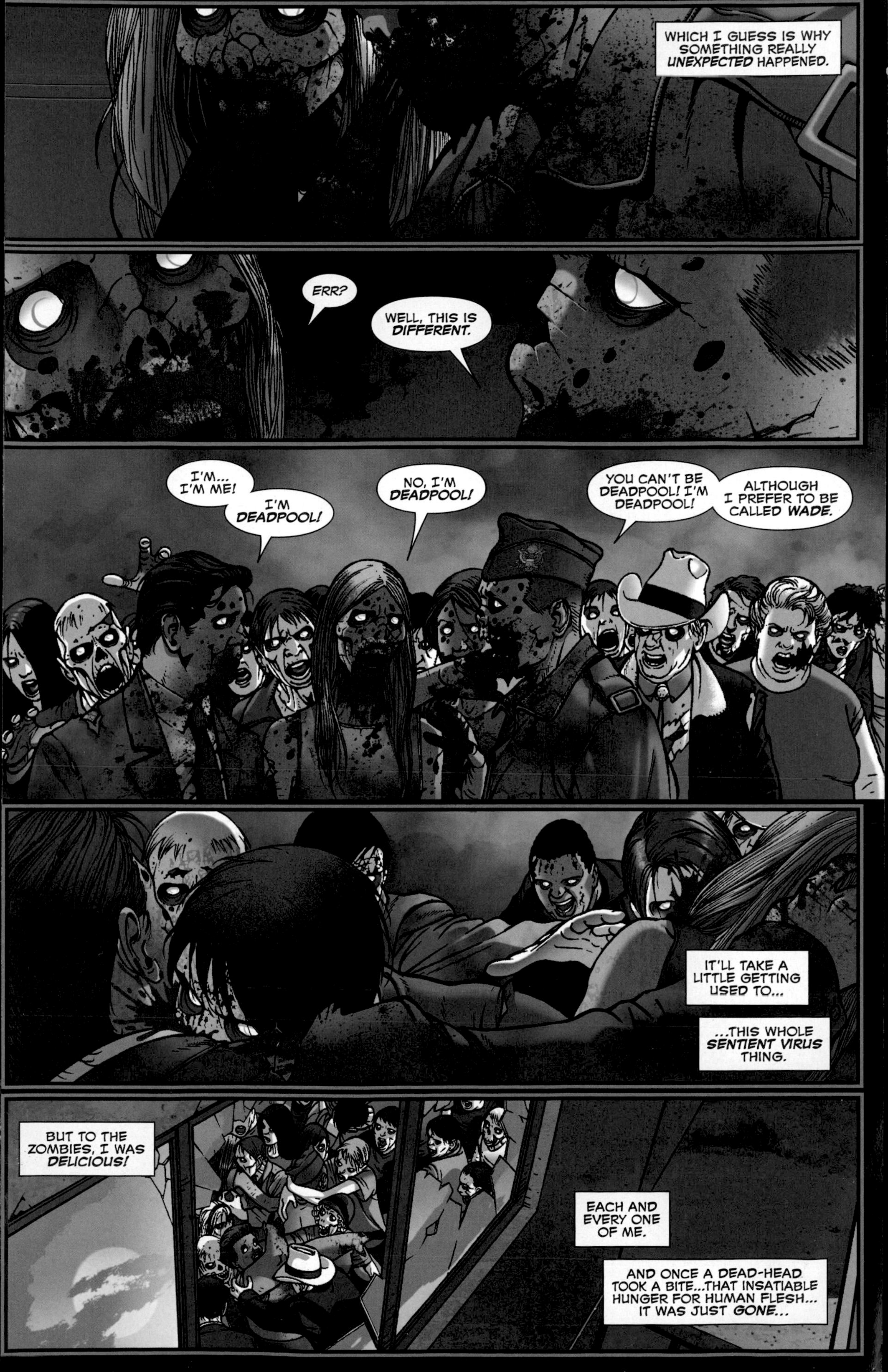
WHICH I GUESS IS WHY SOMETHING REALLY UNEXPECTED HAPPENED.
ERR?
WELL, THIS IS DIFFERENT.
I'M... I'M ME!
I'M DEADPOOL!
NO, I'M DEADPOOL!
YOU CAN'T BE DEADPOOL! I'M DEADPOOL!
ALTHOUGH I PREFER TO BE CALLED WADE.
IT'LL TAKE A LITTLE GETTING USED TO...
...THIS WHOLE SENTIENT VIRUS THING.
BUT TO THE ZOMBIES, I WAS DELICIOUS!
EACH AND EVERY ONE OF ME.
AND ONCE A DEAD-HEAD TOOK A BITE...THAT INSATIABLE HUNGER FOR HUMAN FLESH... IT WAS JUST GONE...

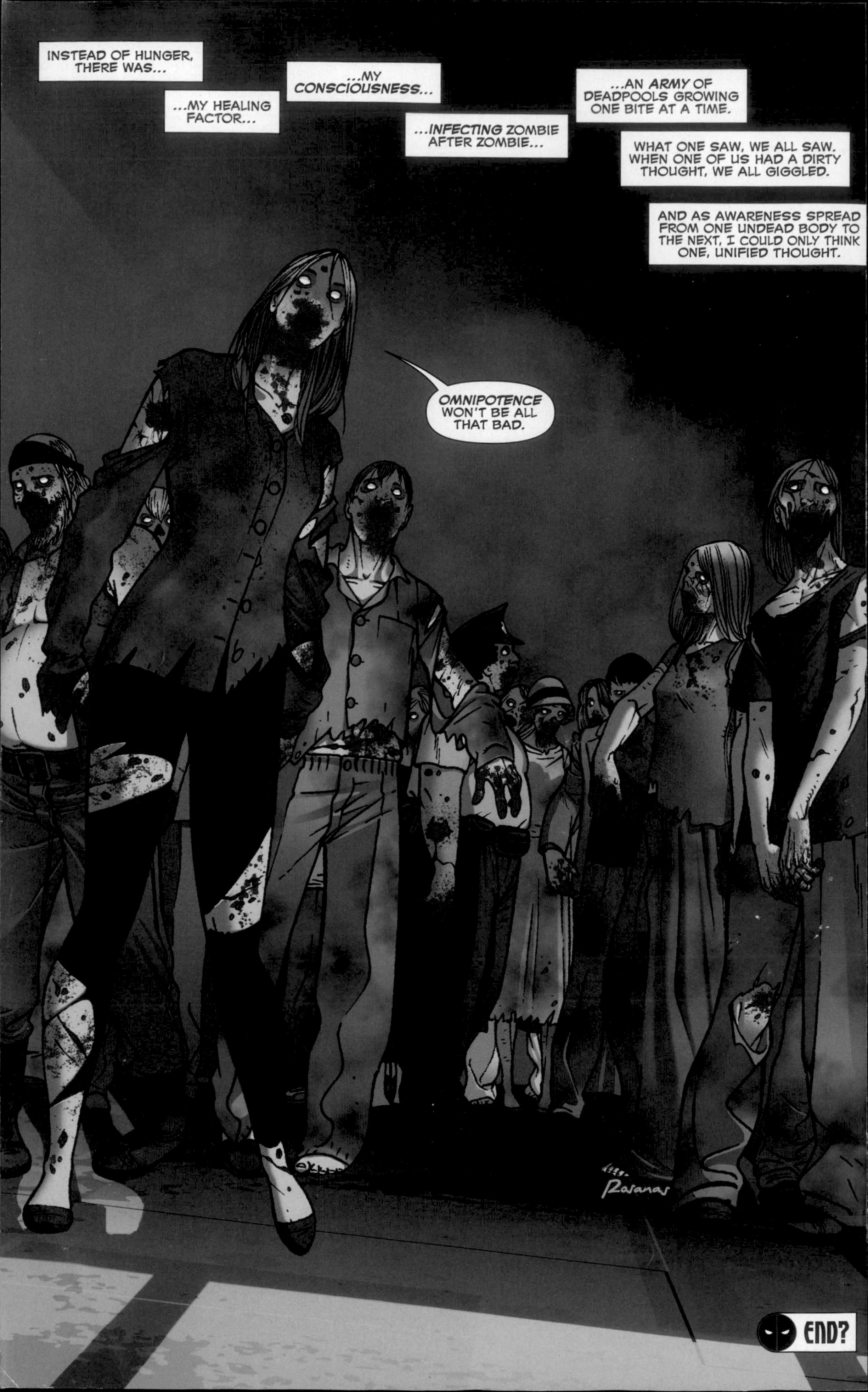
INSTEAD OF HUNGER, THERE WAS...
...MY HEALING FACTOR...
...MY CONSCIOUSNESS...
...INFECTING ZOMBIE AFTER ZOMBIE...
...AN ARMY OF DEADPOOLS GROWING ONE BITE AT A TIME.
WHAT ONE SAW, WE ALL SAW. WHEN ONE OF US HAD A DIRTY THOUGHT, WE ALL GIGGLED.
AND AS AWARENESS SPREAD FROM ONE UNDEAD BODY TO THE NEXT, I COULD ONLY THINK ONE, UNIFIED THOUGHT.
OMNIPOTENCE WON'T BE ALL THAT BAD.
Rosanas
END?

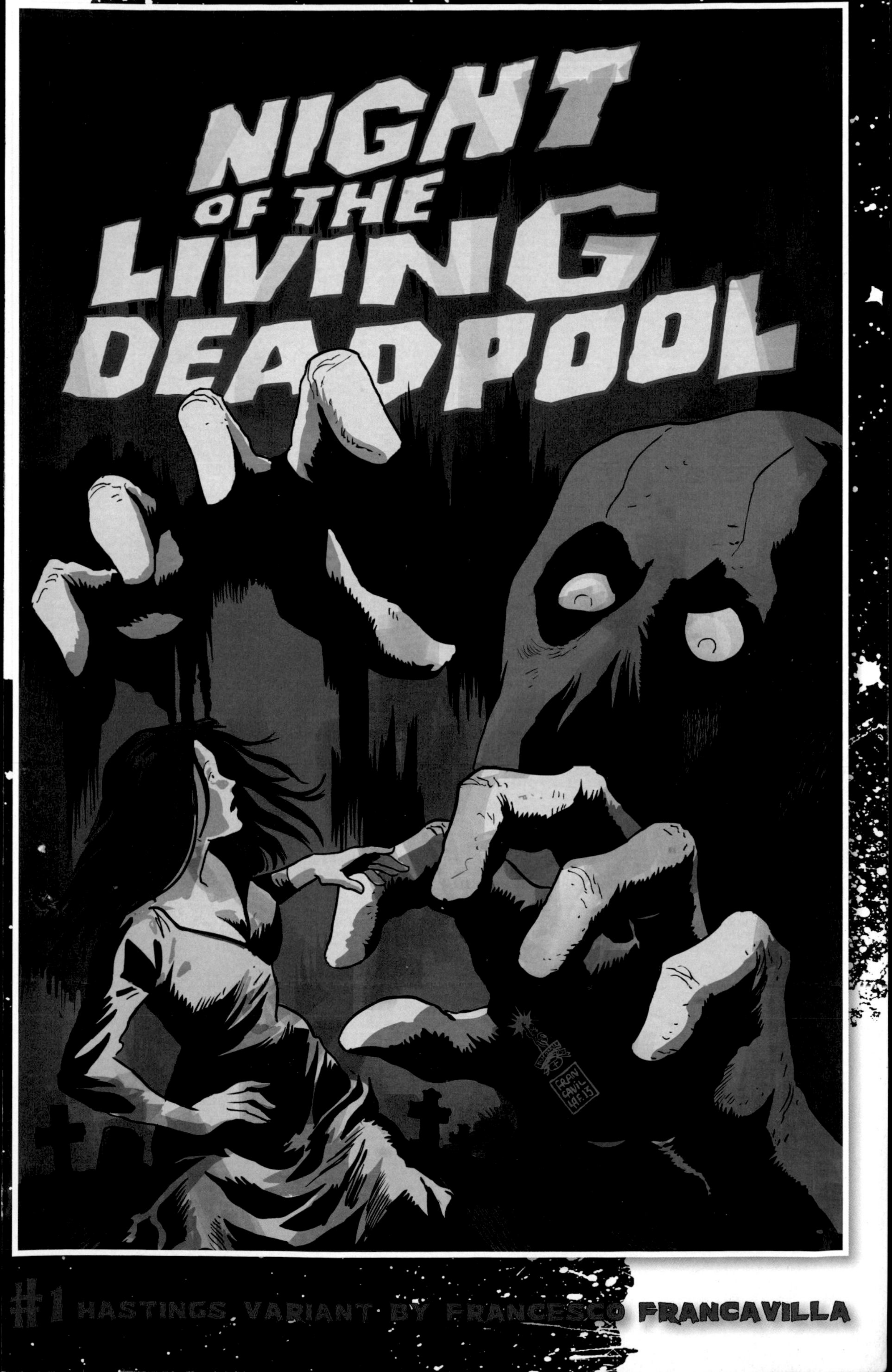
NIGHT
OF THE
LIVING
DEADPOOL

#1 HASTINGS VARIANT BY FRANCESCO FRANCAVILLA

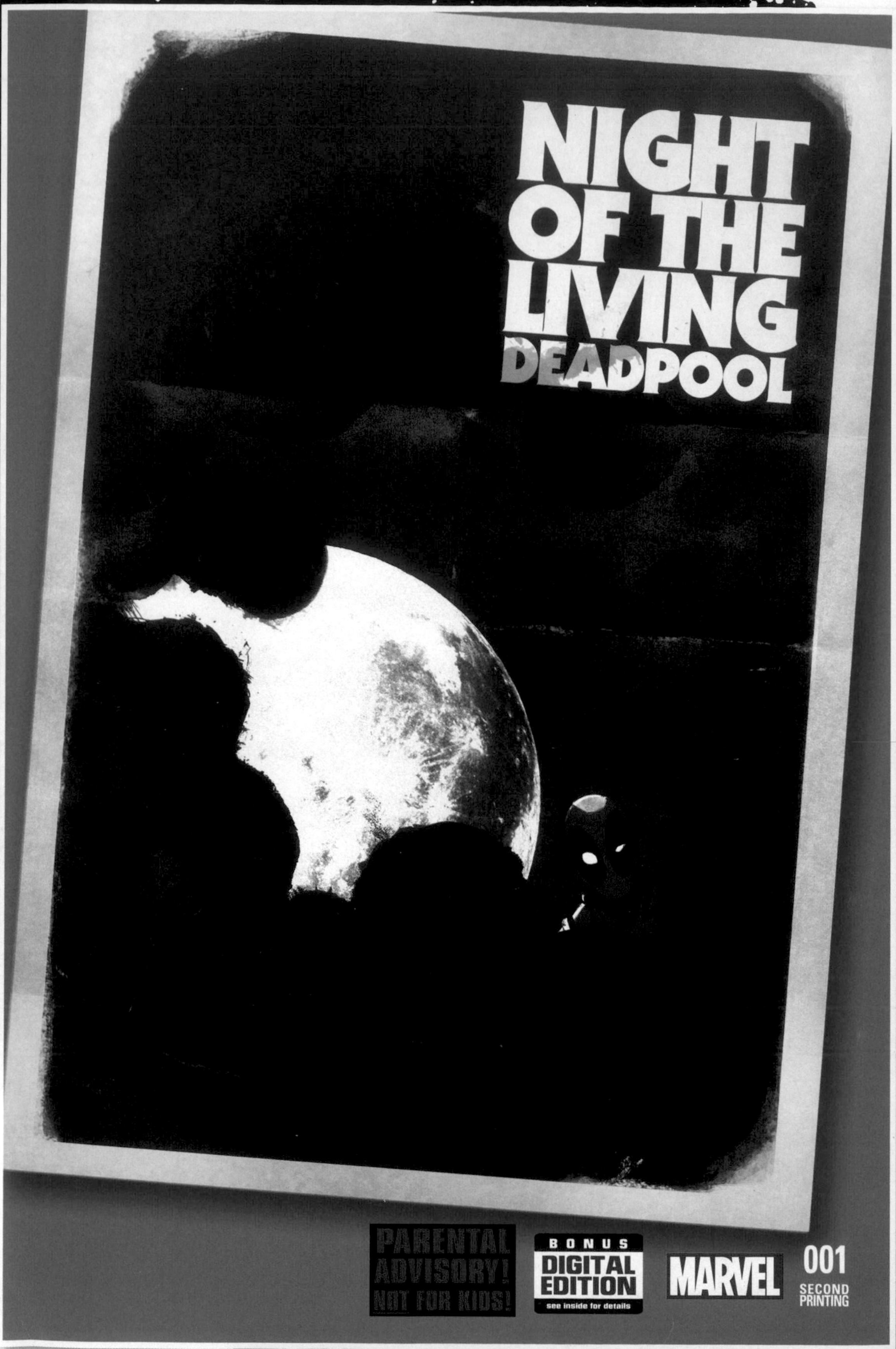

#1 2ND PRINTING VARIANT

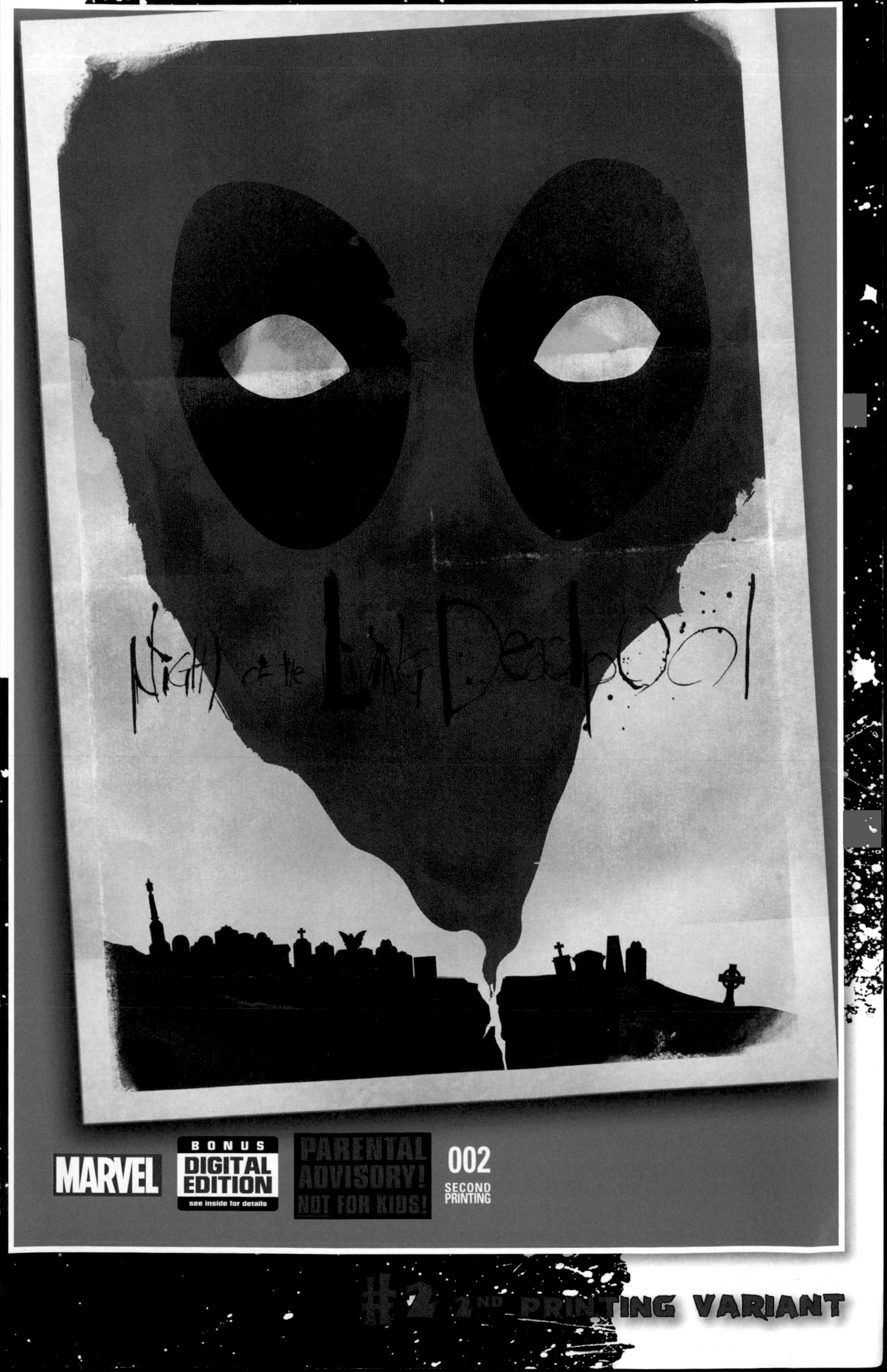
Night of the Living Deadpool
MARVEL
BONUS
DIGITAL EDITION
see inside for details
PARENTAL ADVISORY! NOT FOR KIDS!
002
SECOND PRINTING

#2 2ND PRINTING VARIANT

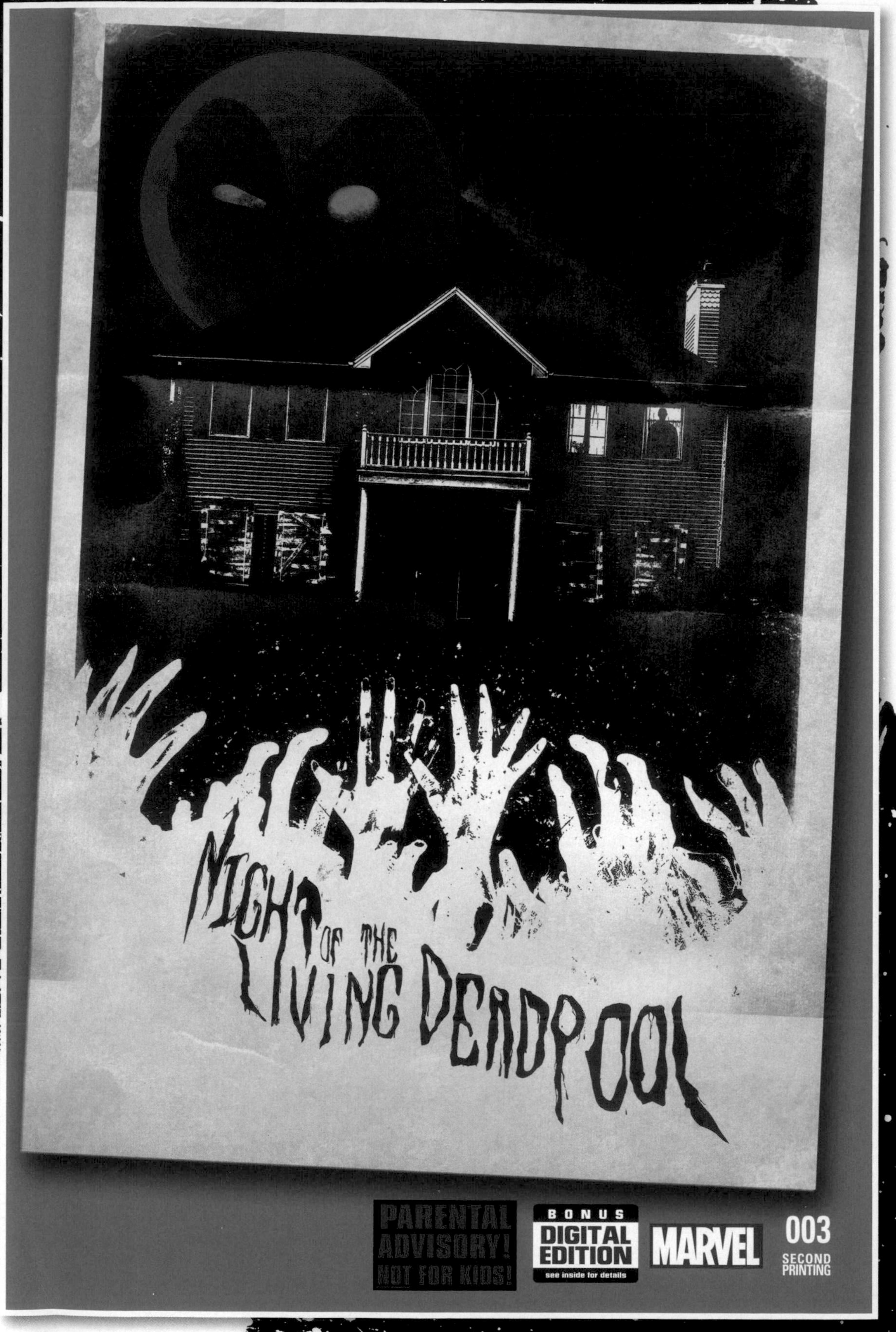

NIGHT OF THE LIVING DEADPOOL
PARENTAL ADVISORY! NOT FOR KIDS!
BONUS
DIGITAL EDITION
see inside for details
MARVEL
003
SECOND PRINTING

#3 2ND PRINTING VARIANT

Been thinking quite a bit about this, and I have a few threads I wanted to run by you.

I think that we should embrace many of the tropes of the zombie apocalypse sub-genre, giving the book a "familiar" feel for readers. You'll see some of those reflected in the ideas below. At the same time, of course, we'll want this to be as fresh as possible, and I think throwing Deadpool into the mix will do that.

TROPES -
Waking after coma to be in the middle of a zombie apocalypse. The first few moments of intense horror after the zombies appear. The mall (although in this case it is a flea market). The graveyard. The roving gangs of human marauders. The lone scientist trying to figure out what happened. The isolationists. The madman who thinks he's doing right, but whose measures are extreme. Etc.

TONE -
I'd like for the zombies to be played straight--dark and scary. They've destroyed the world essentially. Survival is harsh and cruel. But Deadpool, and his reaction to the world, brings a splash of comedy. Think "Last Man on Earth" if they put a comedian in the lead role, but nothing else changed.

HOW DID DEADPOOL GET HERE? -
After an All-You-Can-Eat Chimichanga binge, Deadpool goes into a food coma. He wakes after the apocalypse has occurred.

WHAT MAKES OUR ZOMBIES DIFFERENT? -
These zombies are slow, rotting, flesh-eating creatures, like those in a Romero film. However, the human mind within still sees everything that is happening, but is helpless to stop it. The human consciousness is trapped within, unable to change the zombie's actions. This leads to some real horror, I think, and a reflection of a descent into madness. As the zombies attack living creatures, we may hear them whimpering, begging for forgiveness, begging to be killed, etc. Some of the minds trapped within might actually enjoy what is happening. All of them slowly deteriorate of course. At some point, Deadpool might even capture some of the undead, tying them up and interrogating the host consciousness.

WHAT IS THE CAUSE OF THE ZOMBIE APOCALYPSE? -
Often, the cause of the apocalypse is unknown. A comet passing too close to Earth? A virus? Demons? Voodoo magic? In this case, Deadpool searches for all possible sources for the infestation. In the end, he will discover that the source of the zombie infestation is the same weapons program that created him.

WHERE ARE THE HEROES? -
Since readers will want to know, my suggestion is that we sprinkle hints throughout the series as to what happened to the heroes. I think they all died trying to stop the invasion, leaving Deadpool as the only "hero" left. Some locales may be home bases of heroes/villains, etc. We might even see a couple of heroes who were injured in the Apocalypse but survived....

Maybe Peter Parker, only missing an arm and leg. Maybe Captain America, without his uniform and shield, leading a small ragtag group of survivors. Maybe rumors of The Hulk living out in the wilderness. This story redefines the hero in many ways, and here we'll see a dark reflection of that.

I just feel like we have to do several nods to the Marvel Universe just to make the story work.

DEADPOOL THE HERO -
Like Mad Max in Beyond Thunderdome, Deadpool becomes the savior of a group of survivors. A key part of the story will be his giving up the dream of reversing the cause of the apocalypse and taking up the dream of protecting what few people survive.

DEADPOOL THE ZOMBIE -
In our third act, Deadpool could get infected by a zombie bite. He might even "ride along" in his own undead form until his healing factor brings him back.

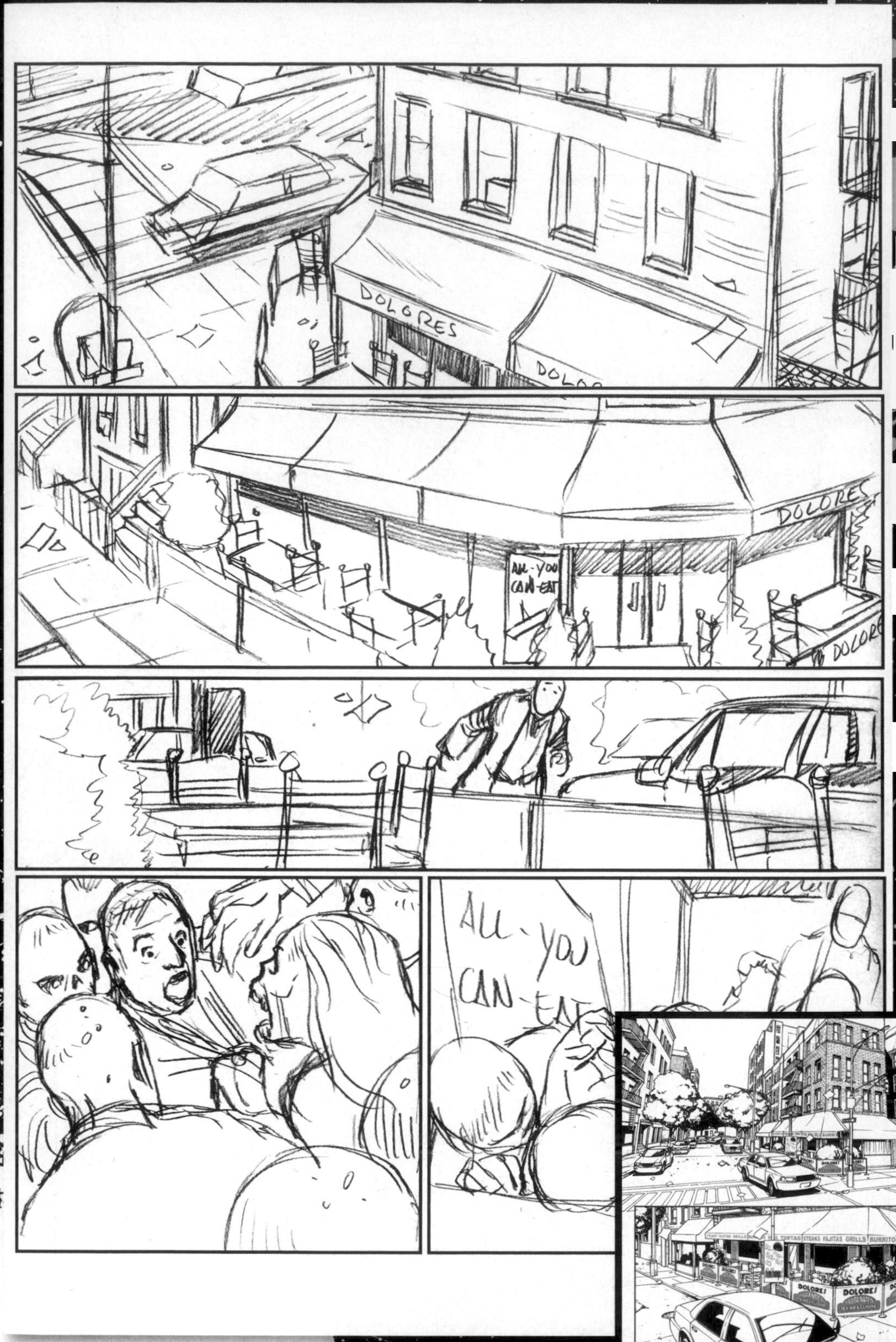
DOLORES
DOLORES
DOLORES
ALL-YOU CAN-EAT
DOLORES
ALL-YOU CAN-EAT

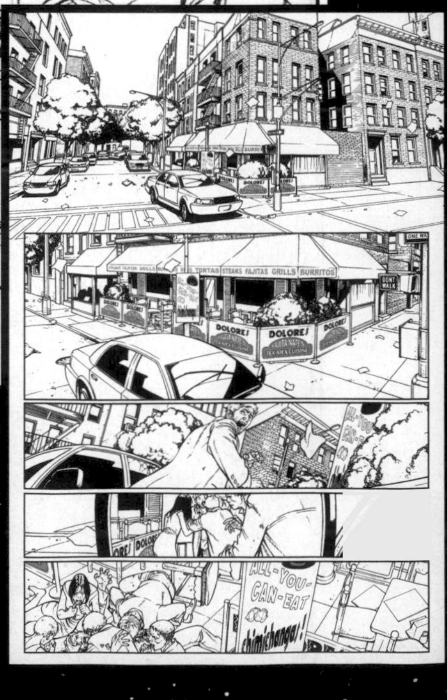
BURRITOS
STEAKS FAJITAS GRILLS BURRITOS
DOLORES
ALL-YOU-CAN-EAT
chimichangas!

#1, PAGE 1 DRAFTS

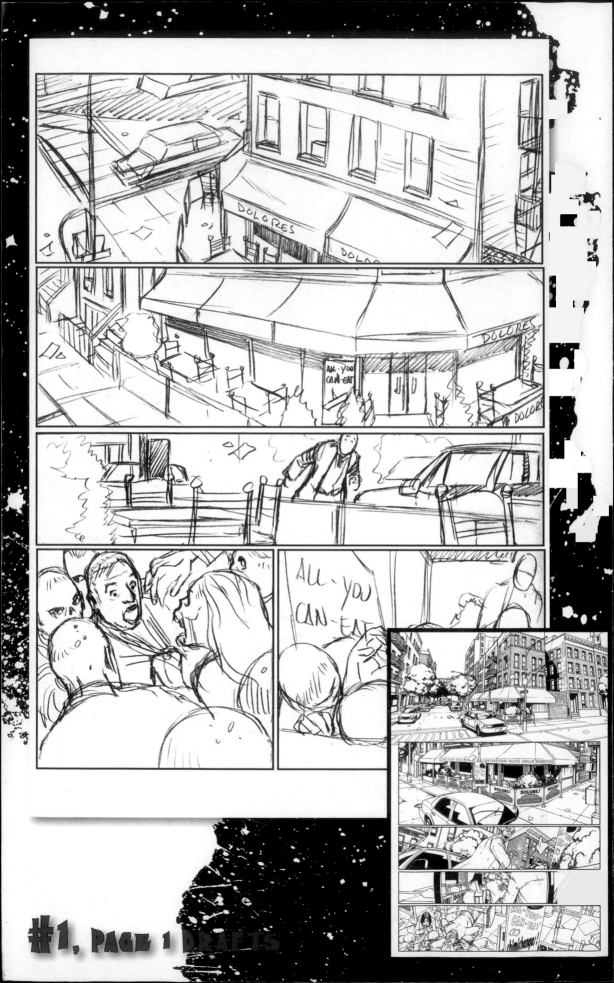

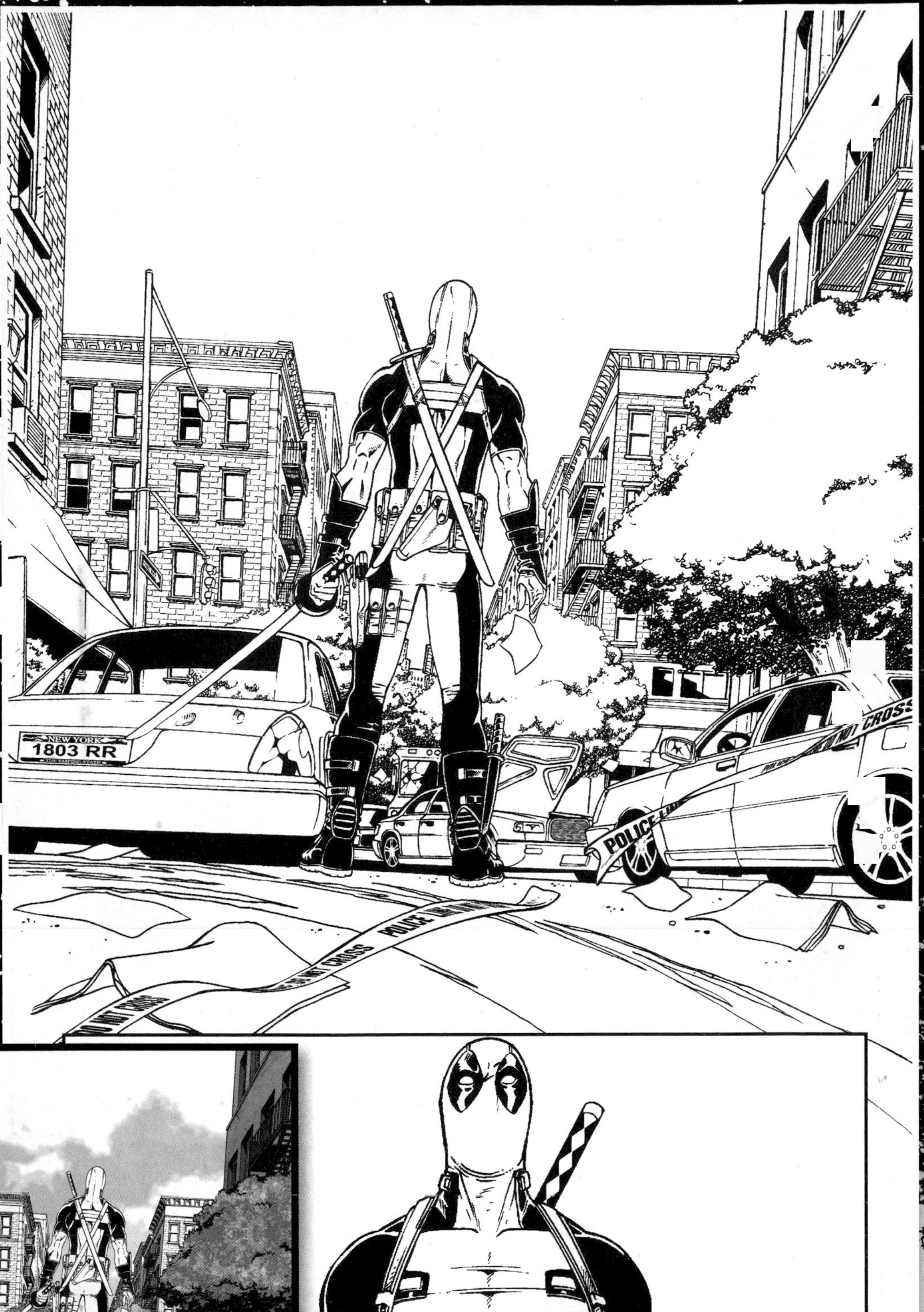
NEW YORK
1803 RR
POLICE
CROSS

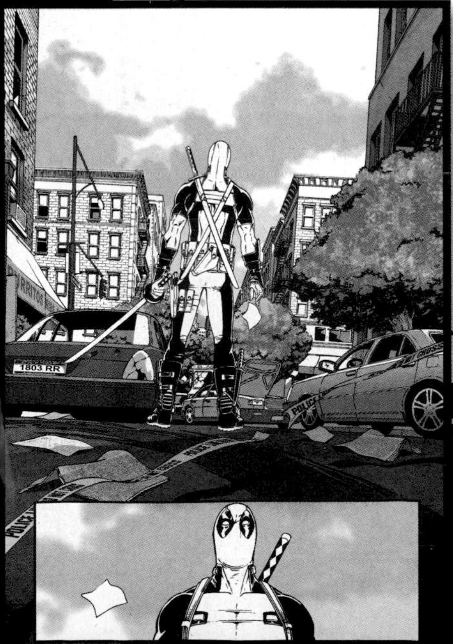
1803 RR

#1, Page 4 Shading

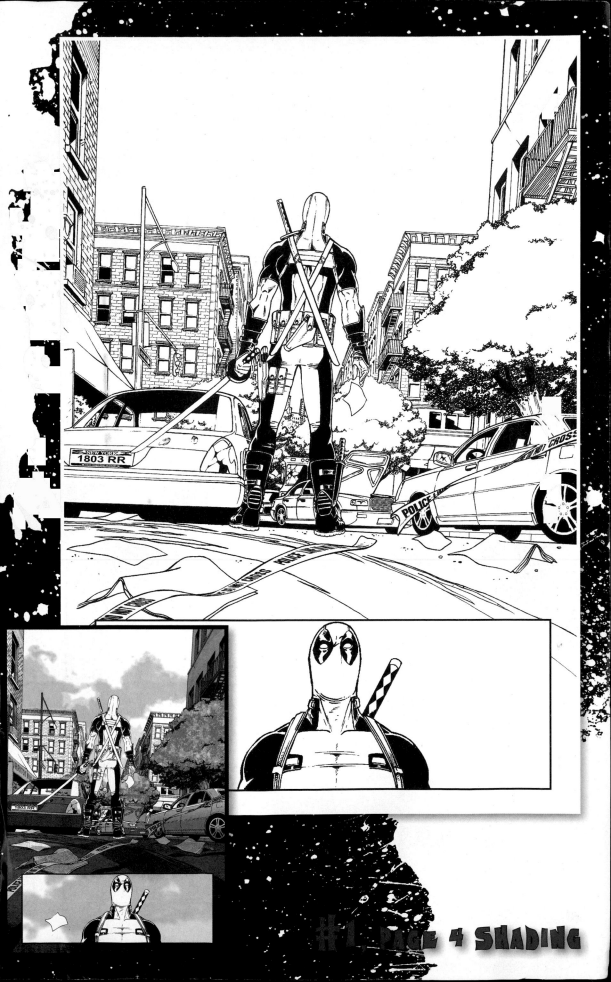

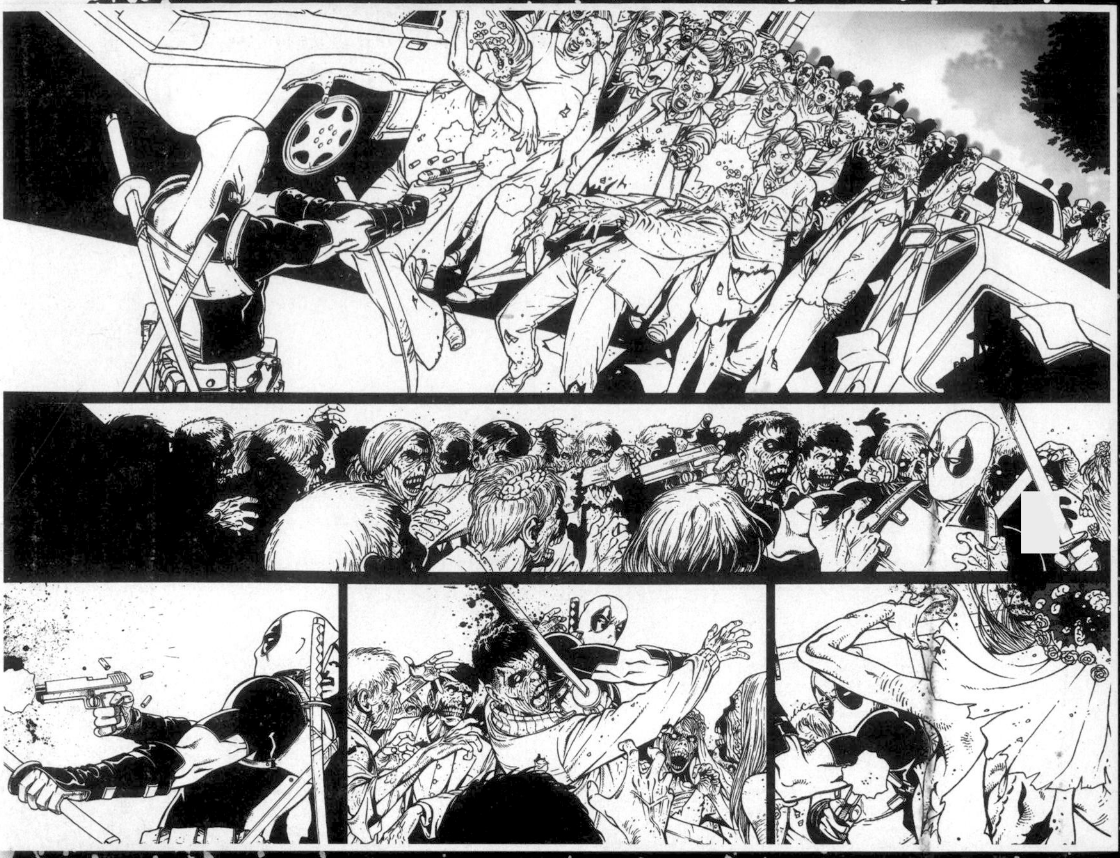

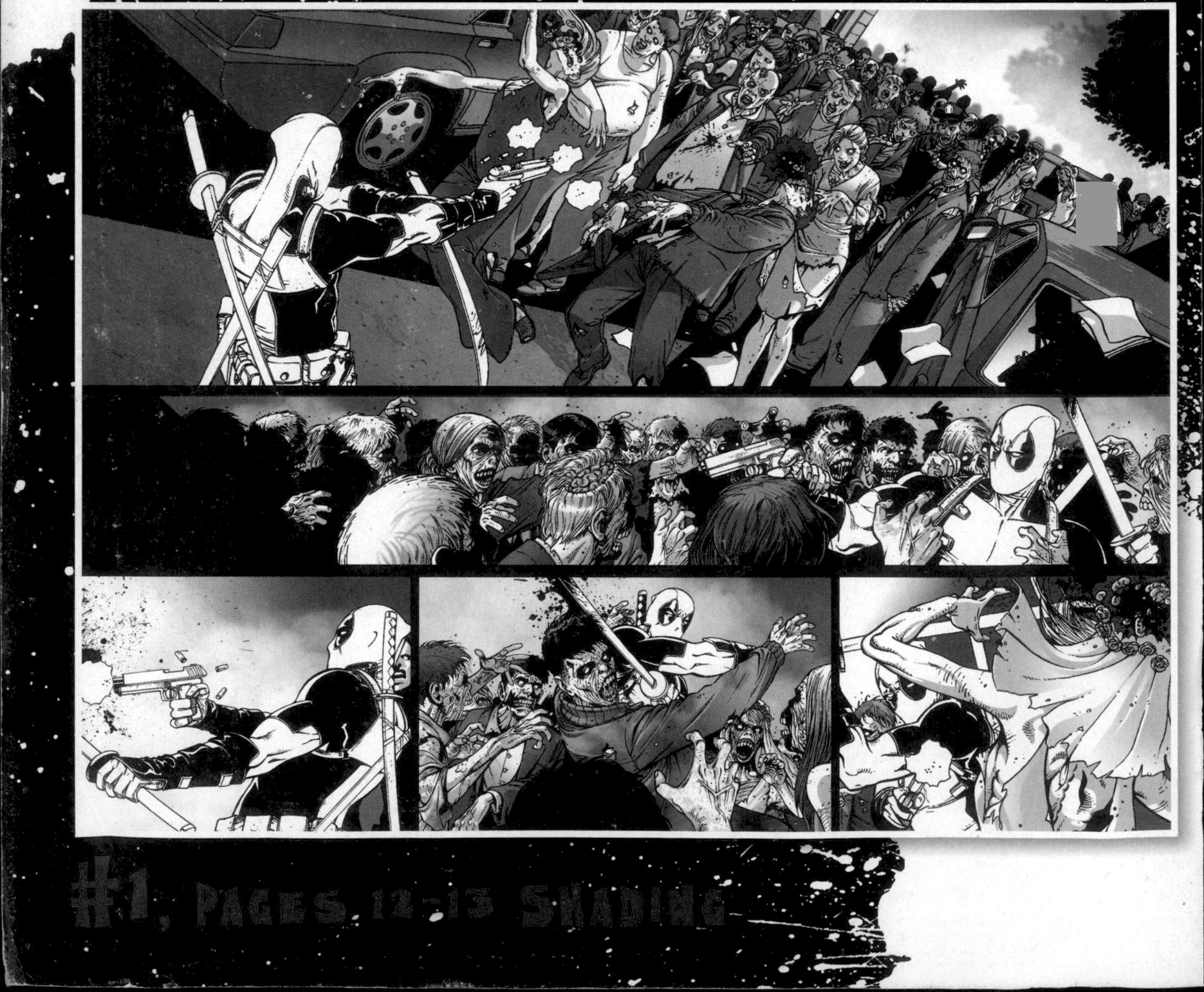

#1, PAGES 12-13 SHADING